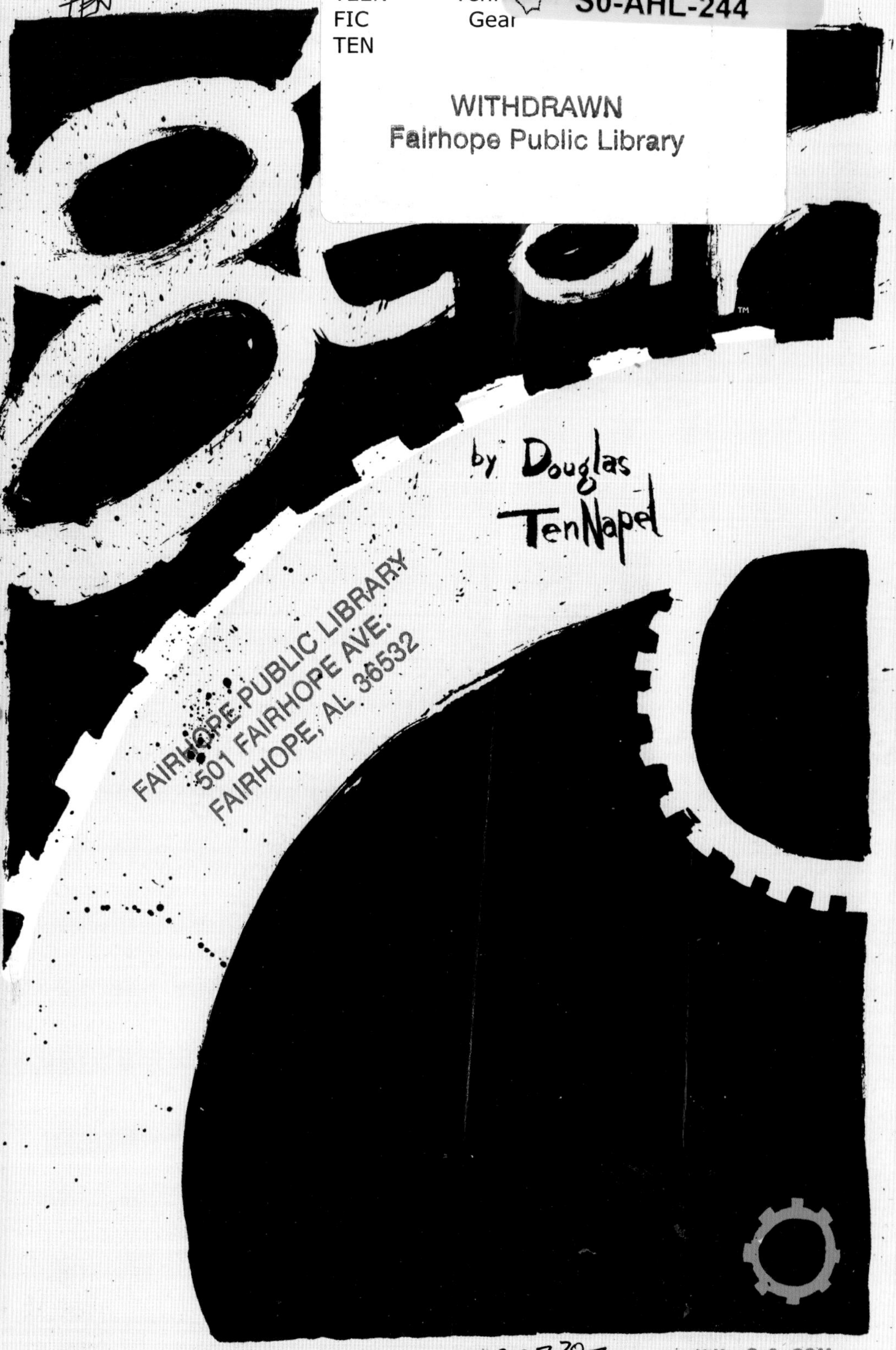
by Douglas TenNapel

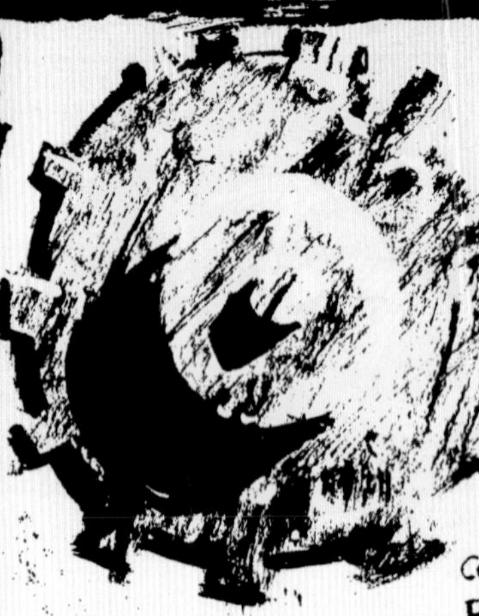

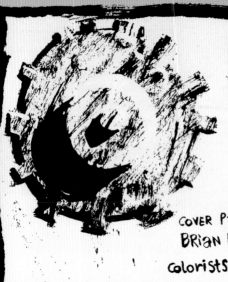

# gear™

Created Written & Drawn by
Douglas TenNapel

Produced by
Peter Alberts &
Rob Schrab

Cover Painting by
Brian Horton

Colorists: Joe Potter
Katherine "Lemm" Garner


Image Comics, Inc.

Erik Larsen - Publisher
Todd McFarlane - President
Marc Silvestri - CEO
Jim Valentino - Vice President
Eric Stephenson - Executive Director
Joe Keatinge - PR & Marketing Coordinator
Thao Le - Accounting
Branwyn Bigglestone - Accounting
Traci Hui - Traffic Manager
Allen Hui - Production Manager
Jonathan Chan - Production Artist
Drew Gill - Production Artist

www.imagecomics.com
www.tennapel.com


This book is dedicated to Simon


**GEAR**. Second Printing. Published by Image Comics, Inc., Office of publication: 1942 University Avenue, Suite 305, Berkeley, California 94704.



**PRINTED IN CHINA**
**ISBN: 978-1-58240-680-0**

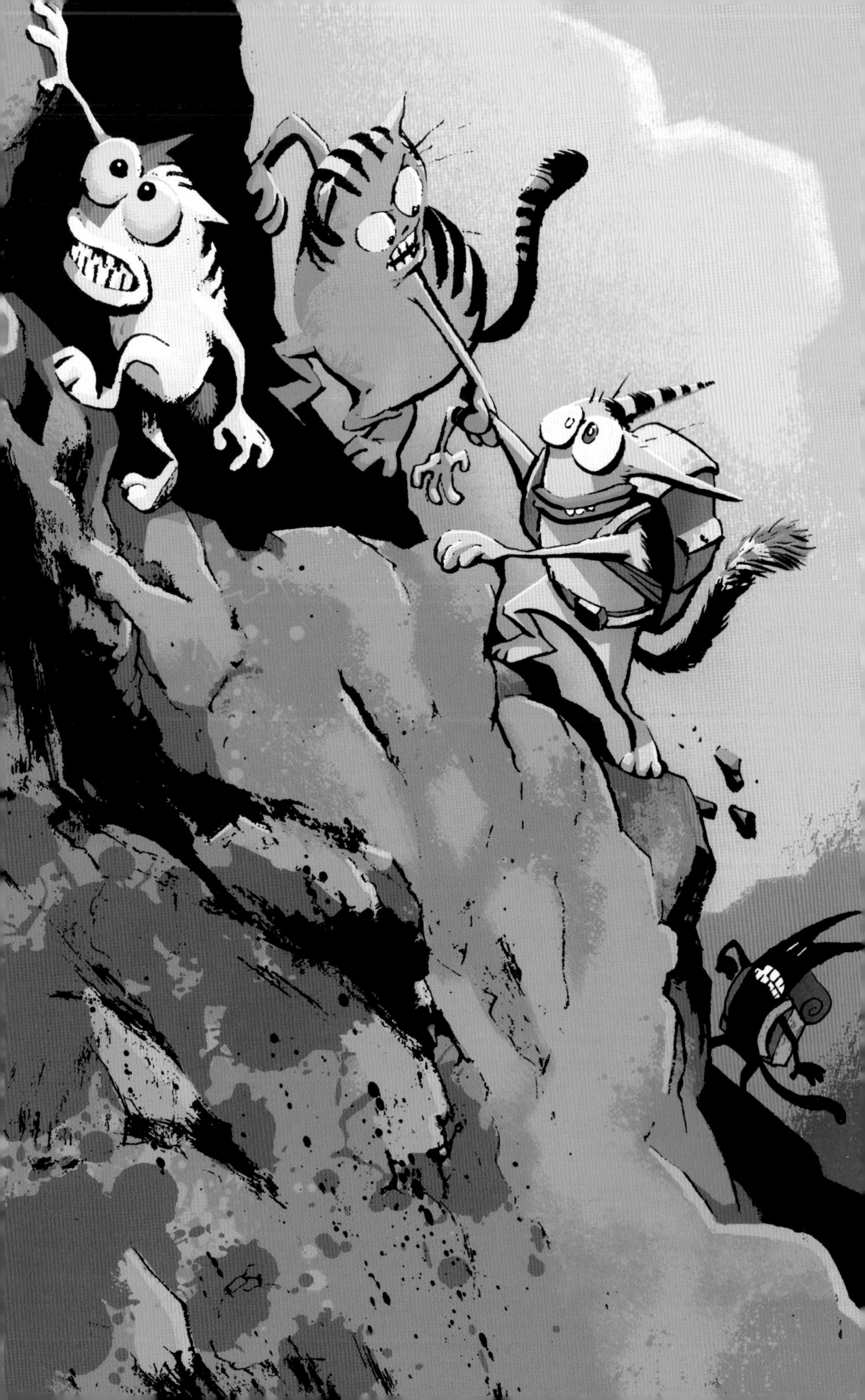

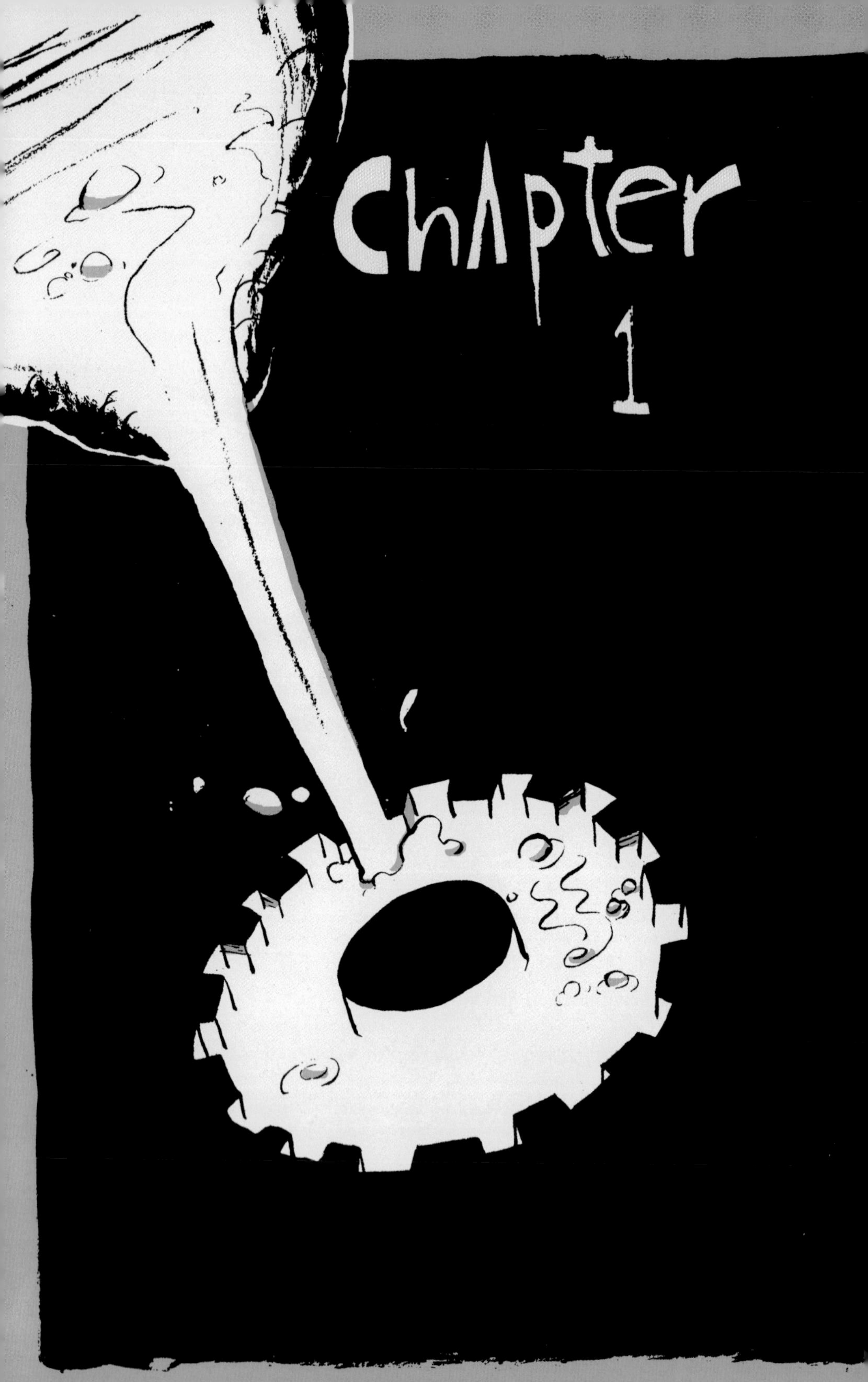
Chapter
1

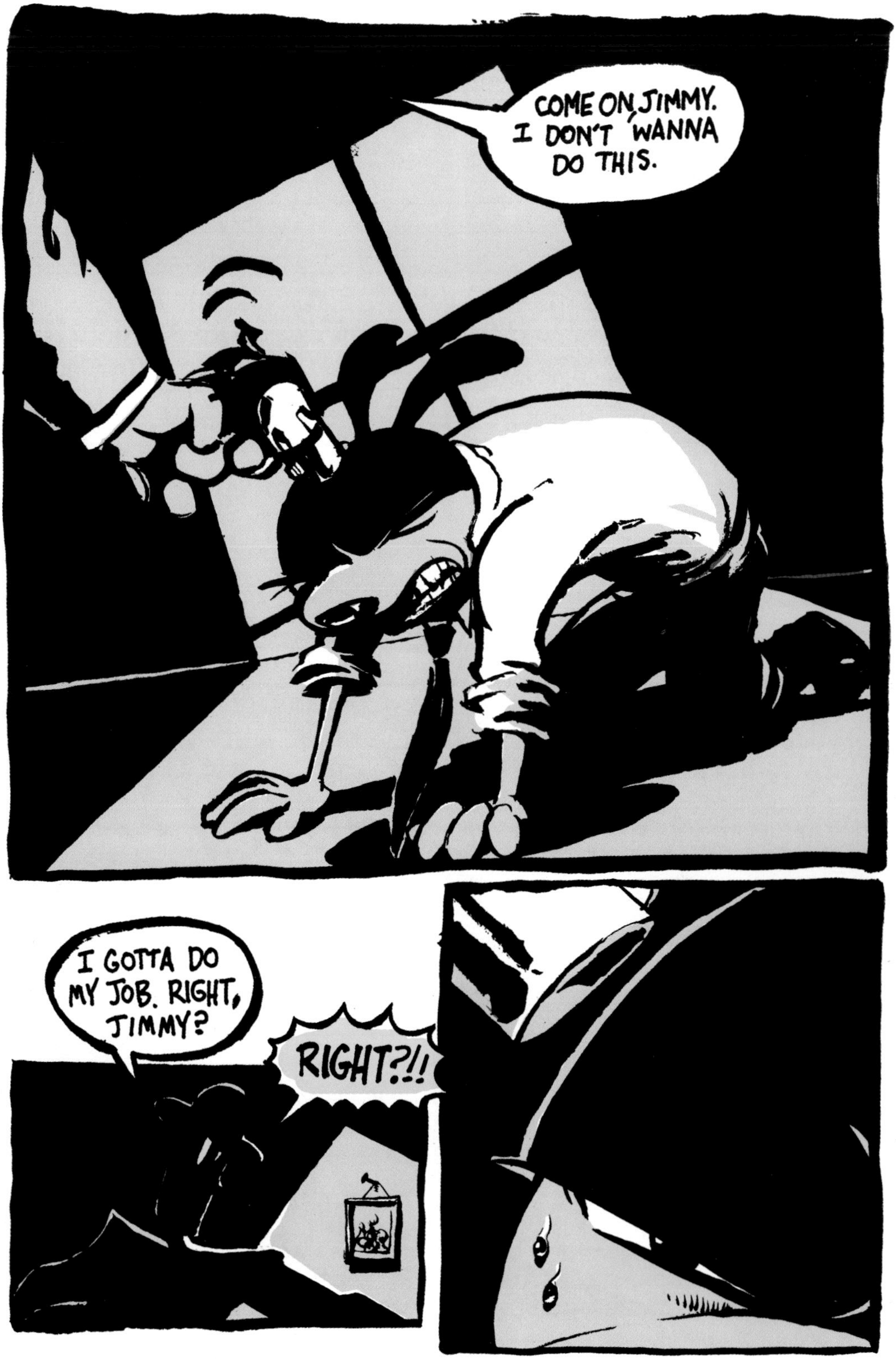
COME ON, JIMMY. I DON'T WANNA DO THIS.
I GOTTA DO MY JOB. RIGHT, JIMMY?
RIGHT?!!

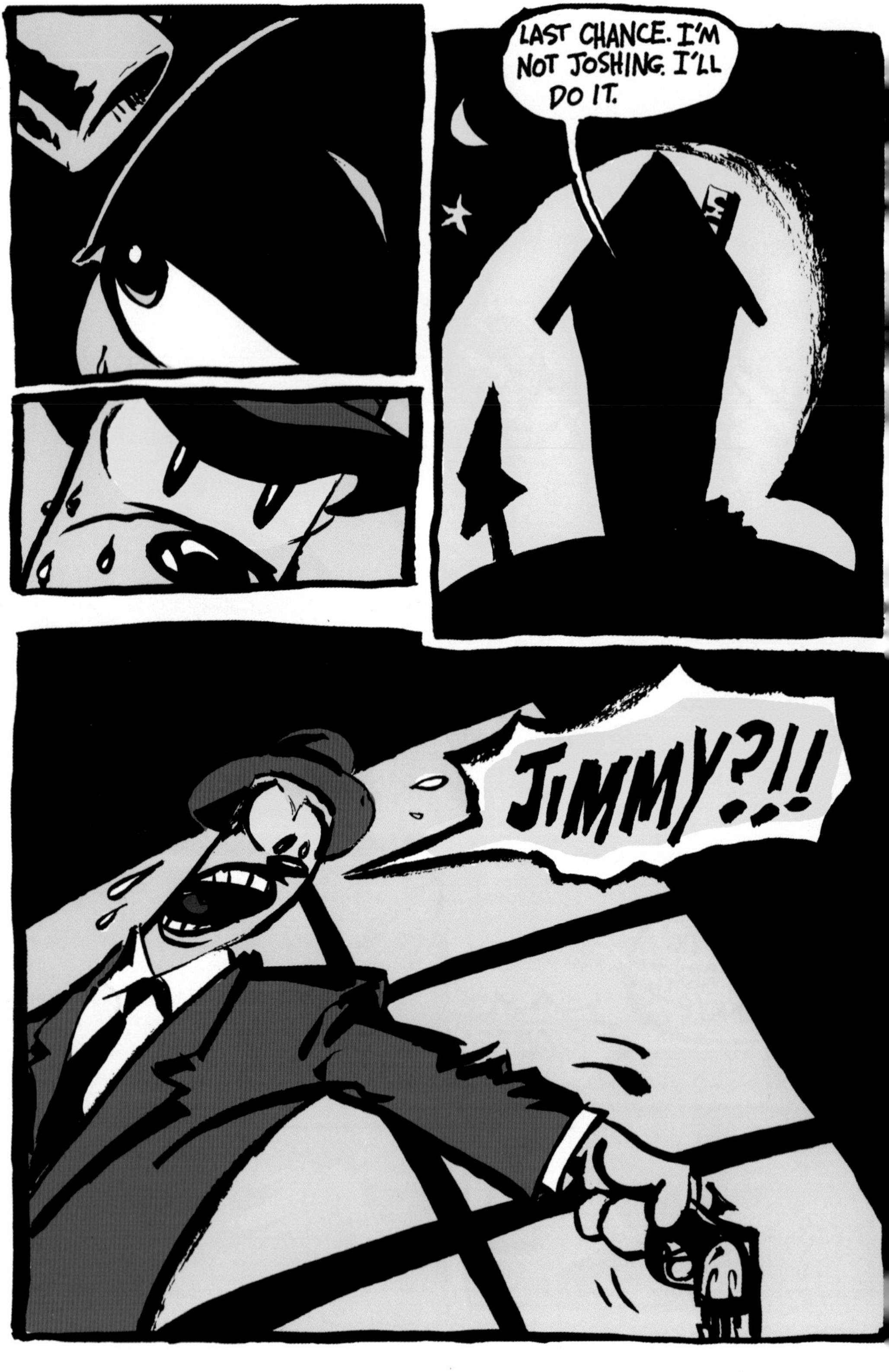
LAST CHANCE. I'M NOT JOSHING. I'LL DO IT.
JIMMY?!!

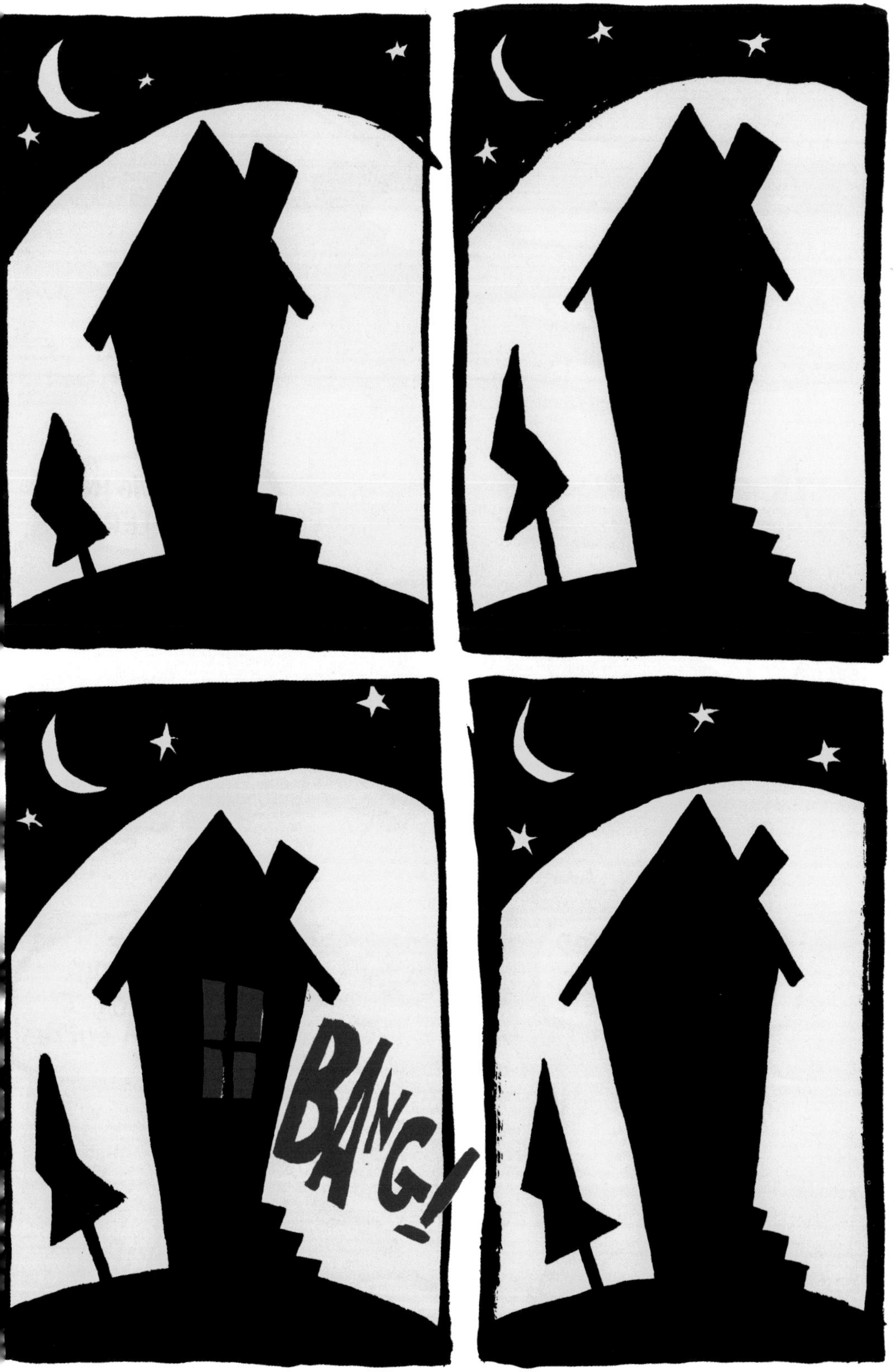
BANG!

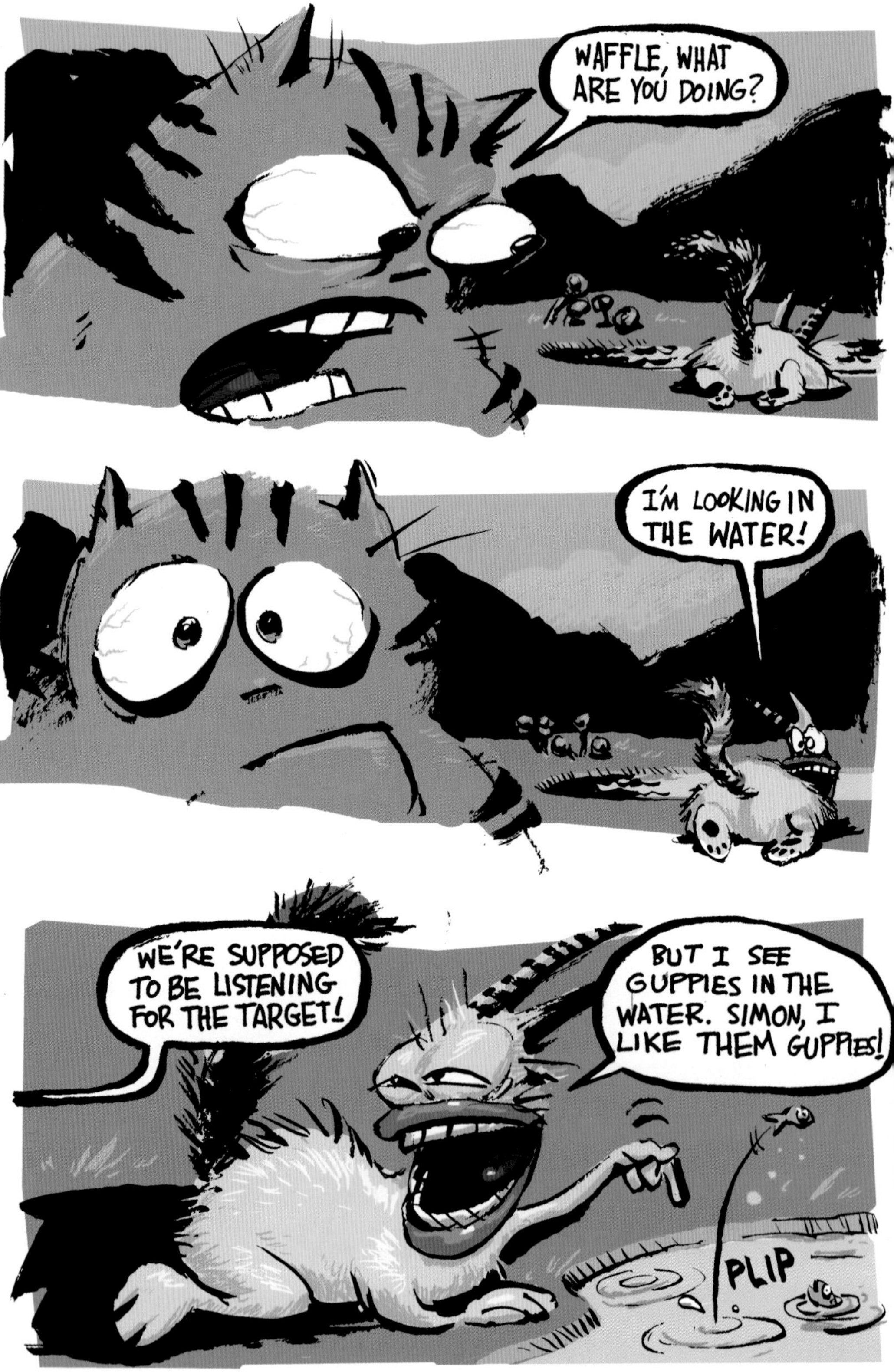
WAFFLE, WHAT ARE YOU DOING?
I'M LOOKING IN THE WATER!
WE'RE SUPPOSED TO BE LISTENING FOR THE TARGET!
BUT I SEE GUPPIES IN THE WATER. SIMON, I LIKE THEM GUPPIES!
PLIP

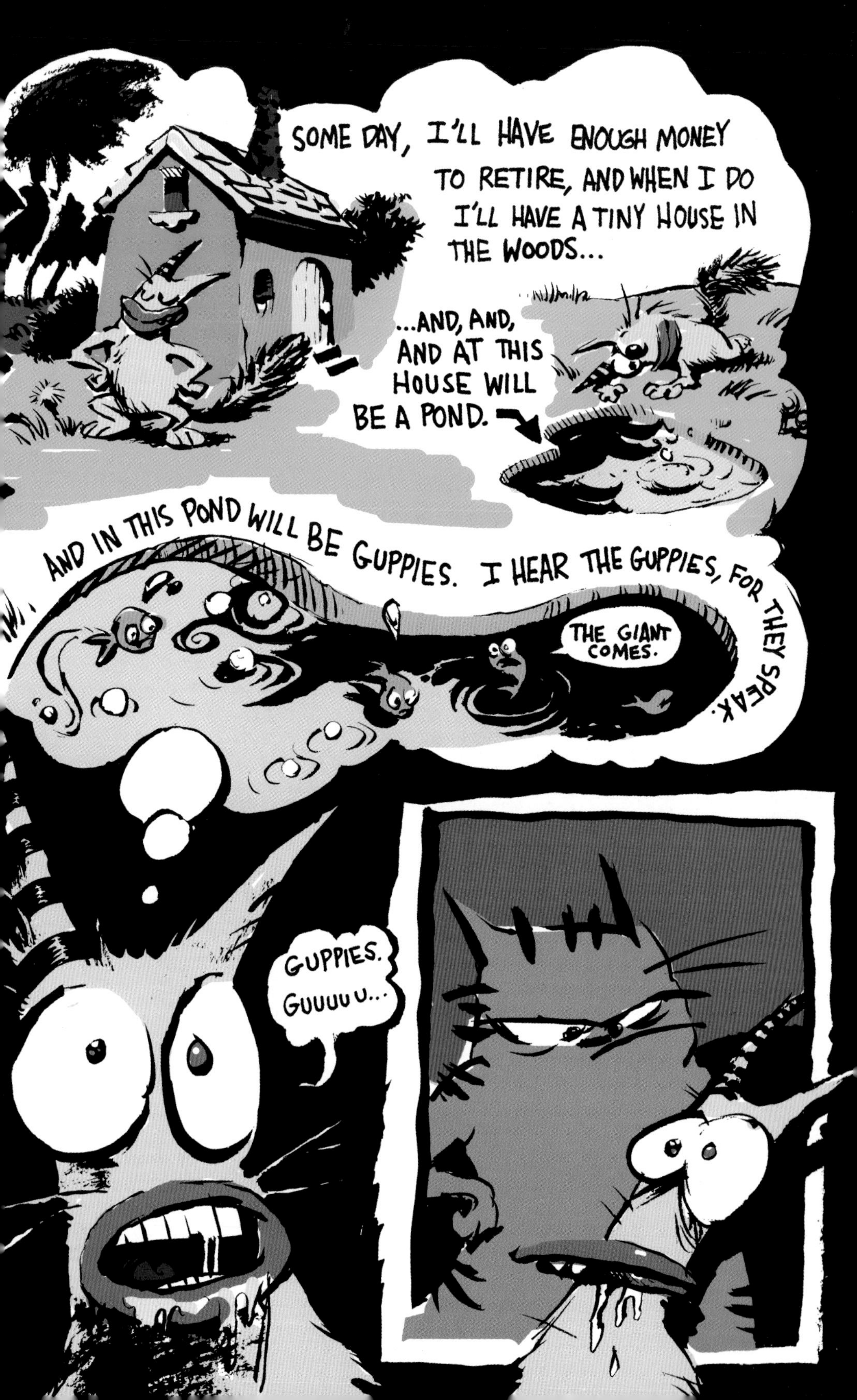
SOME DAY, I'LL HAVE ENOUGH MONEY TO RETIRE, AND WHEN I DO I'LL HAVE A TINY HOUSE IN THE WOODS...
...AND, AND, AND AT THIS HOUSE WILL BE A POND.
AND IN THIS POND WILL BE GUPPIES. I HEAR THE GUPPIES, FOR THEY SPEAK.
THE GIANT COMES.
GUPPIES. GUUUUU...

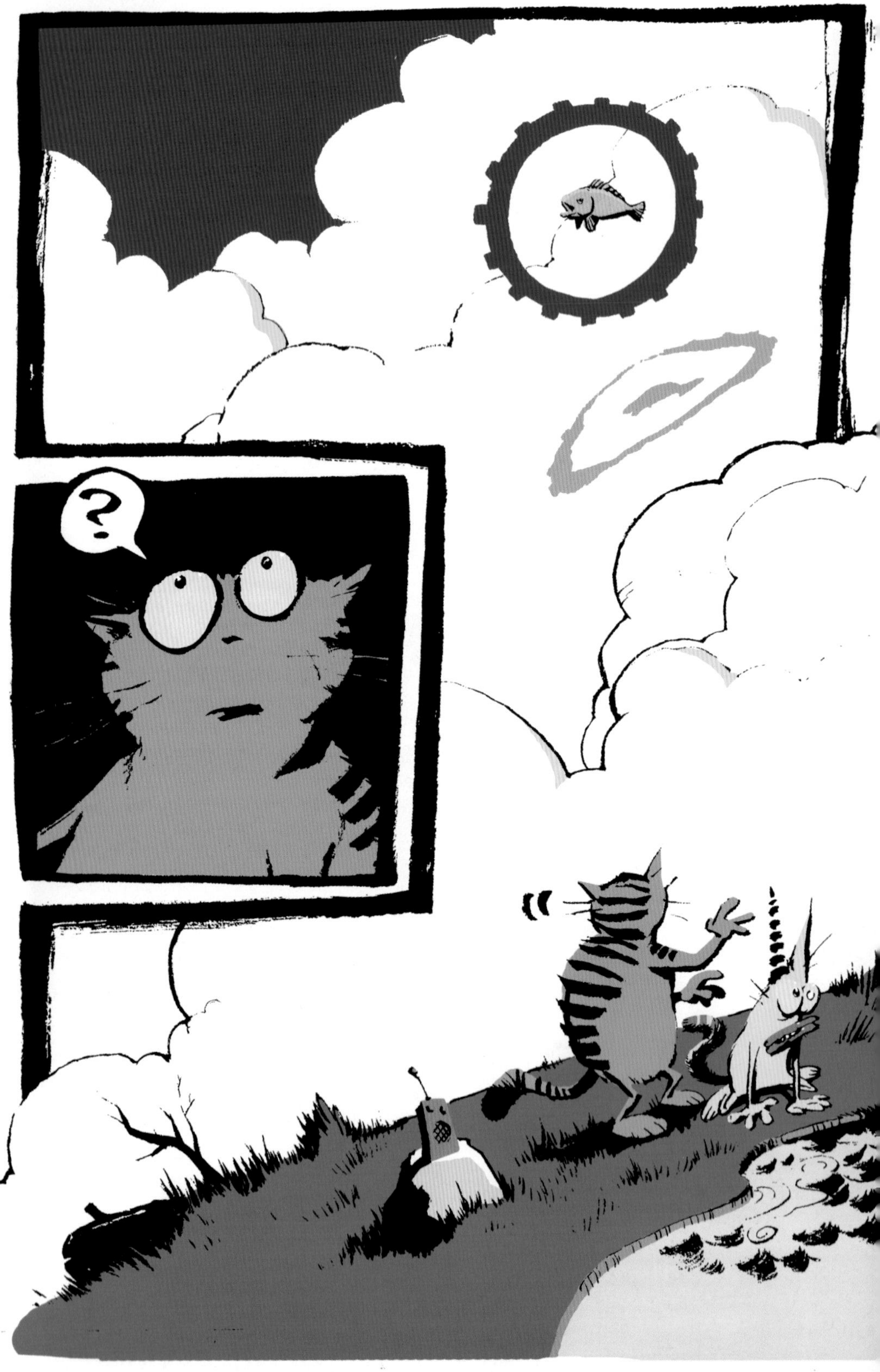
?

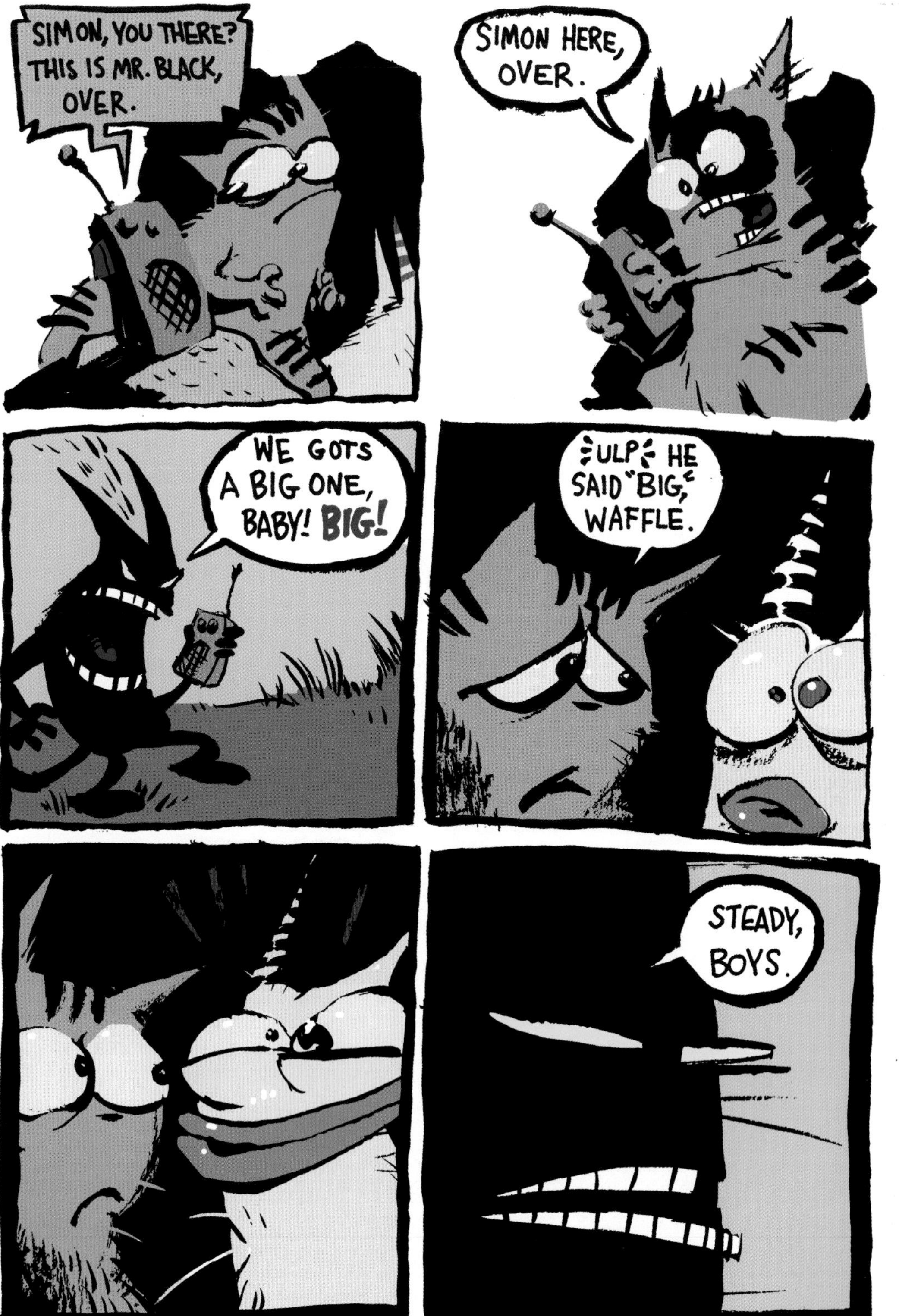
SIMON, YOU THERE? THIS IS MR. BLACK, OVER.
SIMON HERE, OVER.
WE GOTS A BIG ONE, BABY! BIG!
ULP HE SAID "BIG," WAFFLE.
STEADY, BOYS.

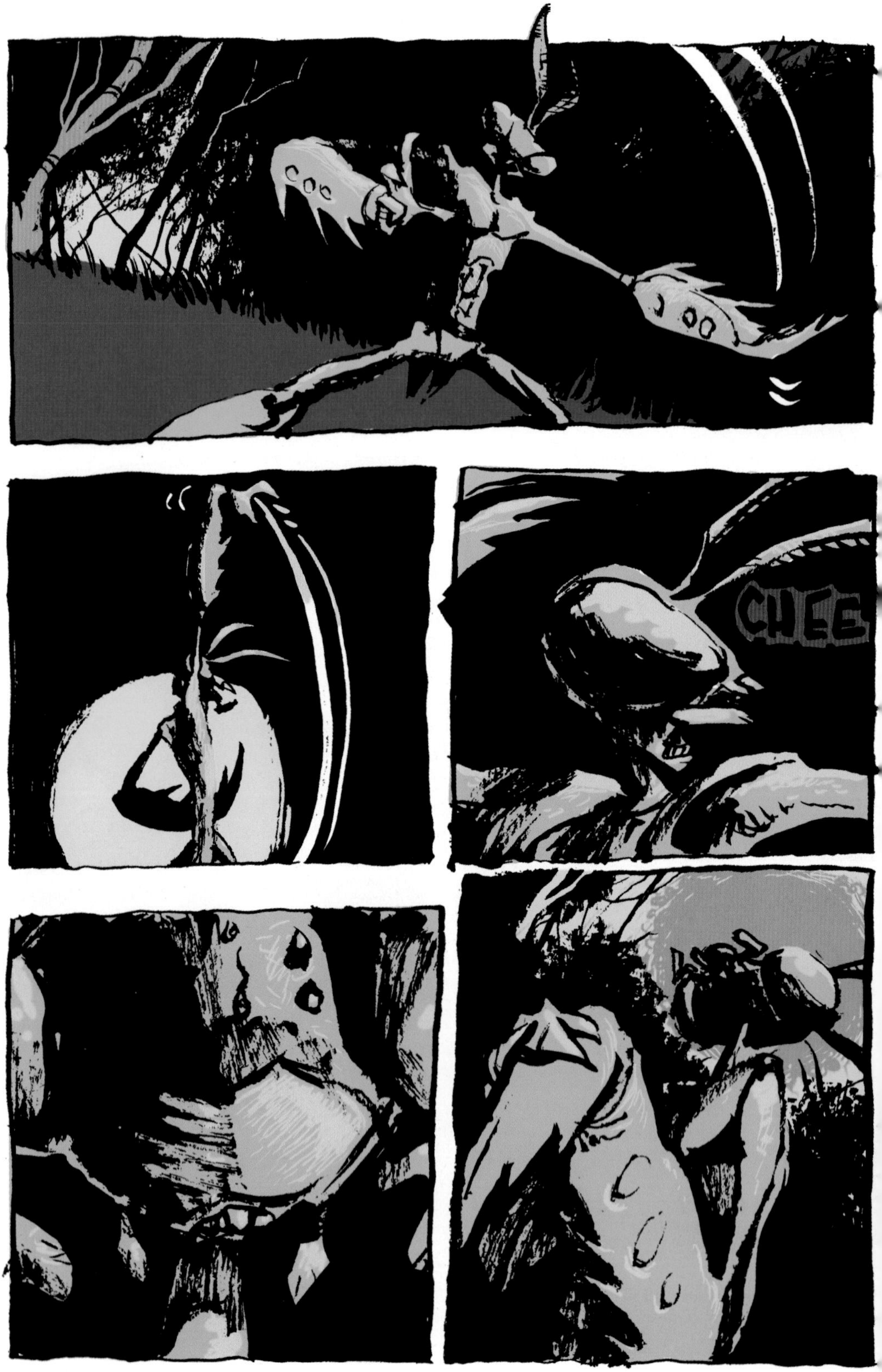
CHEE

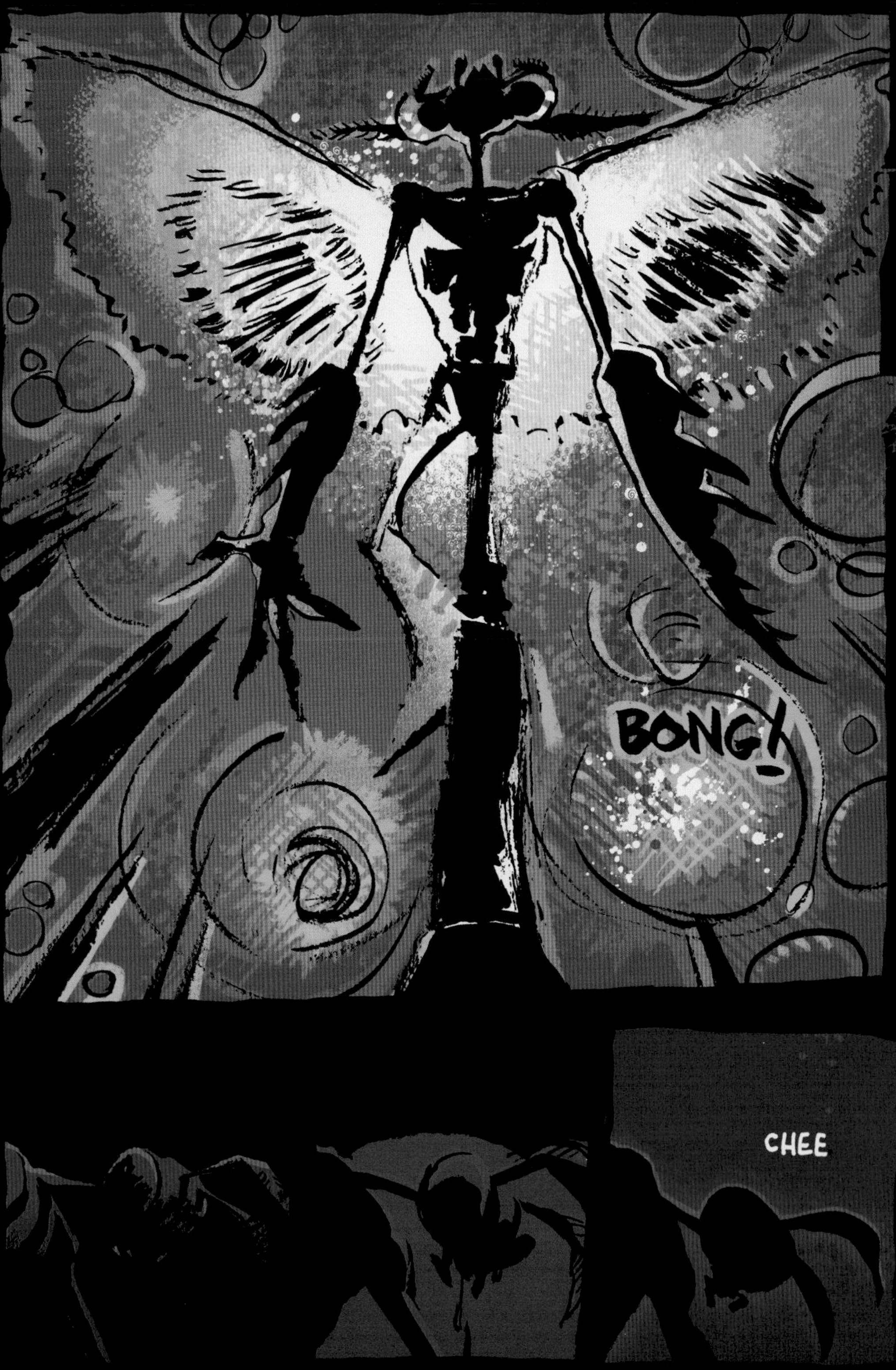
BONG!
CHEE

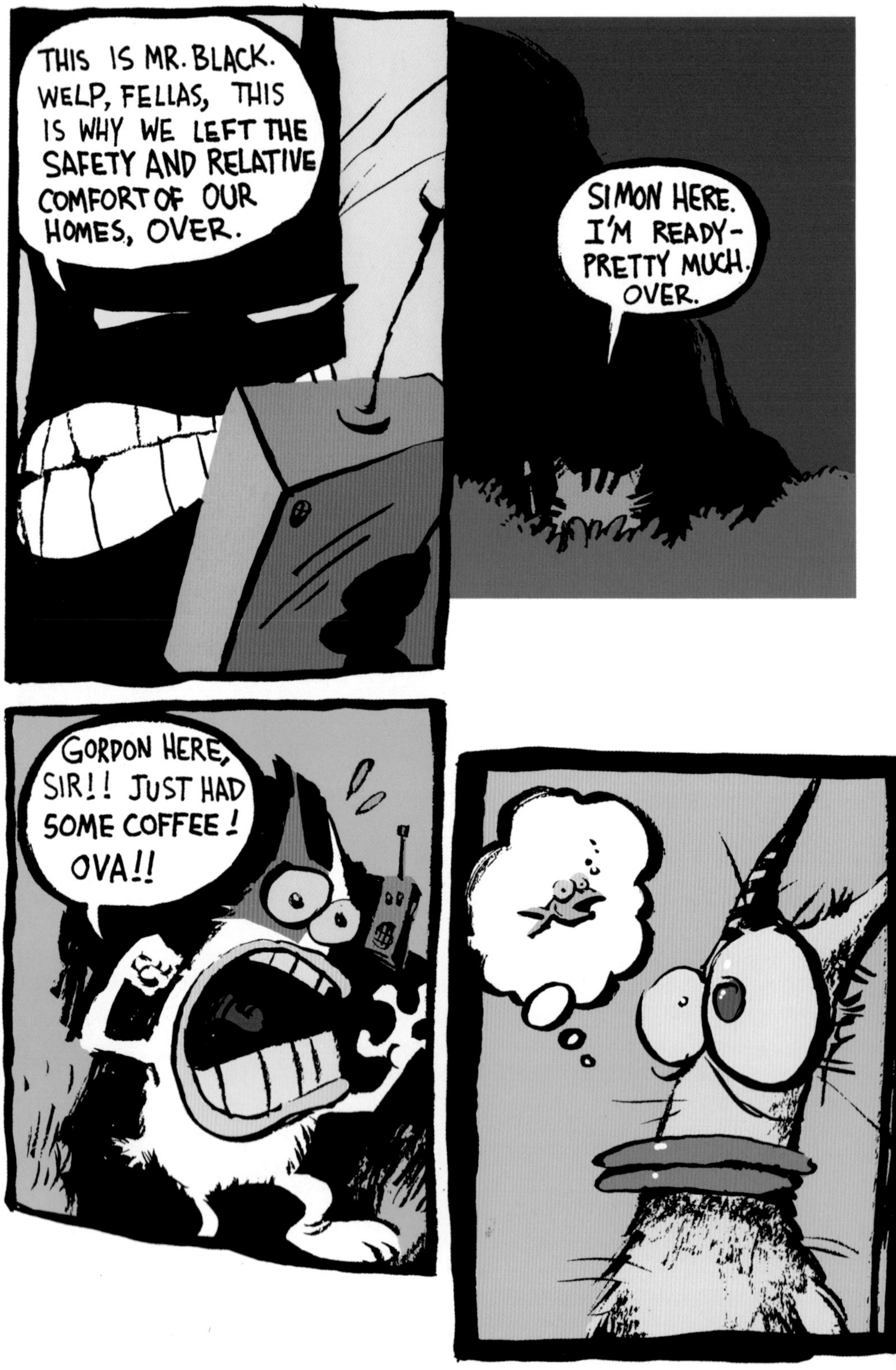
THIS IS MR. BLACK. WELP, FELLAS, THIS IS WHY WE LEFT THE SAFETY AND RELATIVE COMFORT OF OUR HOMES, OVER.
SIMON HERE. I'M READY- PRETTY MUCH. OVER.
GORDON HERE, SIR!! JUST HAD SOME COFFEE! OVA!!

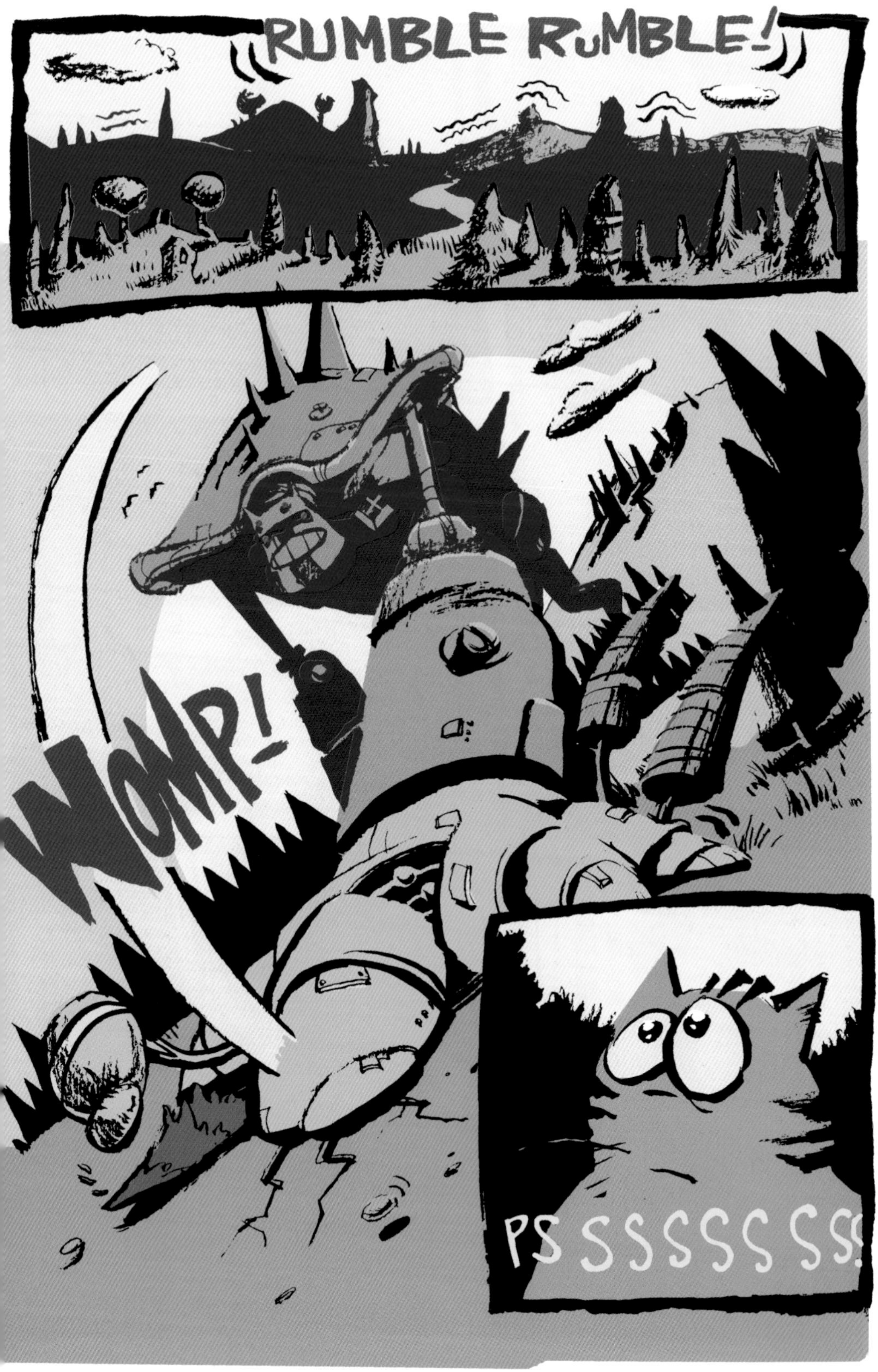
RUMBLE RUMBLE!
WOMP!
PSSSSSSSS!

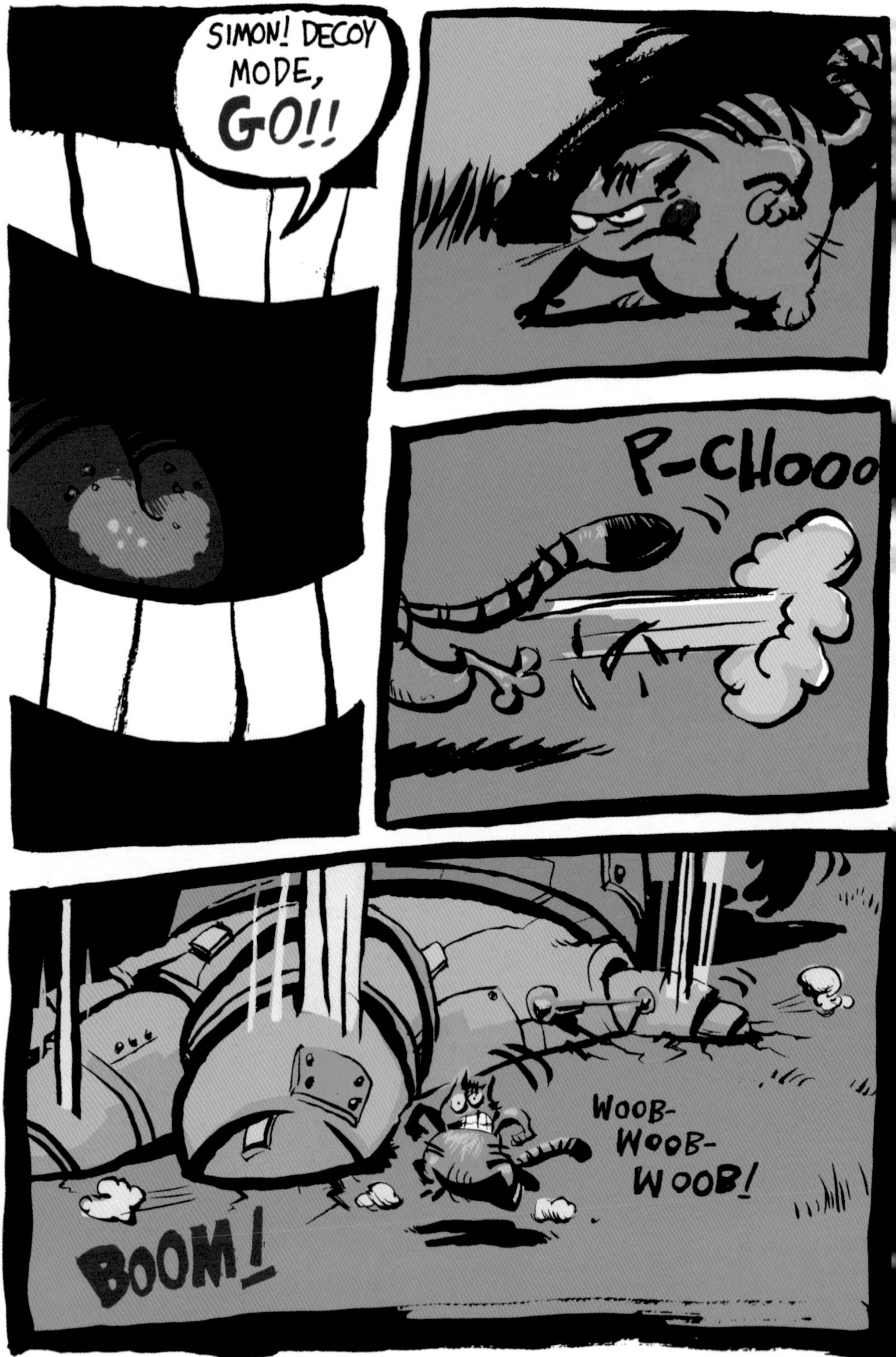
SIMON! DECOY MODE, GO!!
P-CHOOO
BOOM!
WOOB-WOOB-WOOB!

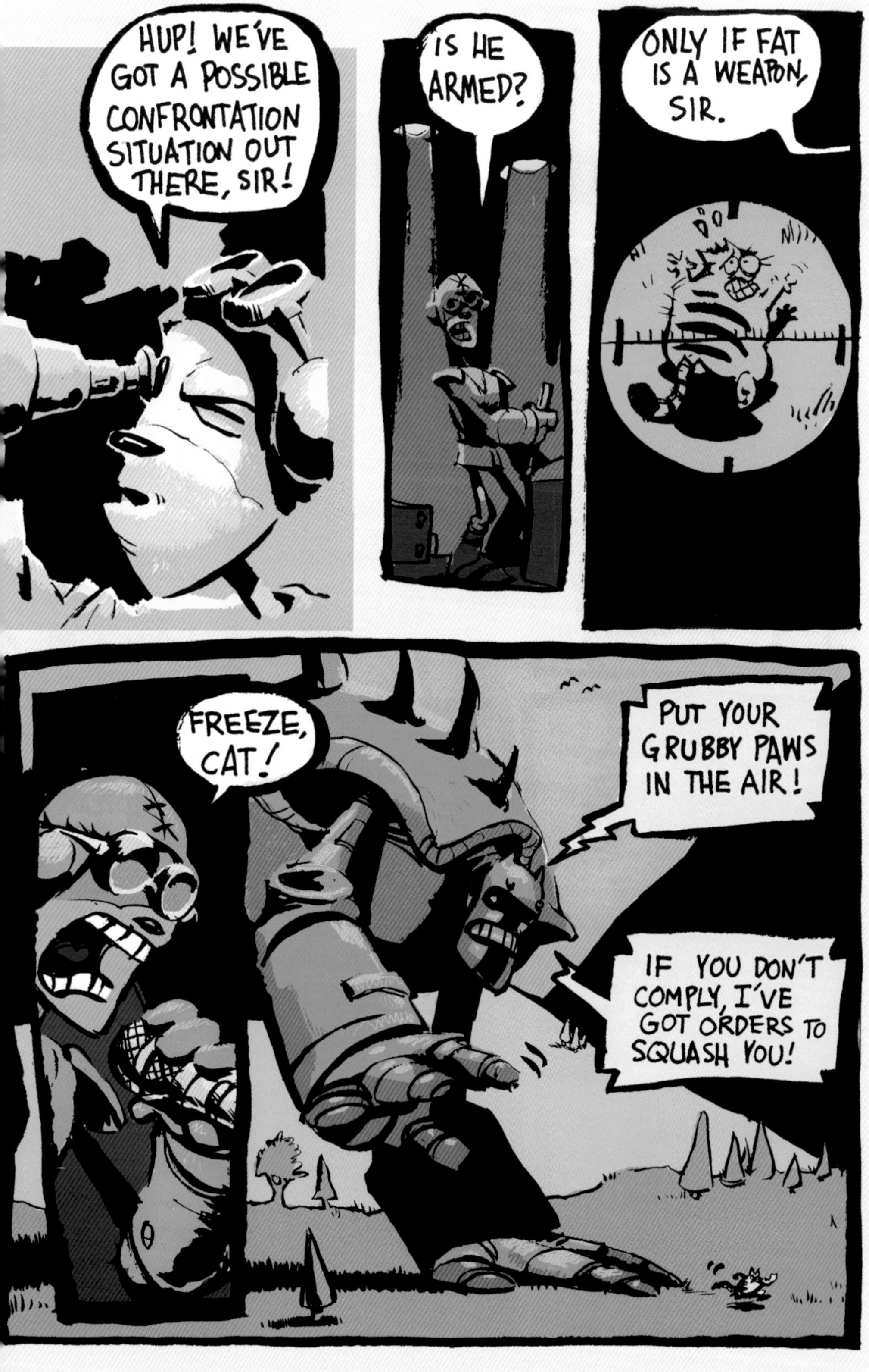
HUP! WE'VE GOT A POSSIBLE CONFRONTATION SITUATION OUT THERE, SIR!
IS HE ARMED?
ONLY IF FAT IS A WEAPON, SIR.
FREEZE, CAT!
PUT YOUR GRUBBY PAWS IN THE AIR!
IF YOU DON'T COMPLY, I'VE GOT ORDERS TO SQUASH YOU!

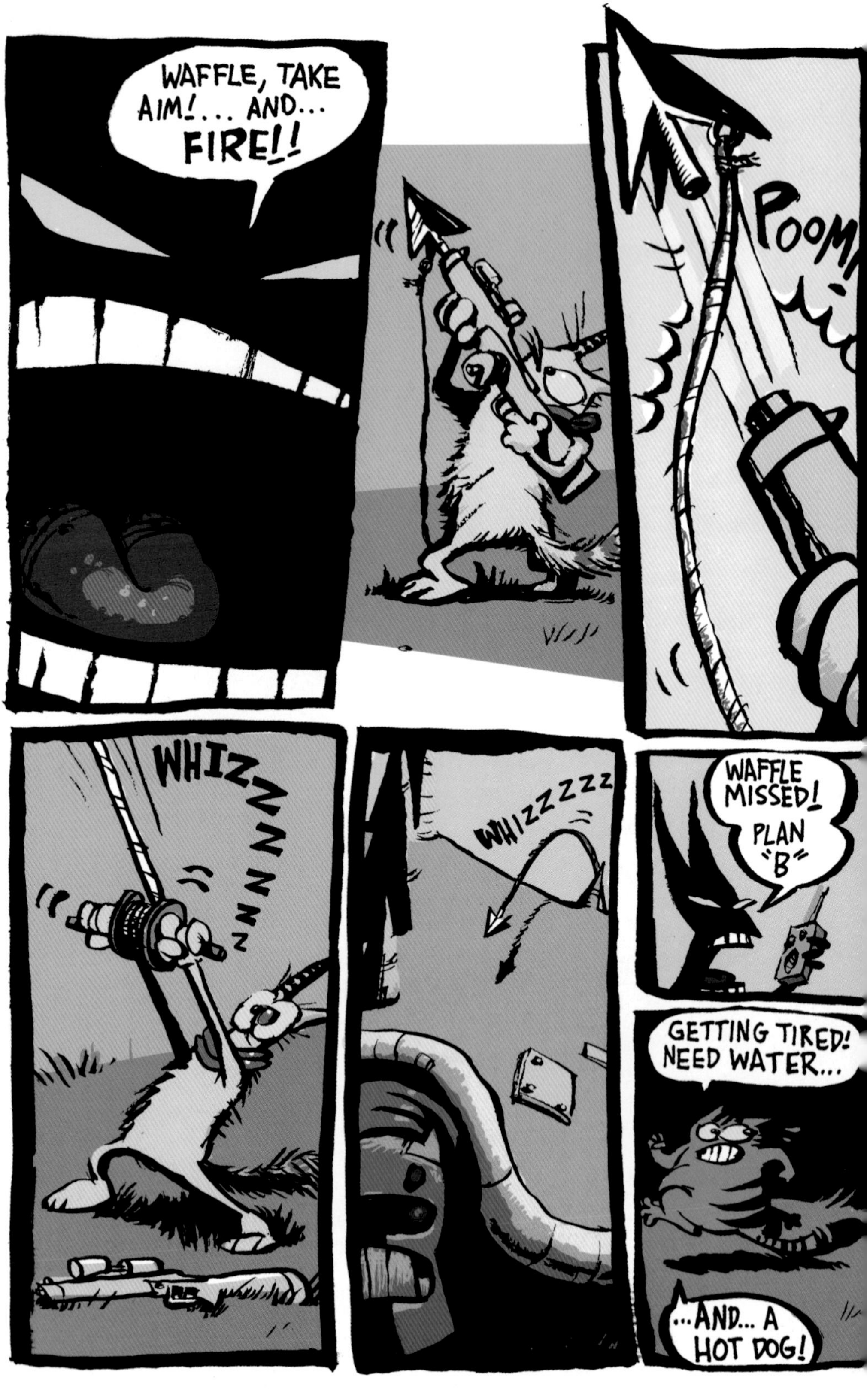
WAFFLE, TAKE AIM!... AND... FIRE!!
POOM!
WHIZZZZZZ
WHIZZZZZ
WAFFLE MISSED! PLAN "B"
GETTING TIRED! NEED WATER...
...AND... A HOT DOG!

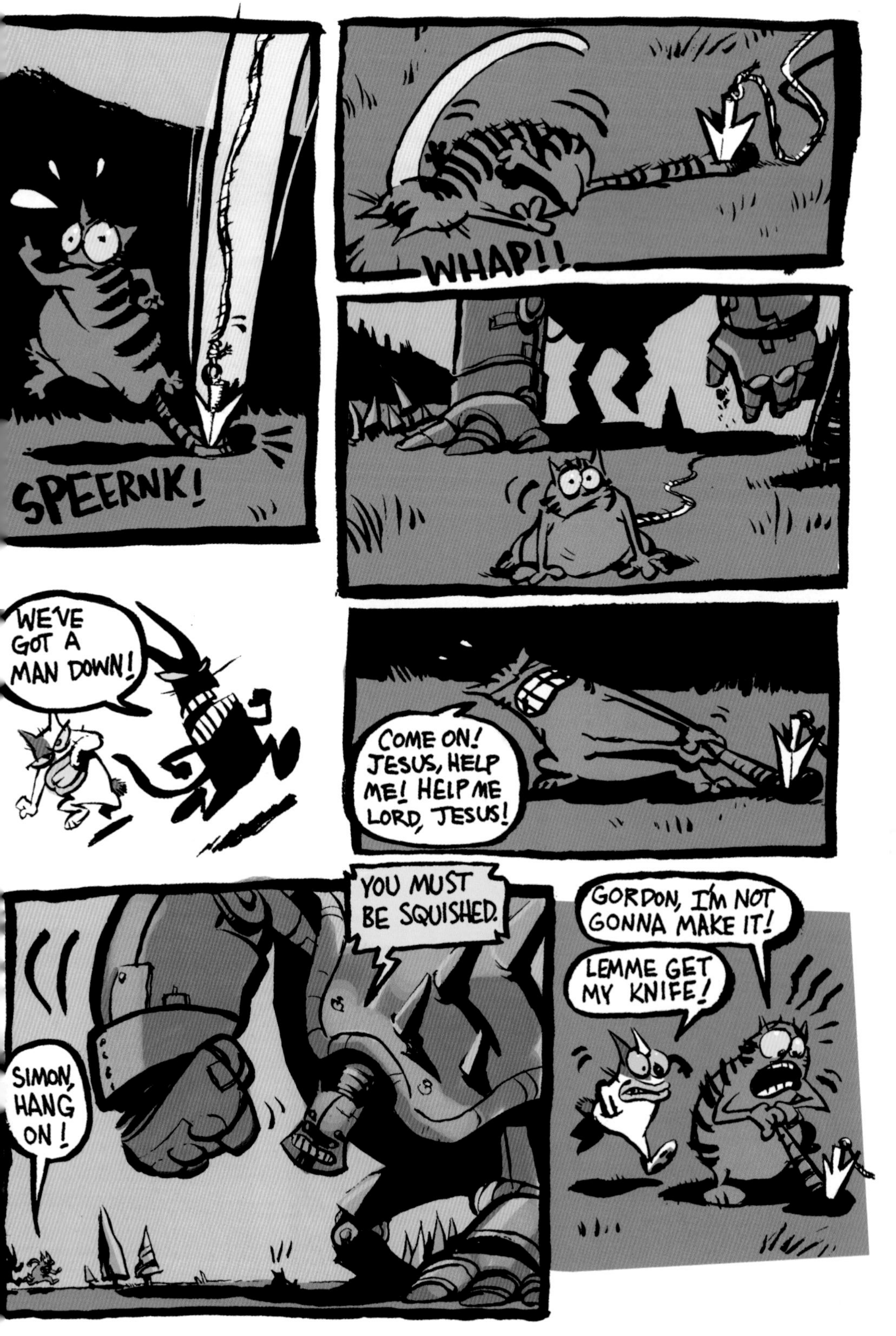
SPEERNK!
WHAP!!
WE'VE GOT A MAN DOWN!
COME ON! JESUS, HELP ME! HELP ME LORD, JESUS!
YOU MUST BE SQUISHED.
SIMON, HANG ON!
GORDON, I'M NOT GONNA MAKE IT!
LEMME GET MY KNIFE!

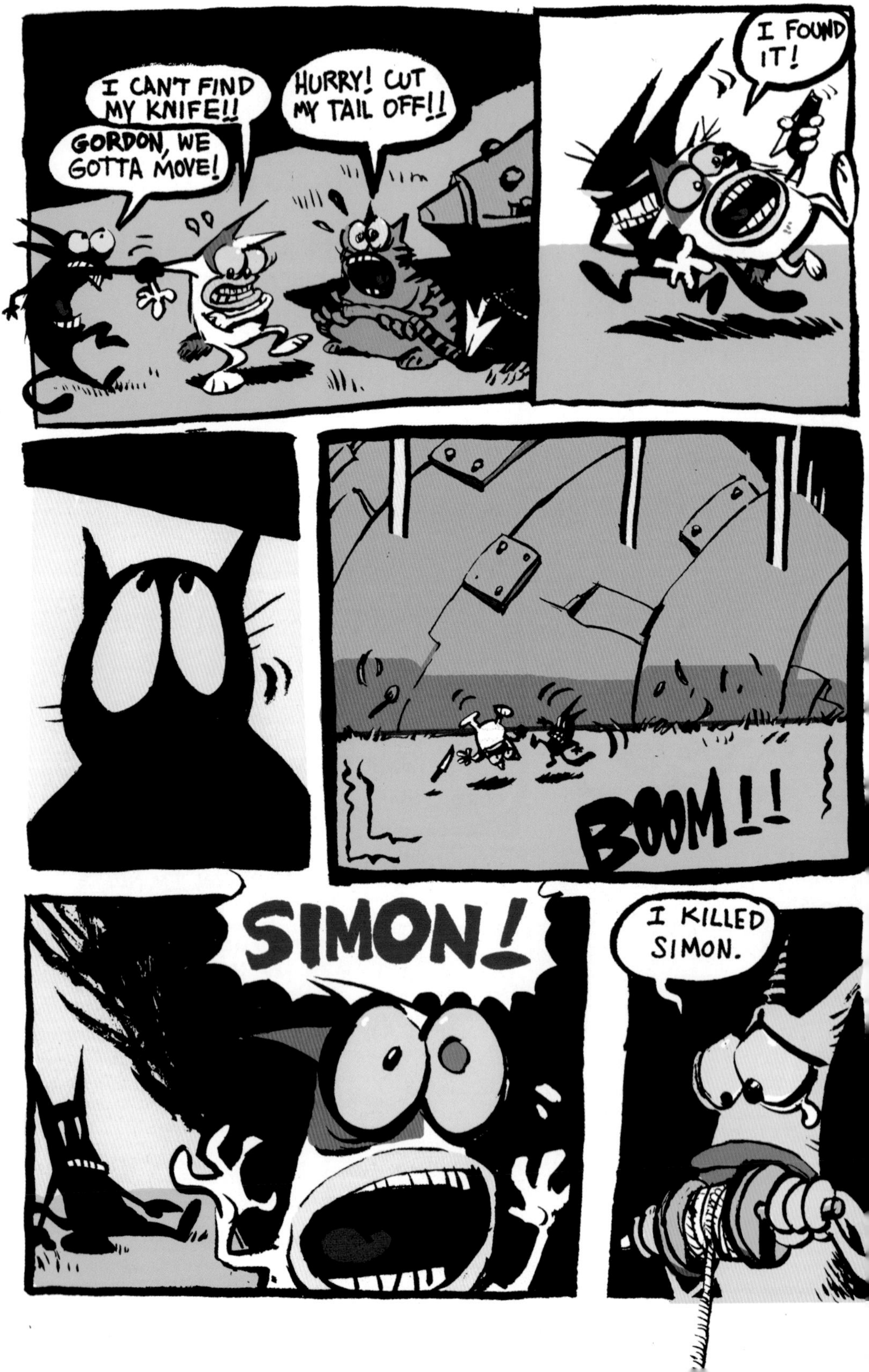

I CAN'T FIND MY KNIFE!!
GORDON, WE GOTTA MOVE!
HURRY! CUT MY TAIL OFF!!
I FOUND IT!
BOOM!!
SIMON!
I KILLED SIMON.

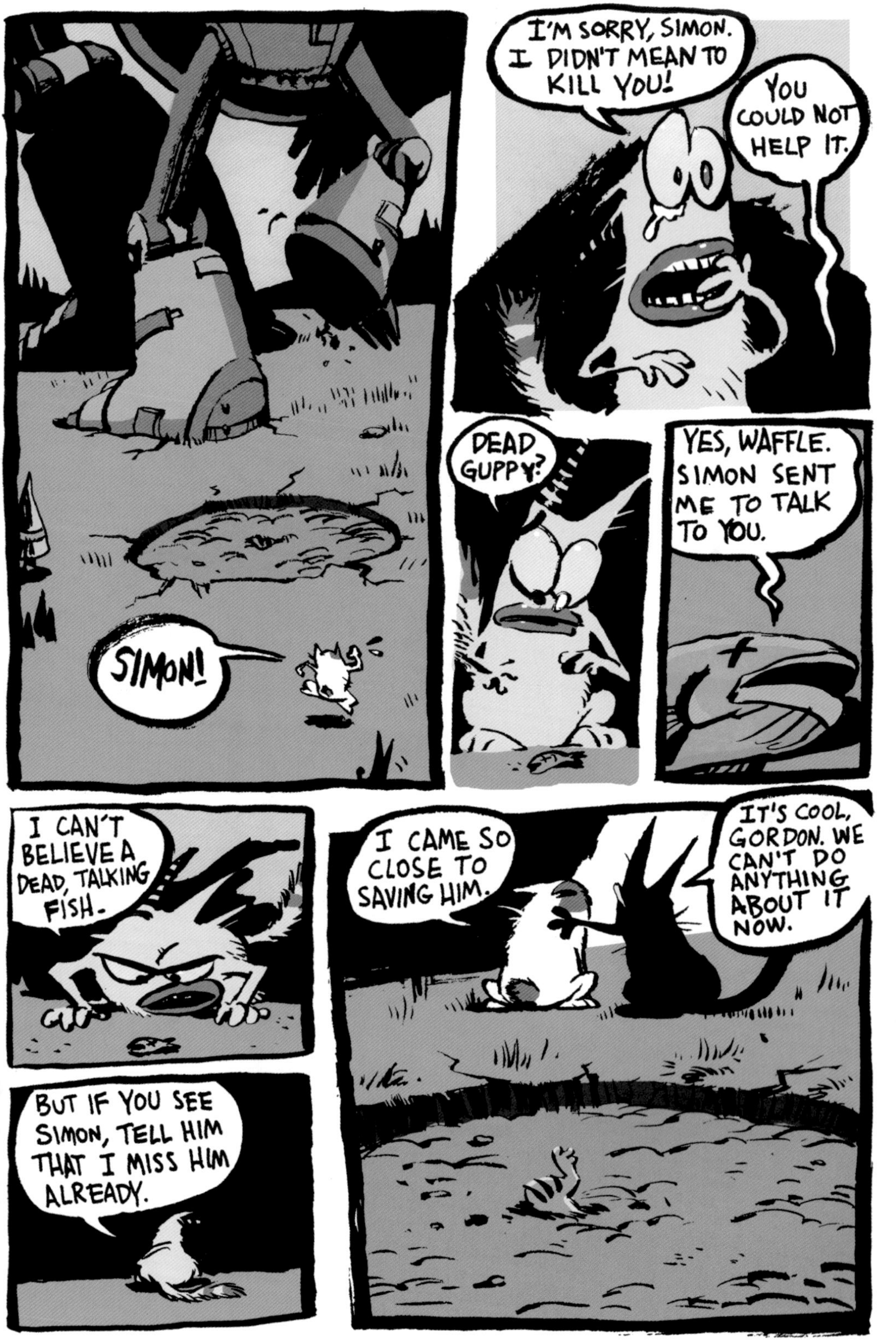
SIMON!
I'M SORRY, SIMON. I DIDN'T MEAN TO KILL YOU!
YOU COULD NOT HELP IT.
DEAD GUPPY?
YES, WAFFLE. SIMON SENT ME TO TALK TO YOU.
I CAN'T BELIEVE A DEAD, TALKING FISH.
BUT IF YOU SEE SIMON, TELL HIM THAT I MISS HIM ALREADY.
I CAME SO CLOSE TO SAVING HIM.
IT'S COOL, GORDON. WE CAN'T DO ANYTHING ABOUT IT NOW.

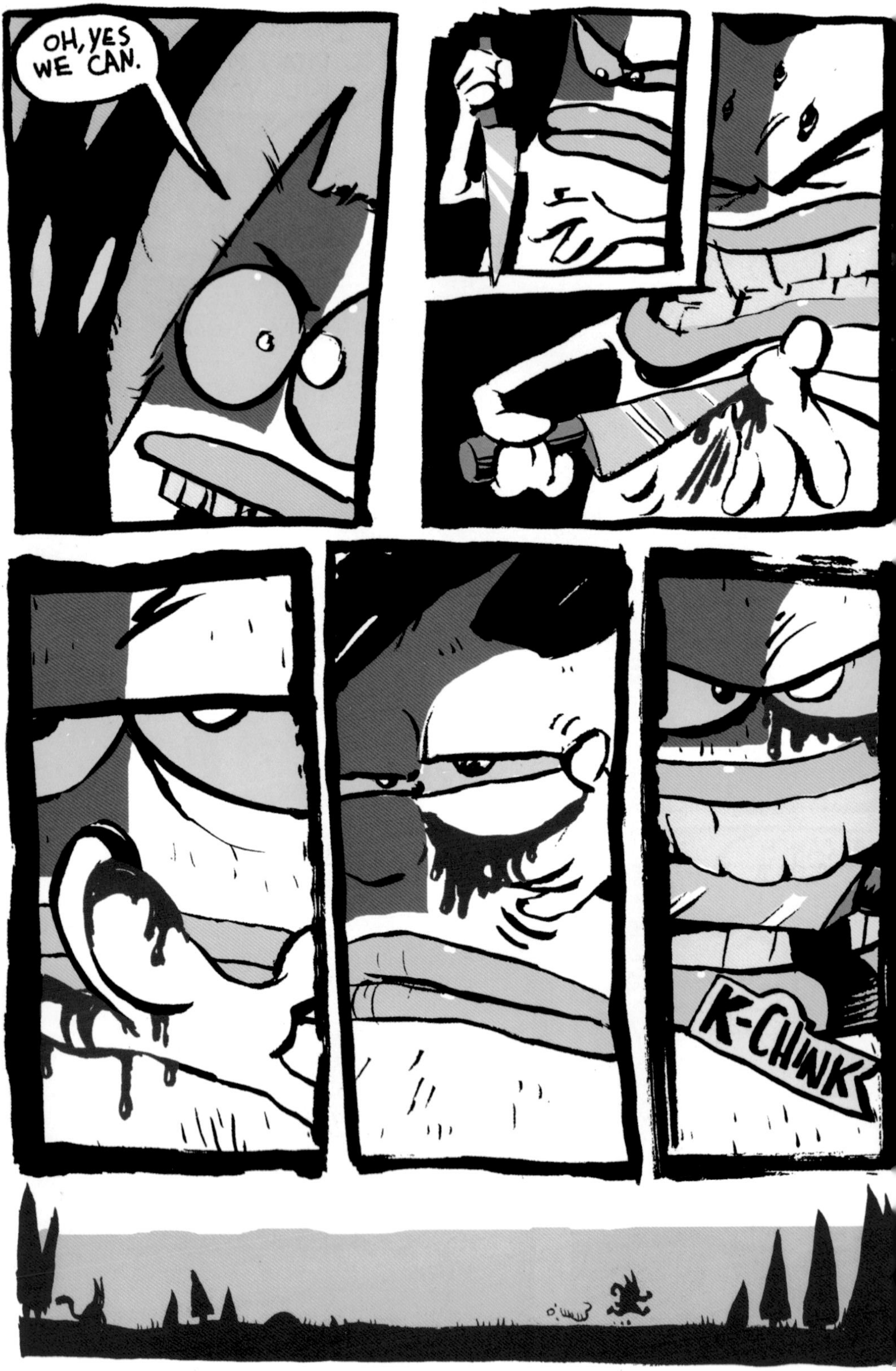
OH, YES WE CAN.
K-CHINK

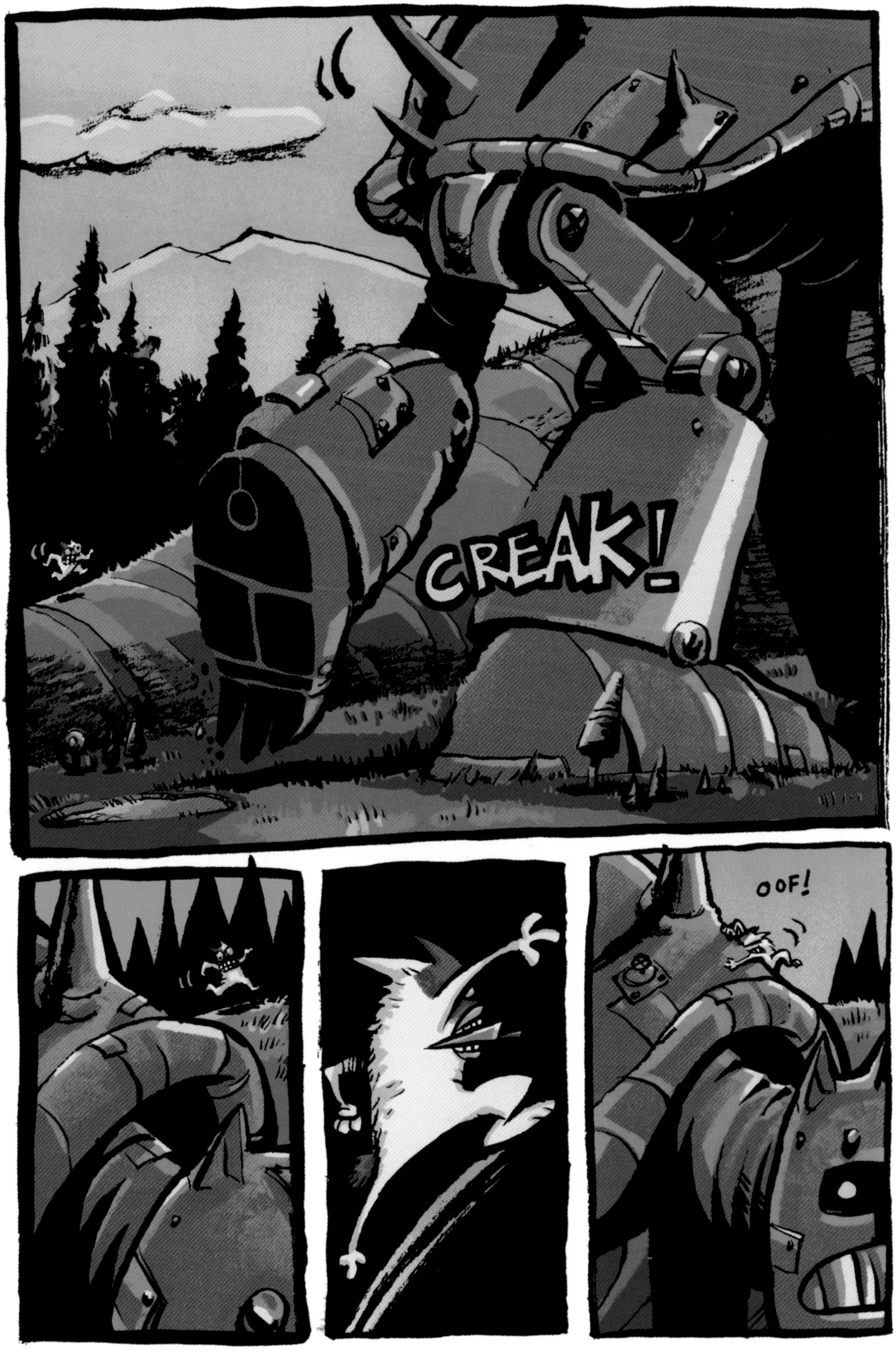
CREAK!
OOF!

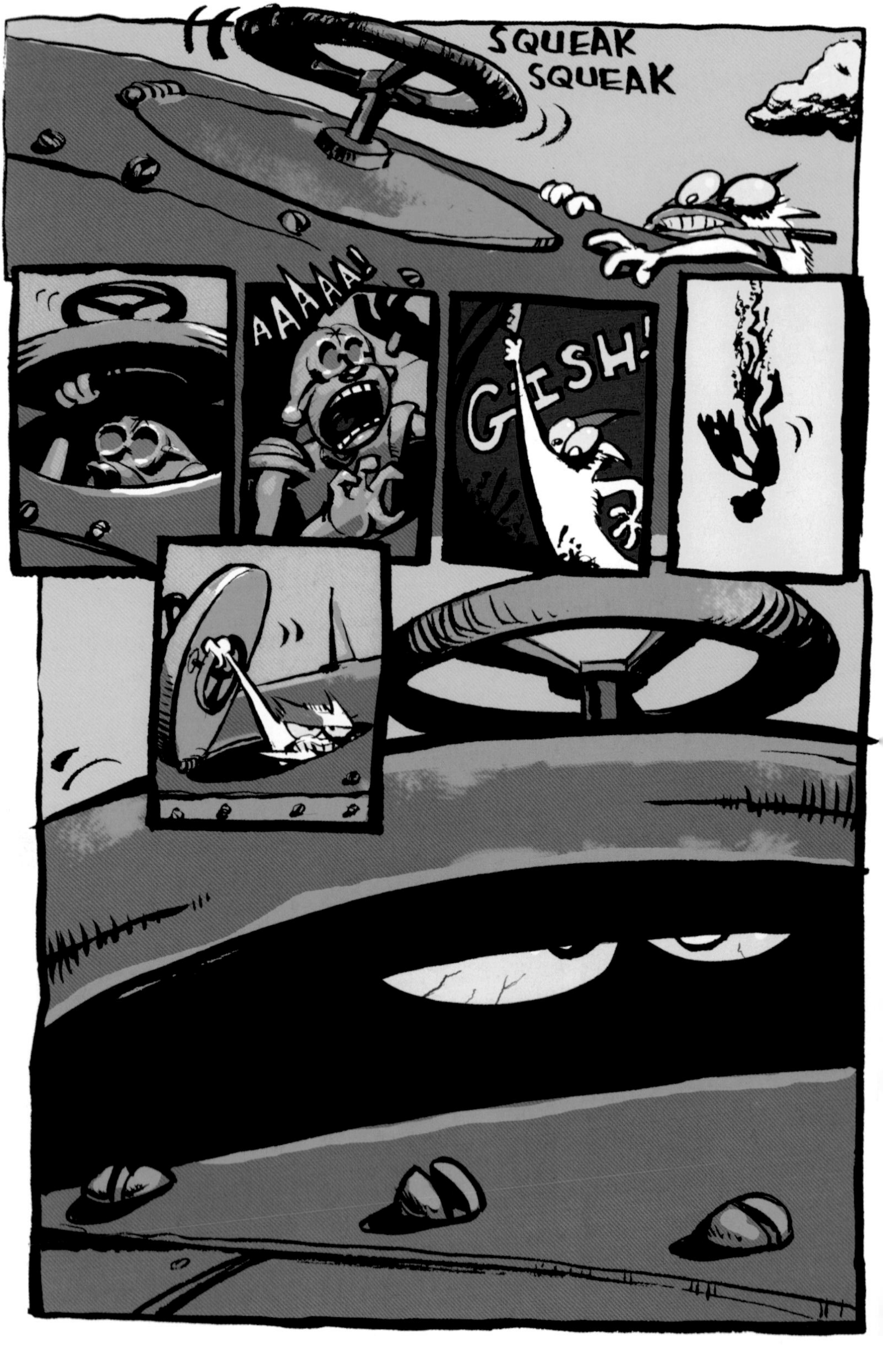
SQUEAK
SQUEAK
AAAAA!
GISH!

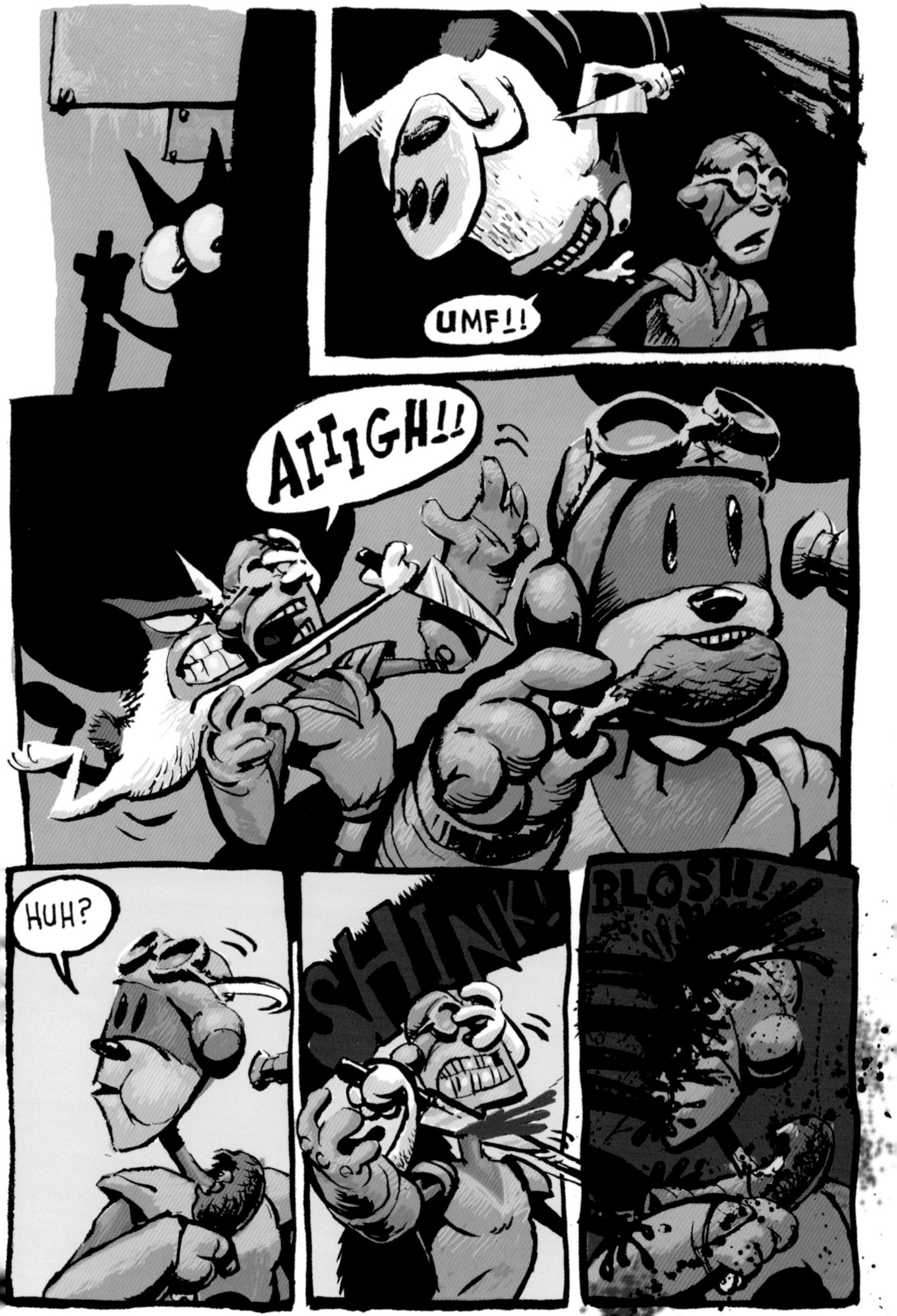
UMF!!
AIIIGH!!
HUH?
SHINK!
BLOSH!

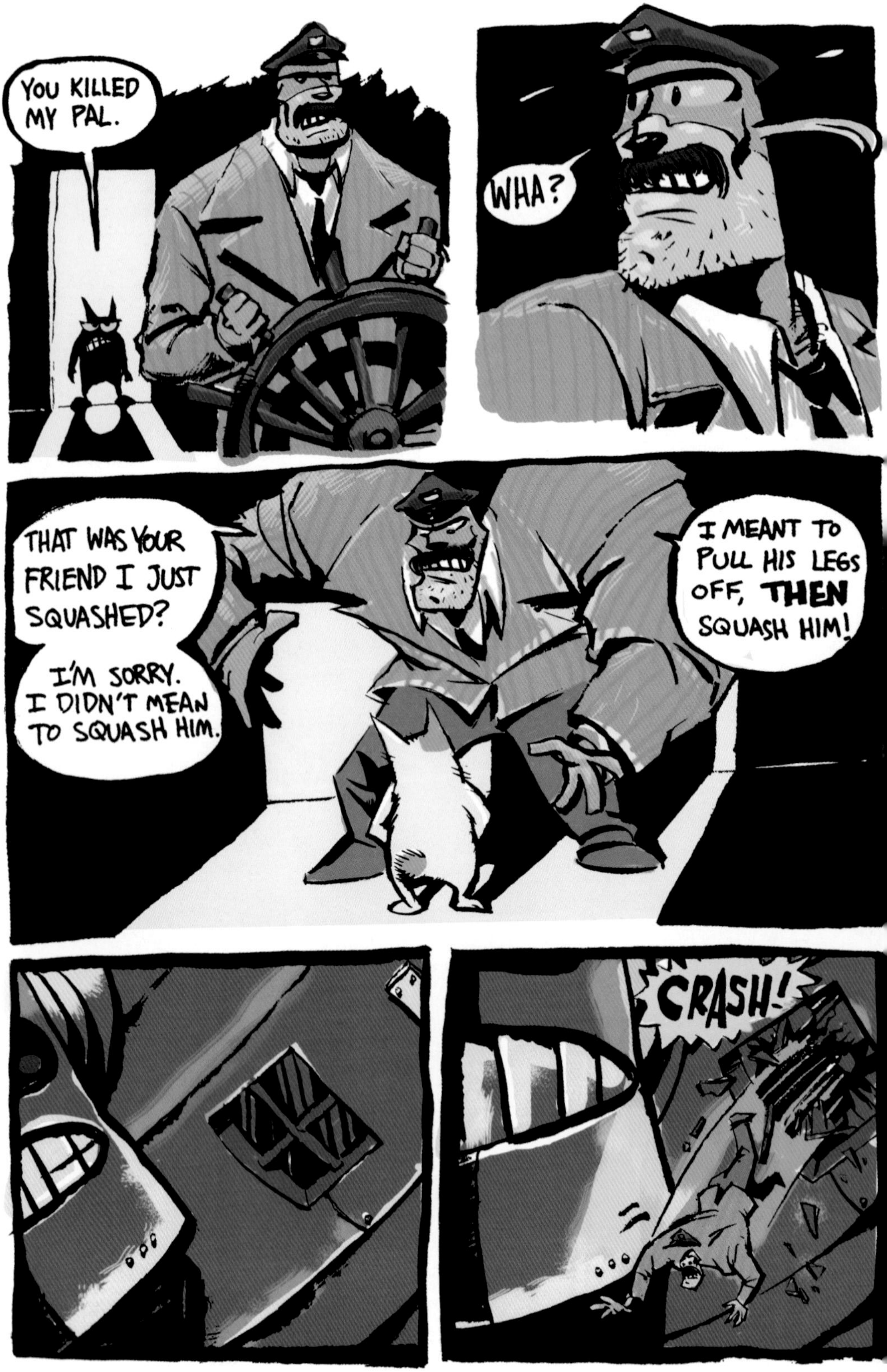
YOU KILLED MY PAL.
WHA?
THAT WAS YOUR FRIEND I JUST SQUASHED?
I'M SORRY. I DIDN'T MEAN TO SQUASH HIM.
I MEANT TO PULL HIS LEGS OFF, THEN SQUASH HIM!
CRASH!

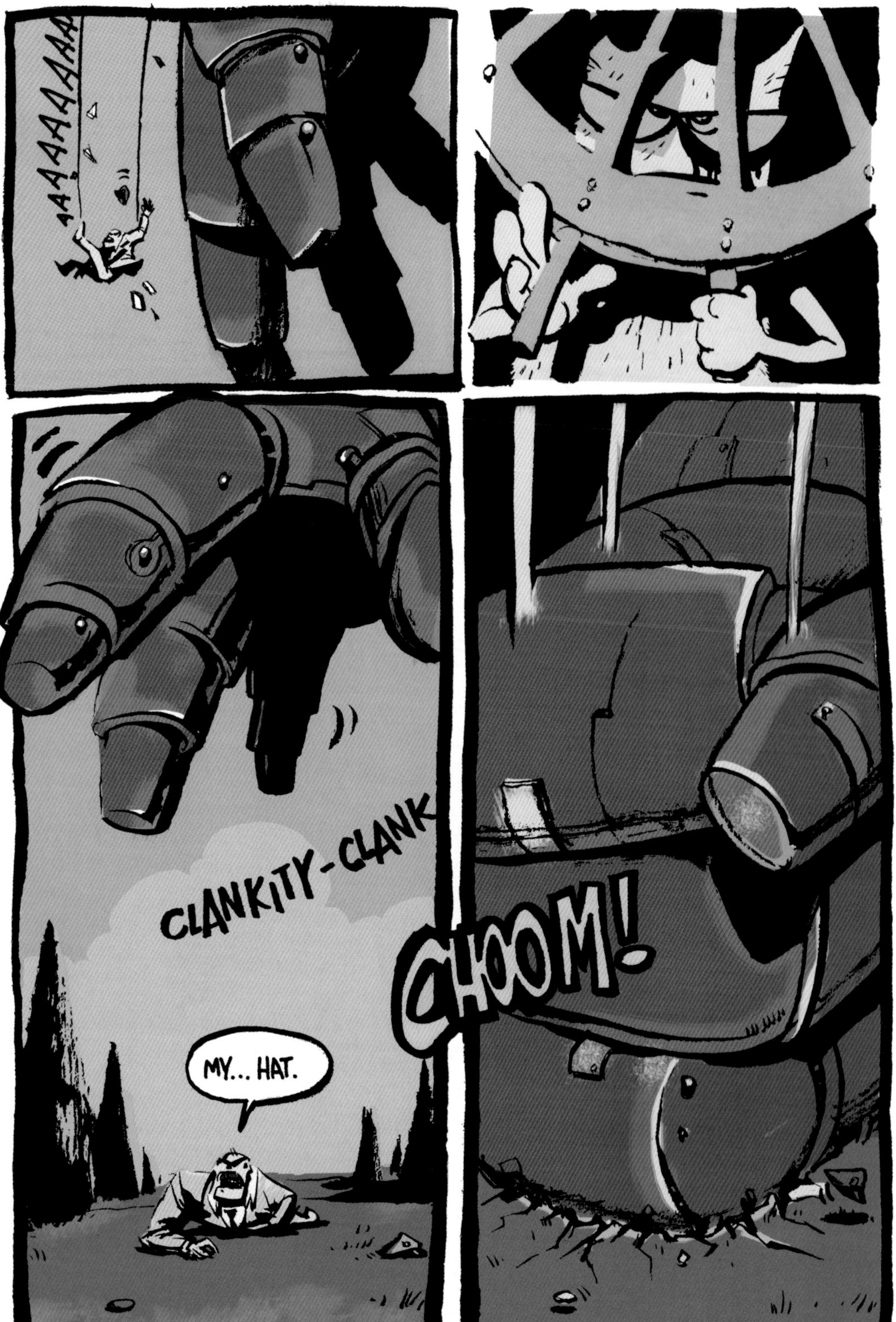
AAAAAAAAAA
CLANKITY-CLANK
MY... HAT.
CHOOM!

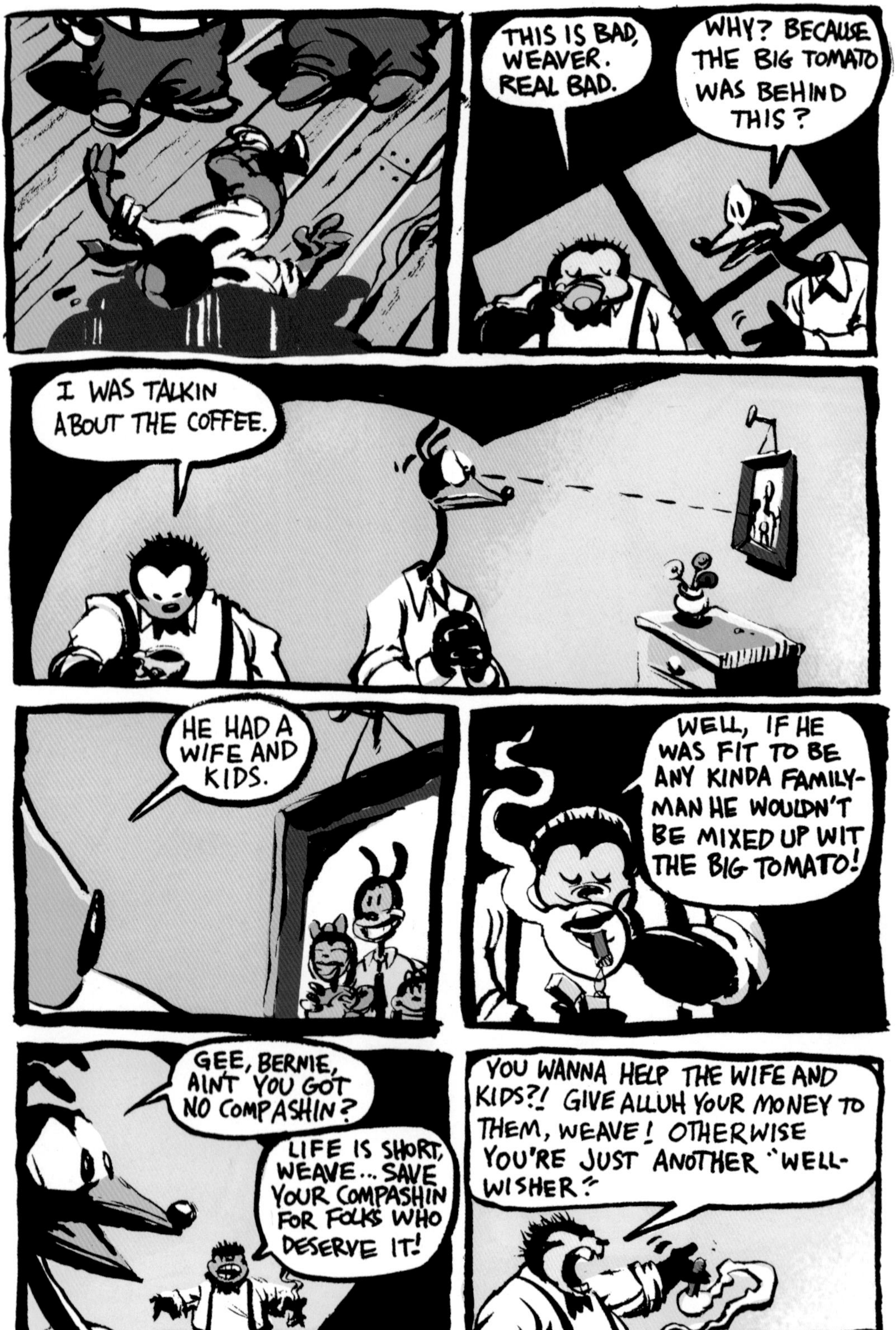
THIS IS BAD, WEAVER. REAL BAD.
WHY? BECAUSE THE BIG TOMATO WAS BEHIND THIS?
I WAS TALKIN ABOUT THE COFFEE.
HE HAD A WIFE AND KIDS.
WELL, IF HE WAS FIT TO BE ANY KINDA FAMILY-MAN HE WOULDN'T BE MIXED UP WIT THE BIG TOMATO!
GEE, BERNIE, AIN'T YOU GOT NO COMPASHIN?
LIFE IS SHORT, WEAVE... SAVE YOUR COMPASHIN FOR FOLKS WHO DESERVE IT!
YOU WANNA HELP THE WIFE AND KIDS?! GIVE ALLUH YOUR MONEY TO THEM, WEAVE! OTHERWISE YOU'RE JUST ANOTHER "WELL-WISHER."

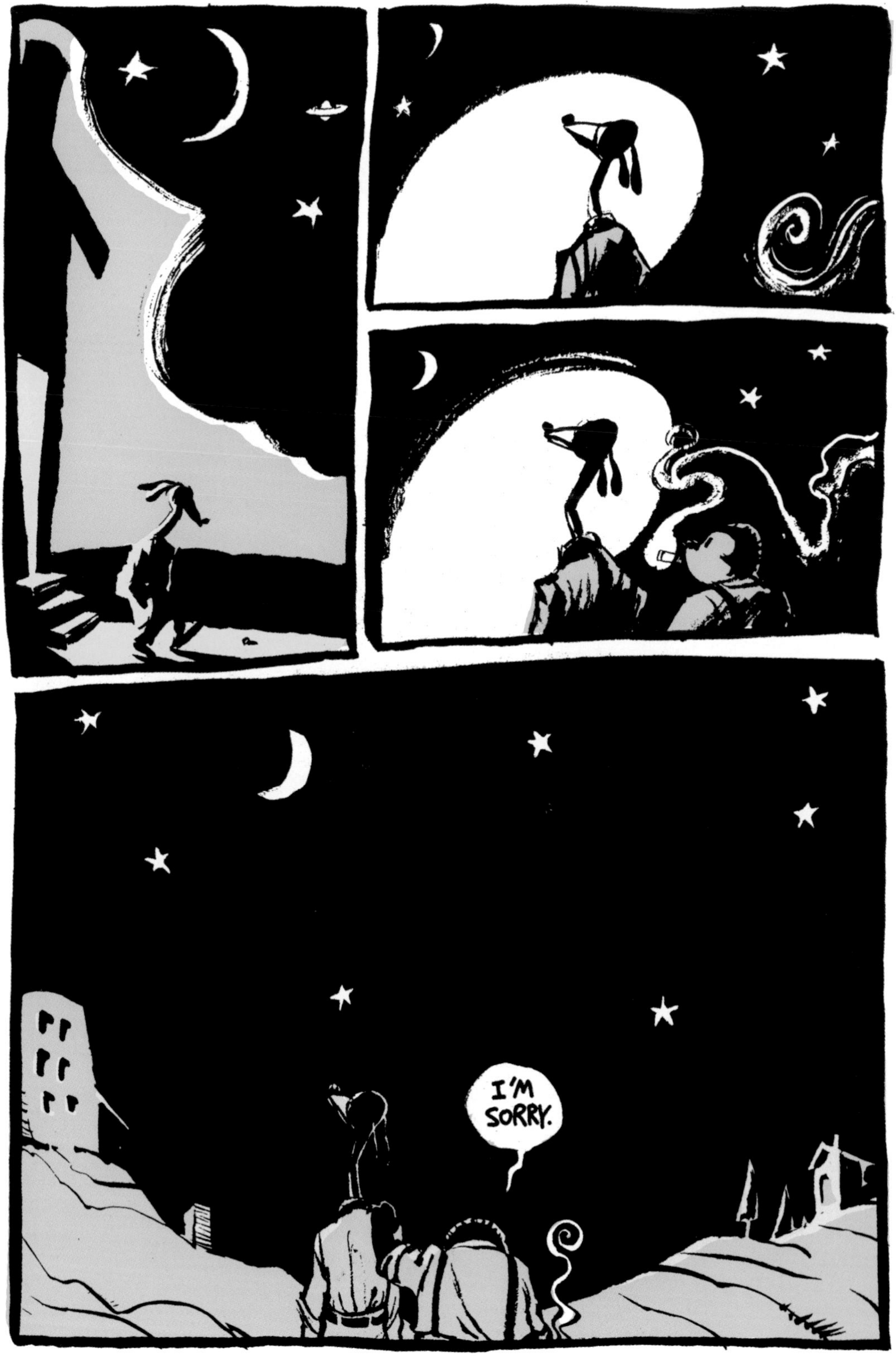
I'M SORRY.

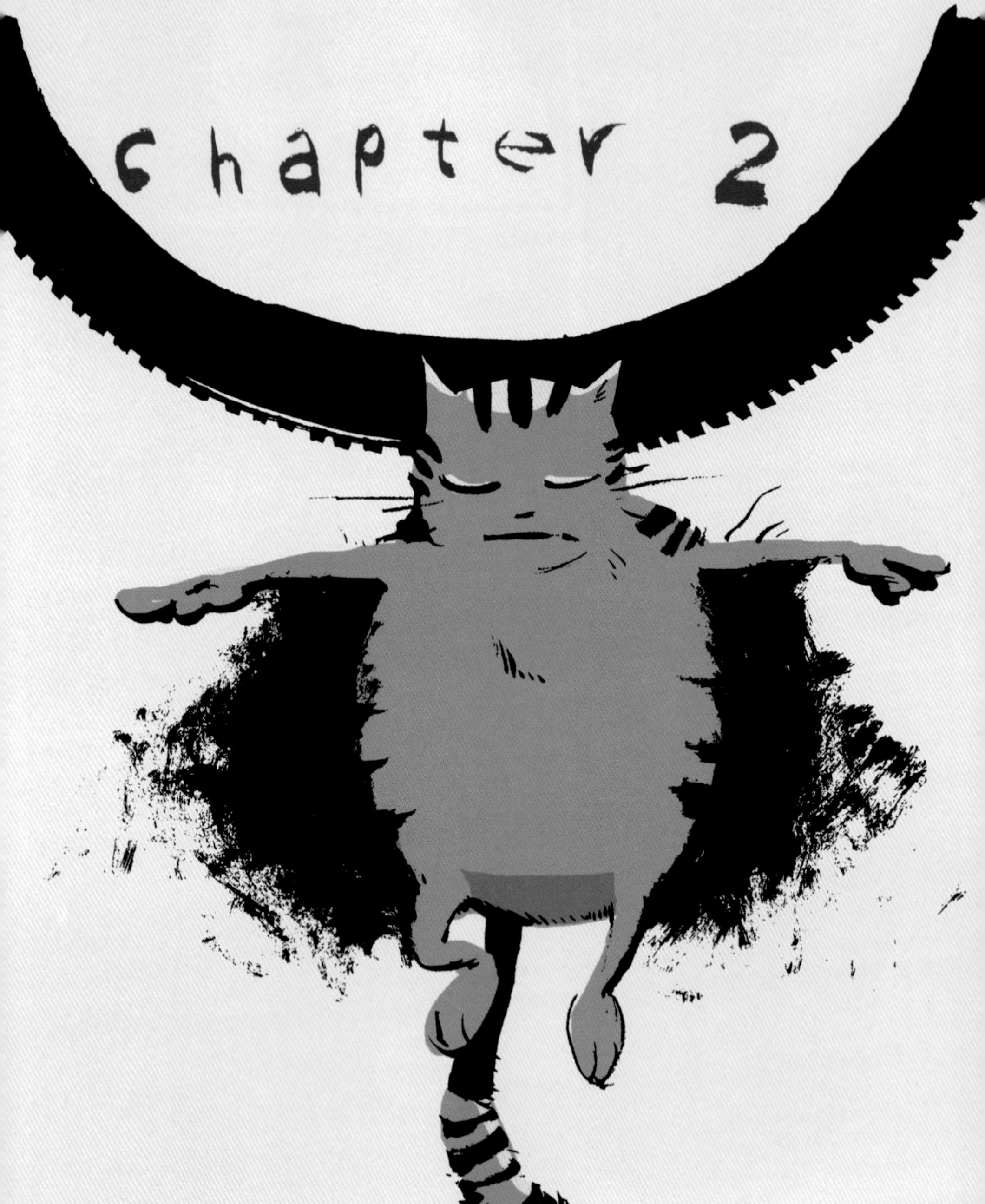
chapter 2

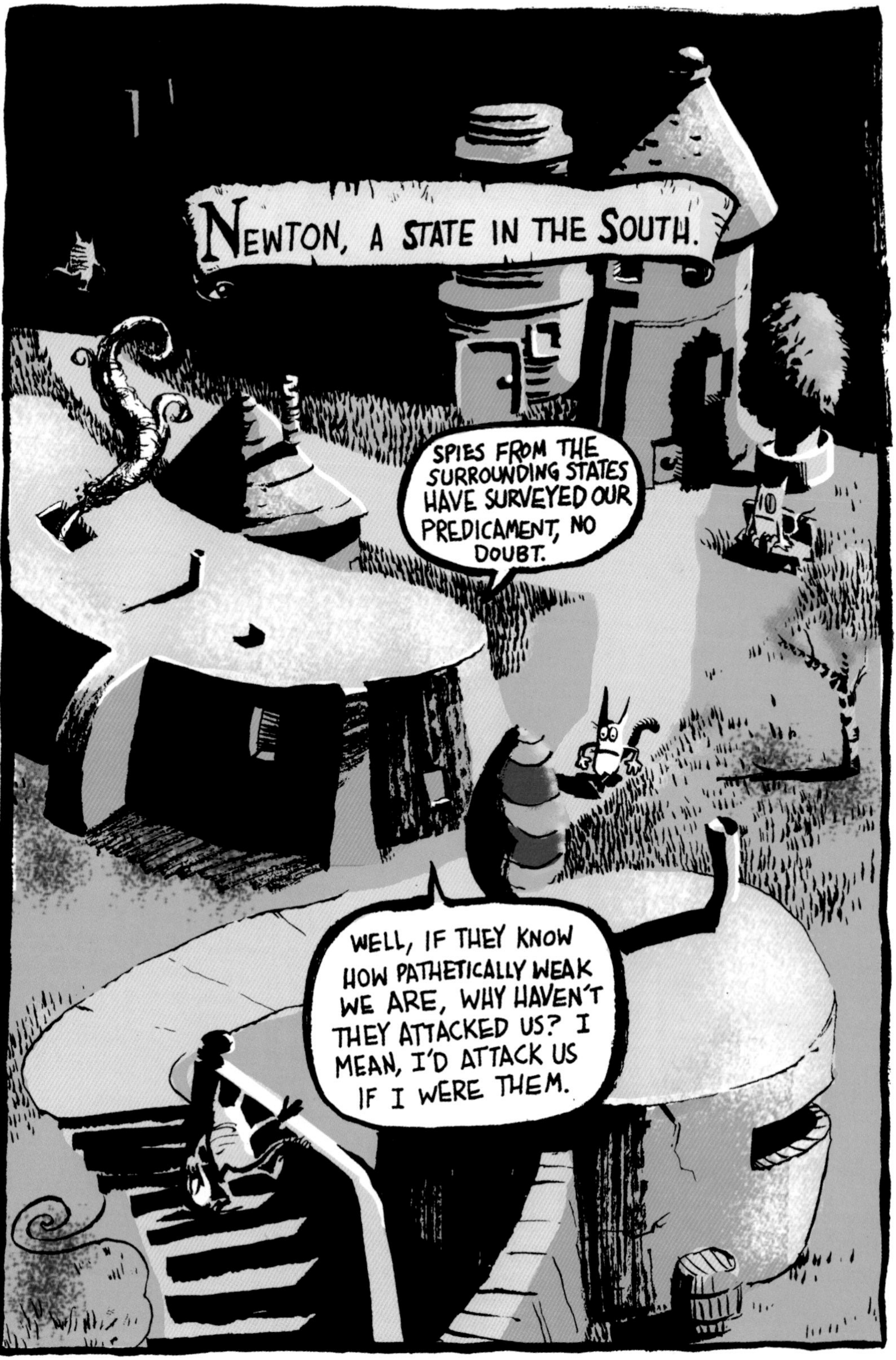
NEWTON, A STATE IN THE SOUTH.
SPIES FROM THE SURROUNDING STATES HAVE SURVEYED OUR PREDICAMENT, NO DOUBT.
WELL, IF THEY KNOW HOW PATHETICALLY WEAK WE ARE, WHY HAVEN'T THEY ATTACKED US? I MEAN, I'D ATTACK US IF I WERE THEM.

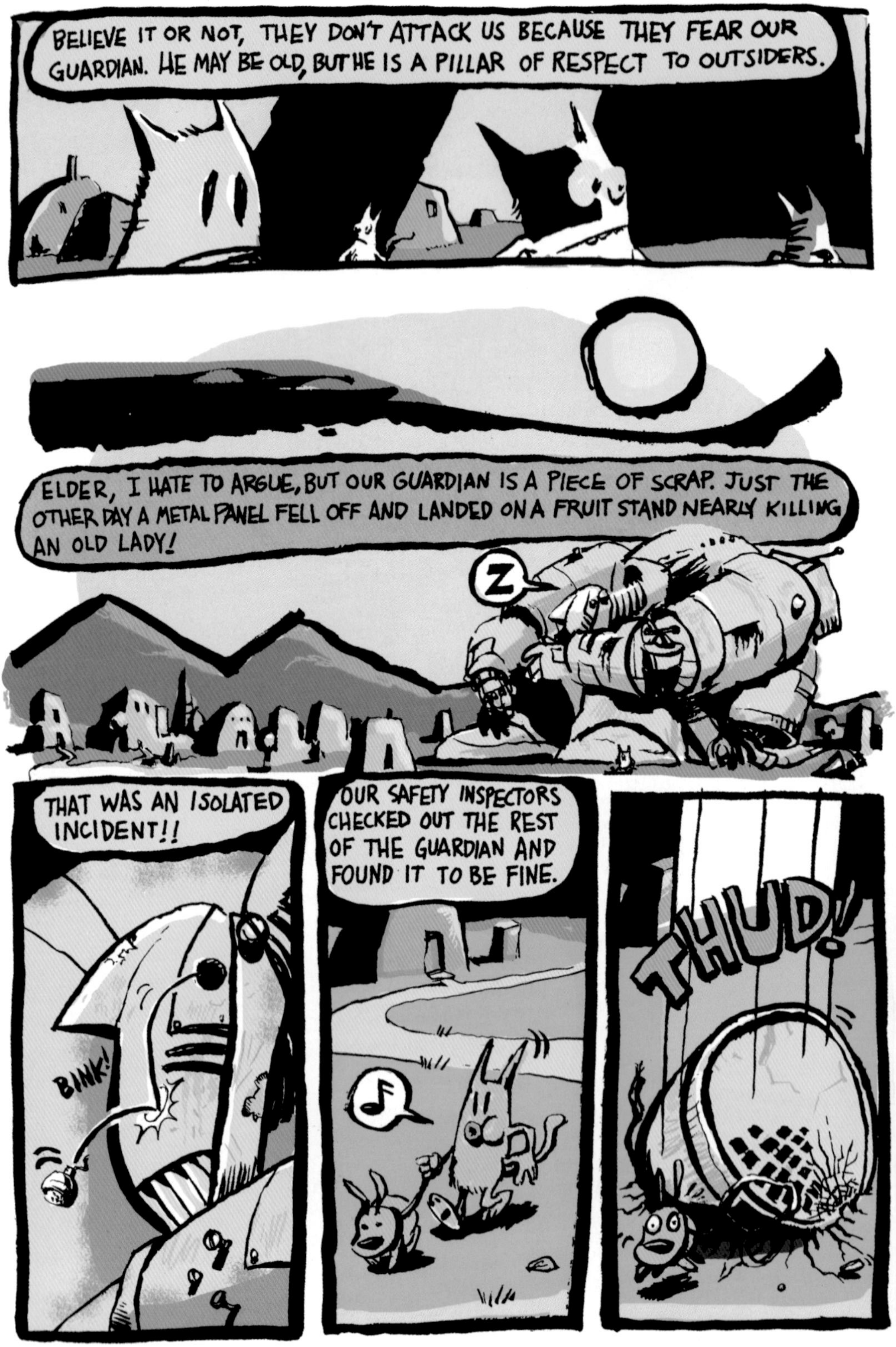
BELIEVE IT OR NOT, THEY DON'T ATTACK US BECAUSE THEY FEAR OUR GUARDIAN. HE MAY BE OLD, BUT HE IS A PILLAR OF RESPECT TO OUTSIDERS.
ELDER, I HATE TO ARGUE, BUT OUR GUARDIAN IS A PIECE OF SCRAP. JUST THE OTHER DAY A METAL PANEL FELL OFF AND LANDED ON A FRUIT STAND NEARLY KILLING AN OLD LADY!
Z
THAT WAS AN ISOLATED INCIDENT!!
BINK!
OUR SAFETY INSPECTORS CHECKED OUT THE REST OF THE GUARDIAN AND FOUND IT TO BE FINE.
THUD!

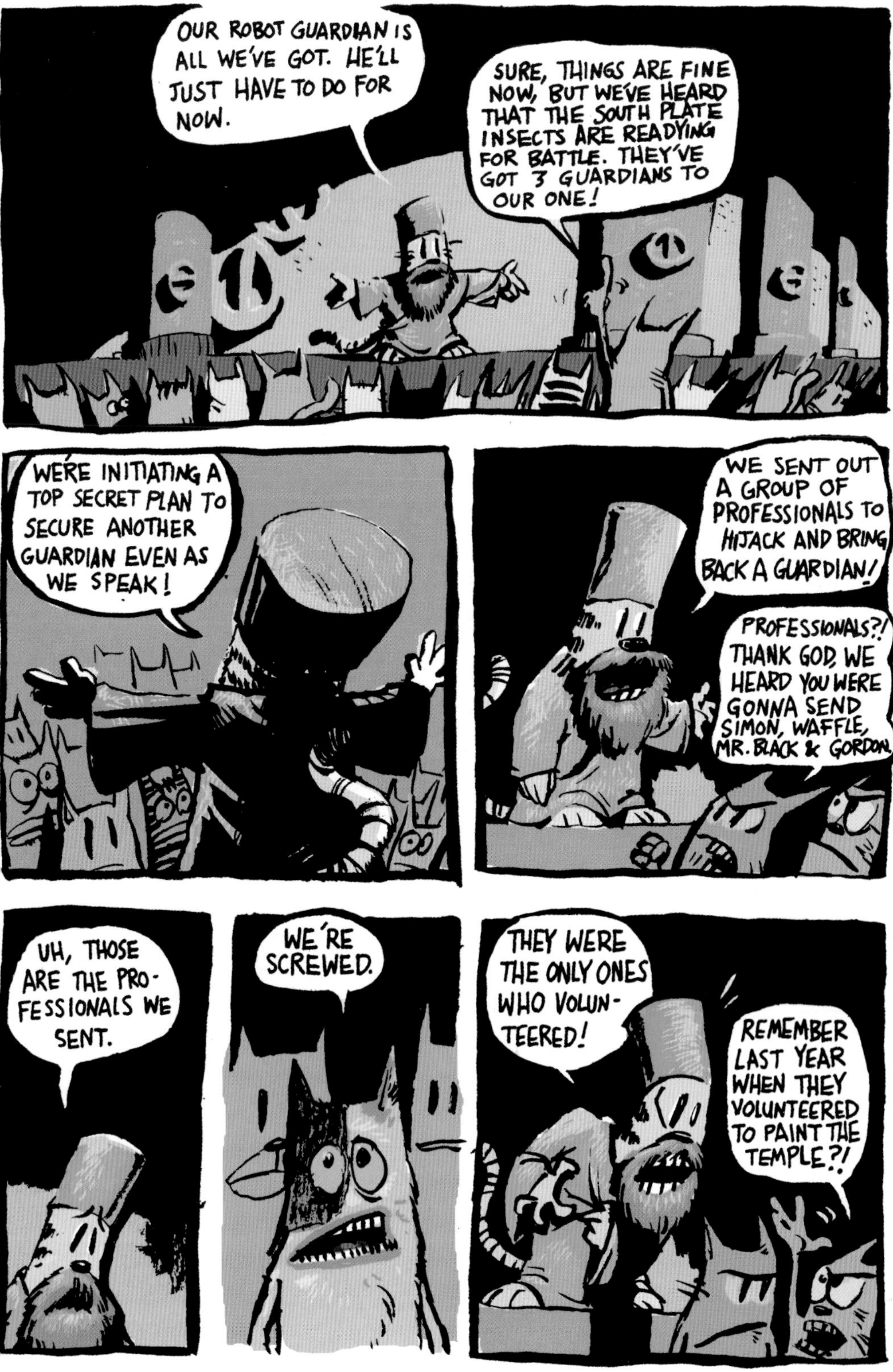
OUR ROBOT GUARDIAN IS ALL WE'VE GOT. HE'LL JUST HAVE TO DO FOR NOW.
SURE, THINGS ARE FINE NOW, BUT WE'VE HEARD THAT THE SOUTH PLATE INSECTS ARE READYING FOR BATTLE. THEY'VE GOT 3 GUARDIANS TO OUR ONE!
WE'RE INITIATING A TOP SECRET PLAN TO SECURE ANOTHER GUARDIAN EVEN AS WE SPEAK!
WE SENT OUT A GROUP OF PROFESSIONALS TO HIJACK AND BRING BACK A GUARDIAN!
PROFESSIONALS?! THANK GOD, WE HEARD YOU WERE GONNA SEND SIMON, WAFFLE, MR. BLACK & GORDON.
UH, THOSE ARE THE PRO-FESSIONALS WE SENT.
WE'RE SCREWED.
THEY WERE THE ONLY ONES WHO VOLUN-TEERED!
REMEMBER LAST YEAR WHEN THEY VOLUNTEERED TO PAINT THE TEMPLE?!

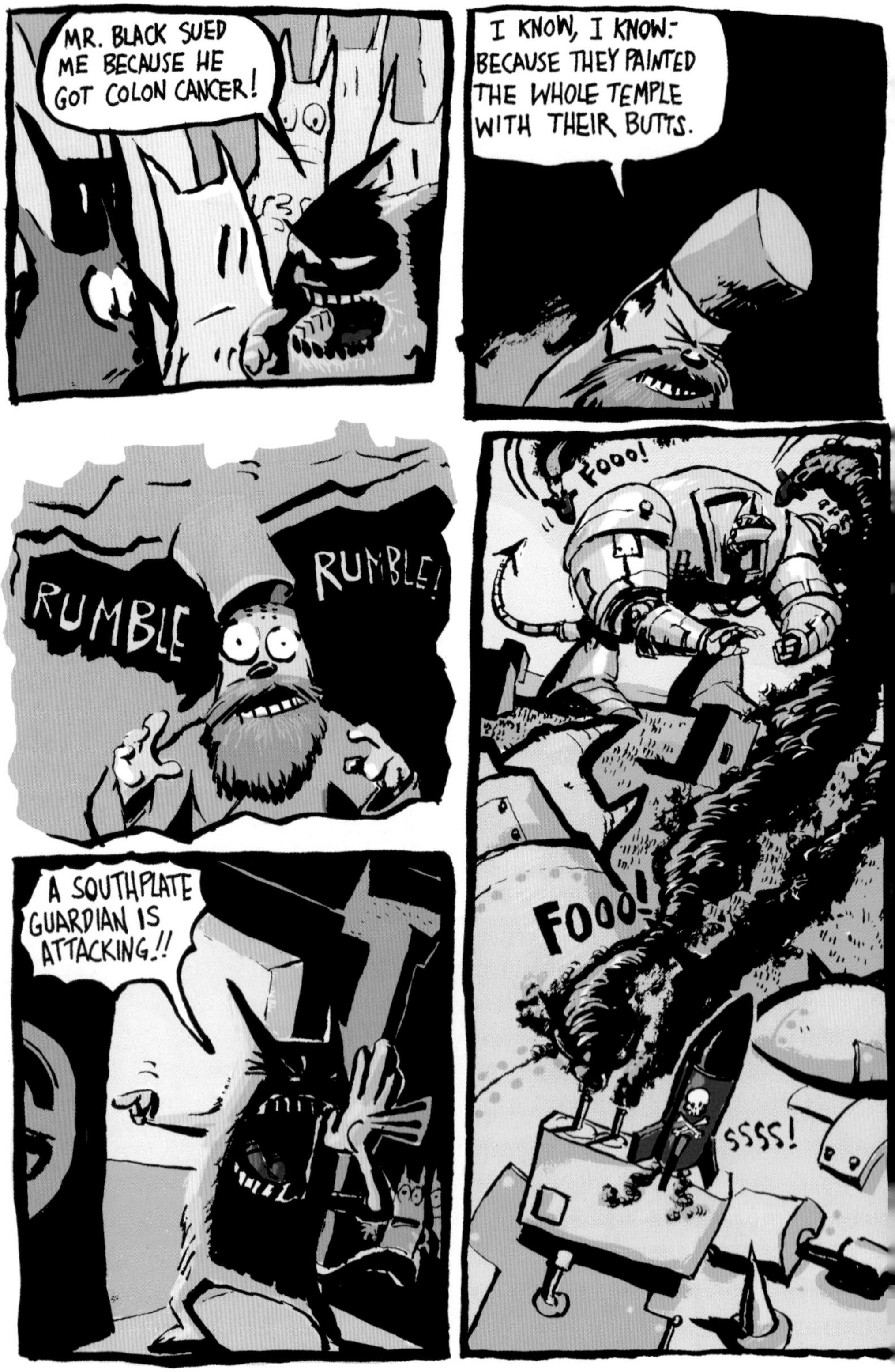
MR. BLACK SUED ME BECAUSE HE GOT COLON CANCER!
I KNOW, I KNOW: BECAUSE THEY PAINTED THE WHOLE TEMPLE WITH THEIR BUTTS.
RUMBLE
RUMBLE!
FOOO!
FOOO!
SSSS!
A SOUTHPLATE GUARDIAN IS ATTACKING!!

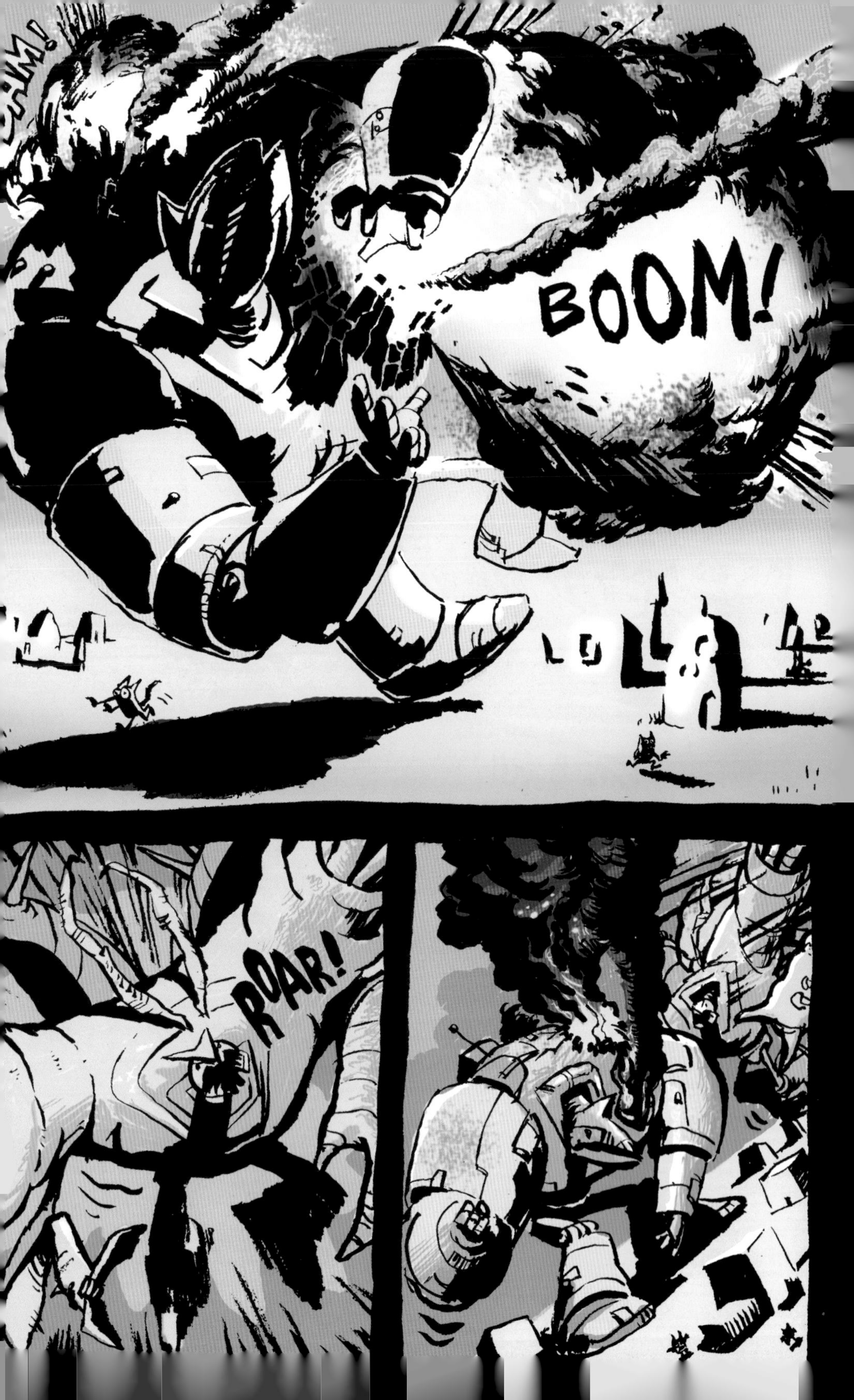
BOOM!
ROAR!

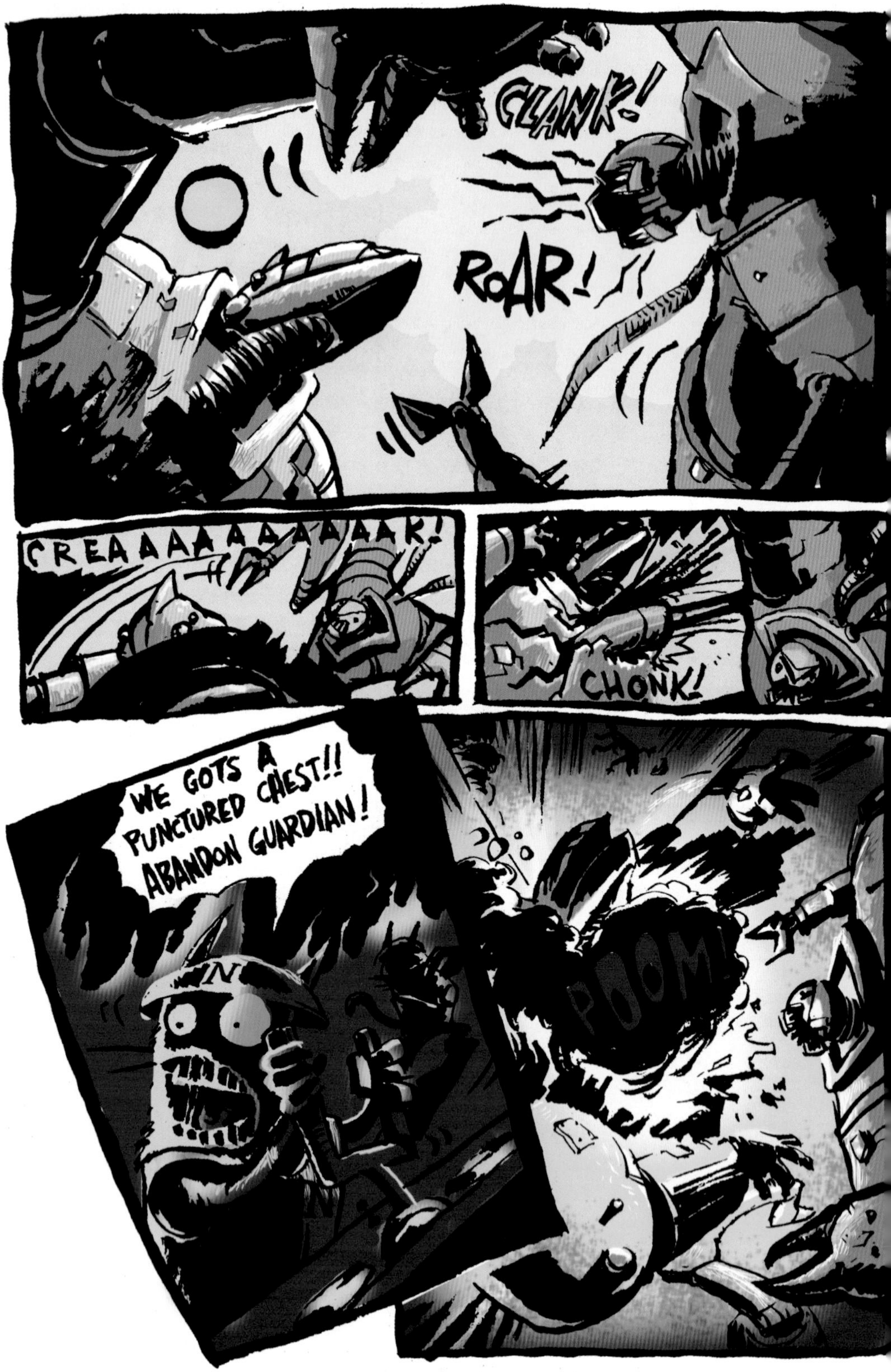
CLANK!
ROAR!
CREAAAAAAAAAAAK!
CHONK!
WE GOTS A PUNCTURED CHEST!! ABANDON GUARDIAN!
POOM!

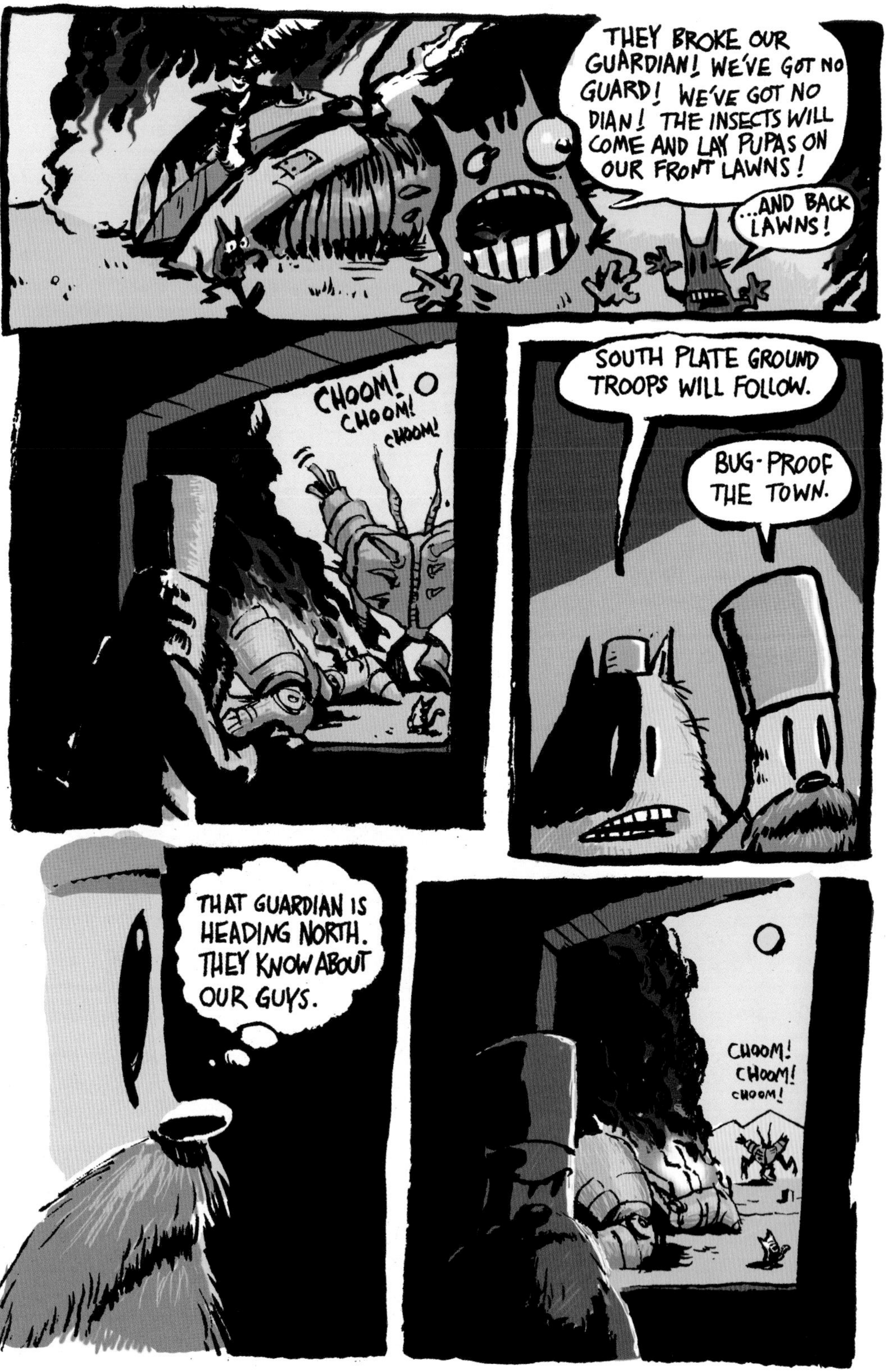
THEY BROKE OUR GUARDIAN! WE'VE GOT NO GUARD! WE'VE GOT NO DIAN! THE INSECTS WILL COME AND LAY PUPAS ON OUR FRONT LAWNS!
...AND BACK LAWNS!
CHOOM! CHOOM! CHOOM!
SOUTH PLATE GROUND TROOPS WILL FOLLOW.
BUG-PROOF THE TOWN.
THAT GUARDIAN IS HEADING NORTH. THEY KNOW ABOUT OUR GUYS.
CHOOM! CHOOM! CHOOM!

I REMEMBER WHEN I WALKED AMONG THE EARTH-BOUND TAKING LIFE FOR GRANTED. I DID NOT PARTICIPATE IN SOME OF THE FINER THINGS. IT WASN'T UNTIL MY SOUL GENTLY SLID FROM ITS MORTAL COIL THAT THESE THINGS BECAME CLEAR TO ME.

I APPROACHED JUDGMENT WITH CONFIDENCE, NOT BECAUSE I LIVED A RIGHTEOUS LIFE BUT BECAUSE I HAD CONFIDENCE IN A FAVORABLE TRIAL.

I FIGURED THAT IF I WAS CAST INTO THE FIERY LAKE, THEN GOD WILL HAVE DONE EVERYTHING IN HIS POWER TO SAVE ME. DURING JUDGEMENT, NONE OF THE BAD THINGS I HAD DONE WERE EVEN MENTIONED. NOT EVEN THE TIME I SQUASHED OVER 50 SNAILS WITH A HAMMER. RATHER, HE ONLY TOLD EVERYONE HOW BRAVE I WAS. THEN I WALKED THROUGH CLOUDS AND DRANK FROM RIVERS OF MILK. THIS WAS SPECIAL MILK, IN THAT IT DIDN'T GIVE ME DIARRHEA. OH YES, AND THERE ARE GUPPIES HERE. MILLIONS OF THEM! THEY FLY ALL AROUND YOUR HEAD SINGING ALL THE WHILE. WHEN I INTRODUCE MYSELF TO THESE HEAVENLY GUPPIES... THEY RECOGNIZED ME AS THE HALF-BROTHER OF WAFFLE. I ASKED ONE OF THEM HOW ALL OF THE GUPPIES KNEW WHO WAFFLE WAS. I ATE THE GUPPY BEFORE HE COULD ANSWER.

I WAS ESCORTED TO MY OWN SCRATCH-POST AND SOLID GOLD LITTER-BOX. I CAN ALSO CRAWL ONTO PARKED CAR ENGINES AND SLEEP IN WARMTH WITHOUT FEAR OF GETTING CHOPPED UP IN A FAN BELT.

I'M SURPRISED AT ALL OF THE FOLKS WHO MADE IT HERE AS OPPOSED TO THOSE WHO DIDN'T.

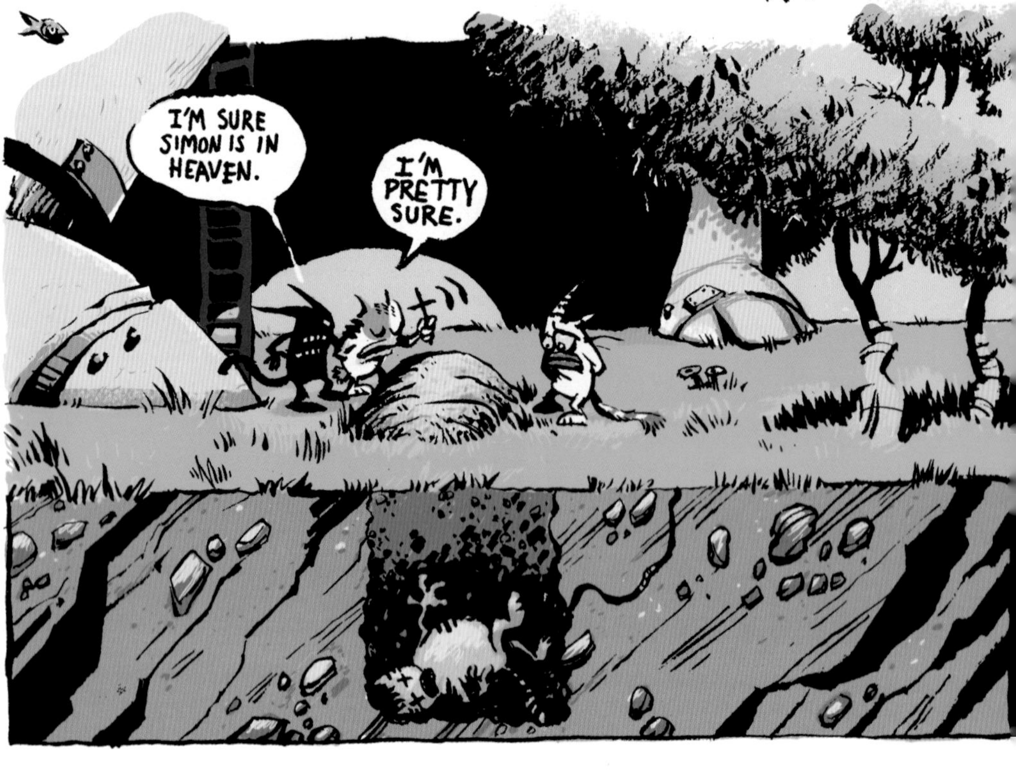
I'M SURE SIMON IS IN HEAVEN.
I'M PRETTY SURE.

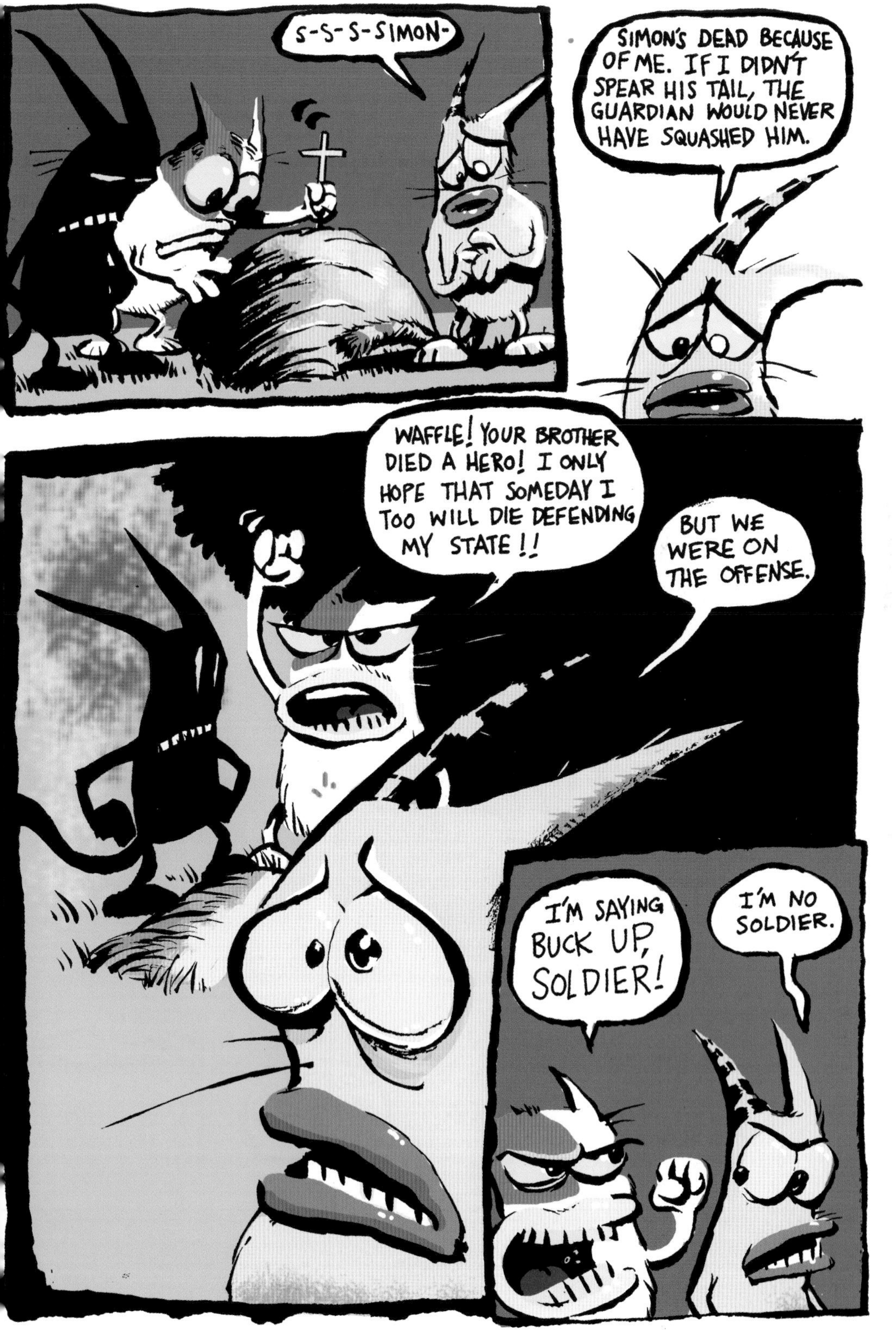
S-S-S-SIMON-
SIMON'S DEAD BECAUSE OF ME. IF I DIDN'T SPEAR HIS TAIL, THE GUARDIAN WOULD NEVER HAVE SQUASHED HIM.
WAFFLE! YOUR BROTHER DIED A HERO! I ONLY HOPE THAT SOMEDAY I TOO WILL DIE DEFENDING MY STATE!!
BUT WE WERE ON THE OFFENSE.
I'M SAYING BUCK UP, SOLDIER!
I'M NO SOLDIER.

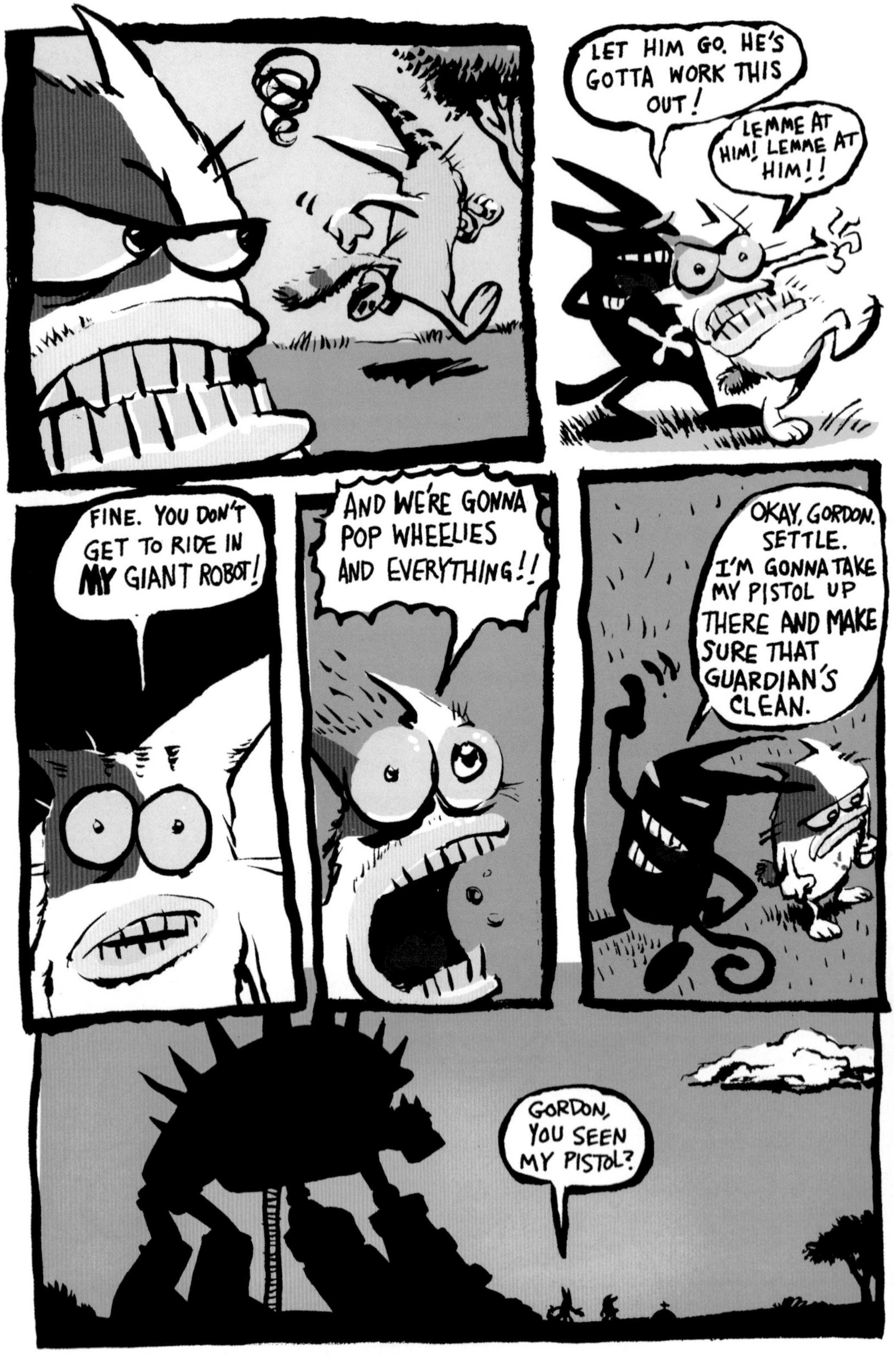
LET HIM GO. HE'S GOTTA WORK THIS OUT!
LEMME AT HIM! LEMME AT HIM!!
FINE. YOU DON'T GET TO RIDE IN MY GIANT ROBOT!
AND WE'RE GONNA POP WHEELIES AND EVERYTHING!!
OKAY, GORDON. SETTLE. I'M GONNA TAKE MY PISTOL UP THERE AND MAKE SURE THAT GUARDIAN'S CLEAN.
GORDON, YOU SEEN MY PISTOL?

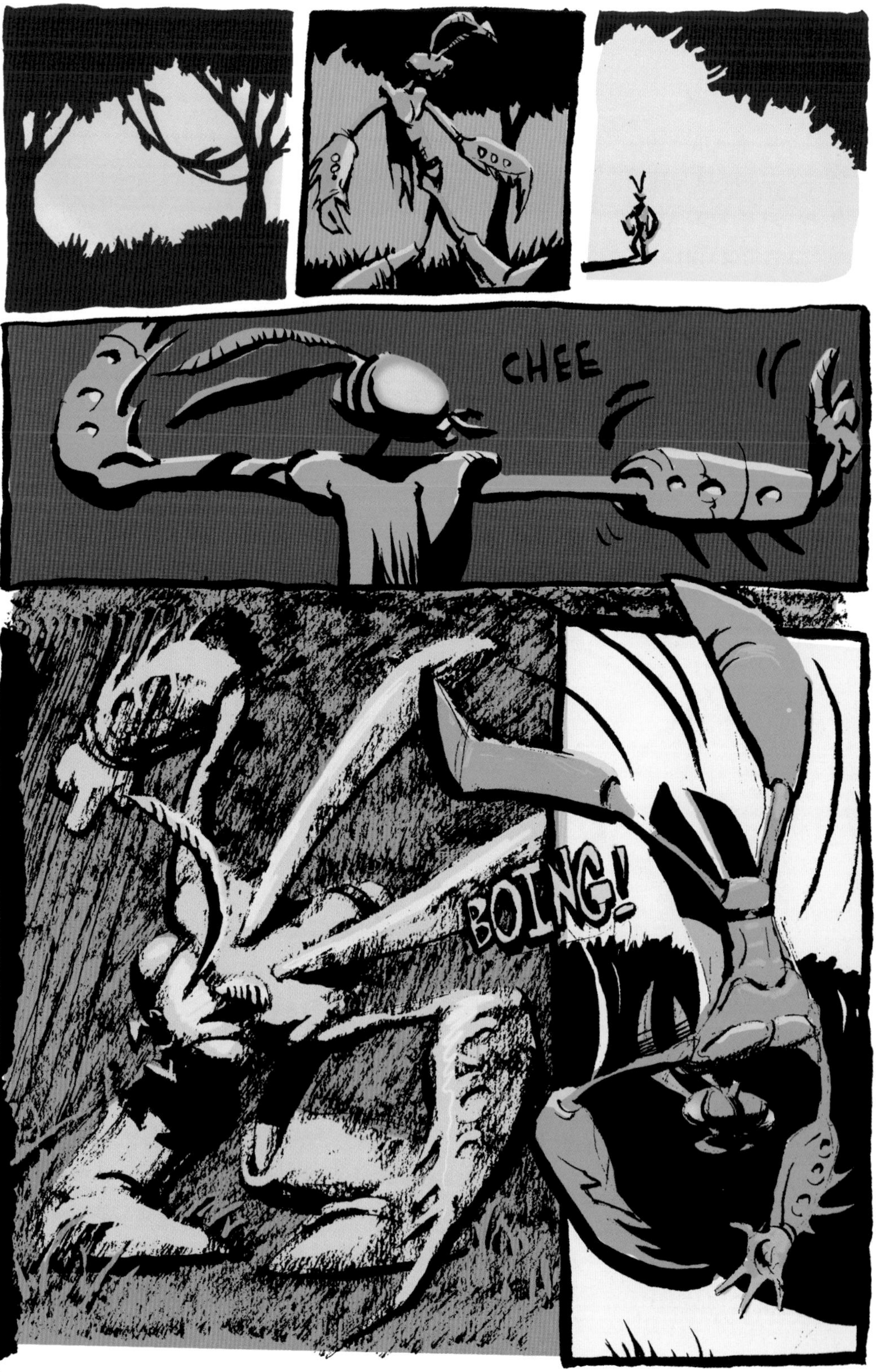
CHEE
BOING!

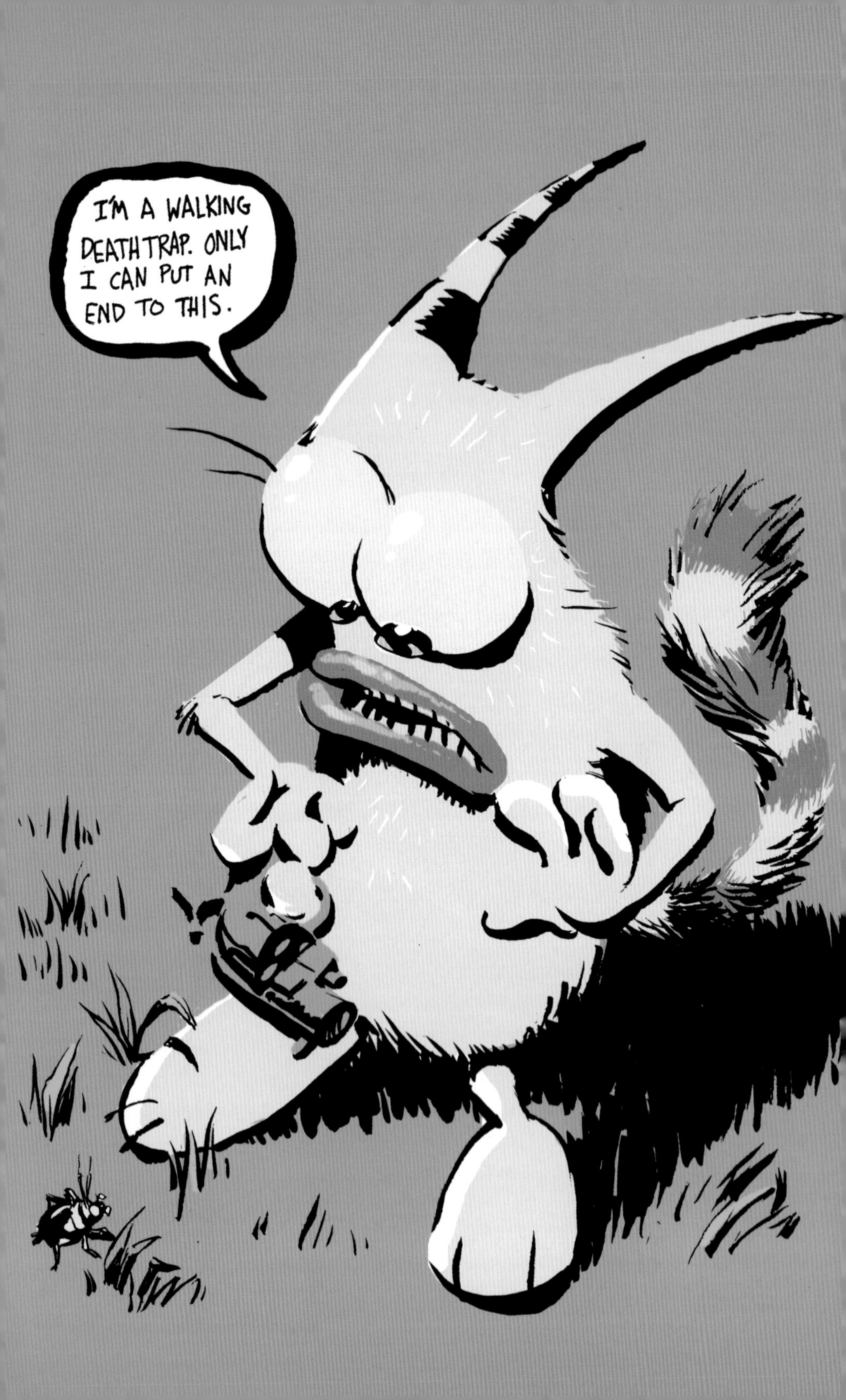
I'M A WALKING DEATHTRAP. ONLY I CAN PUT AN END TO THIS.

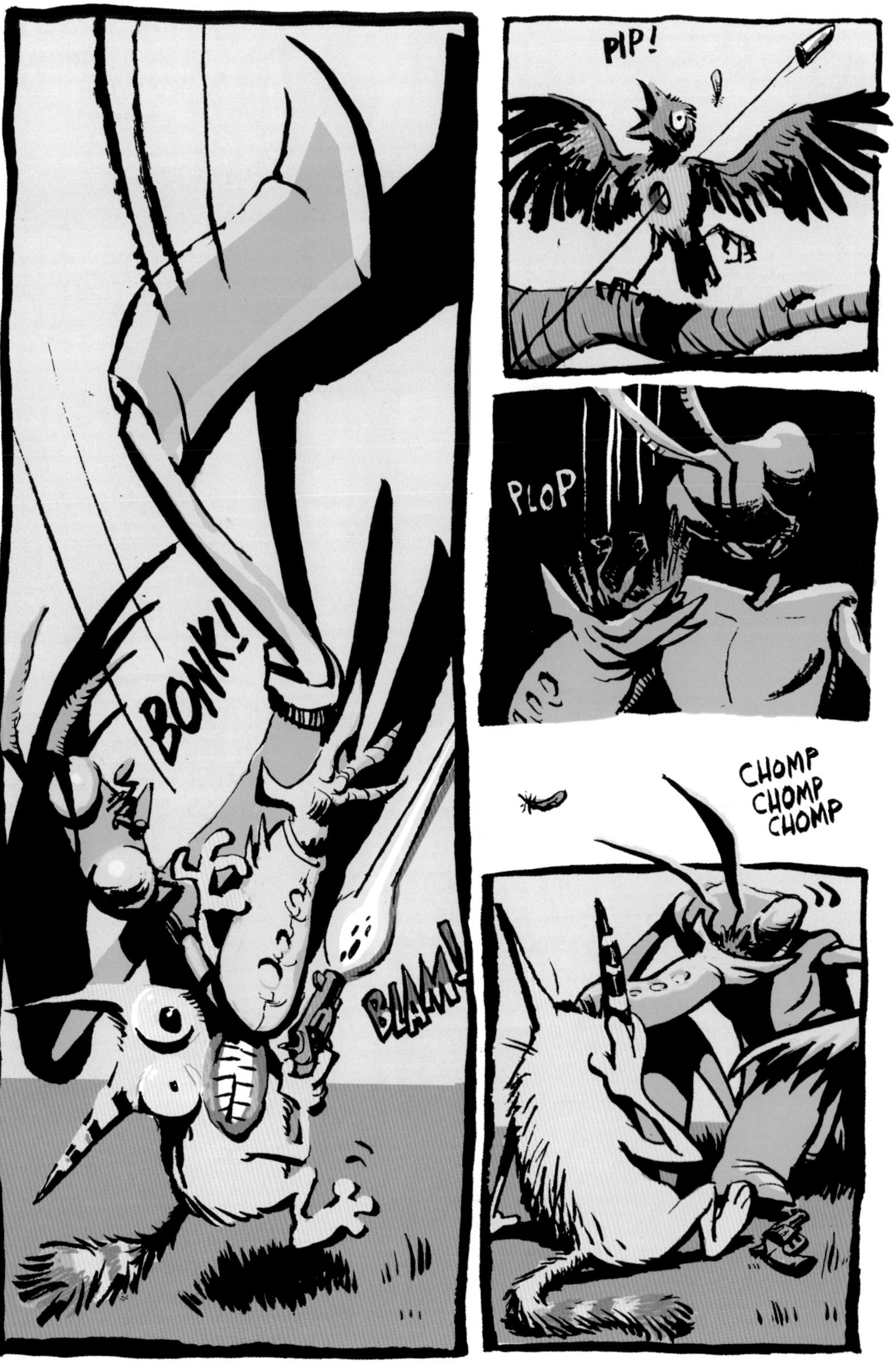
BONK!
BLAM!
PIP!
PLOP
CHOMP
CHOMP
CHOMP

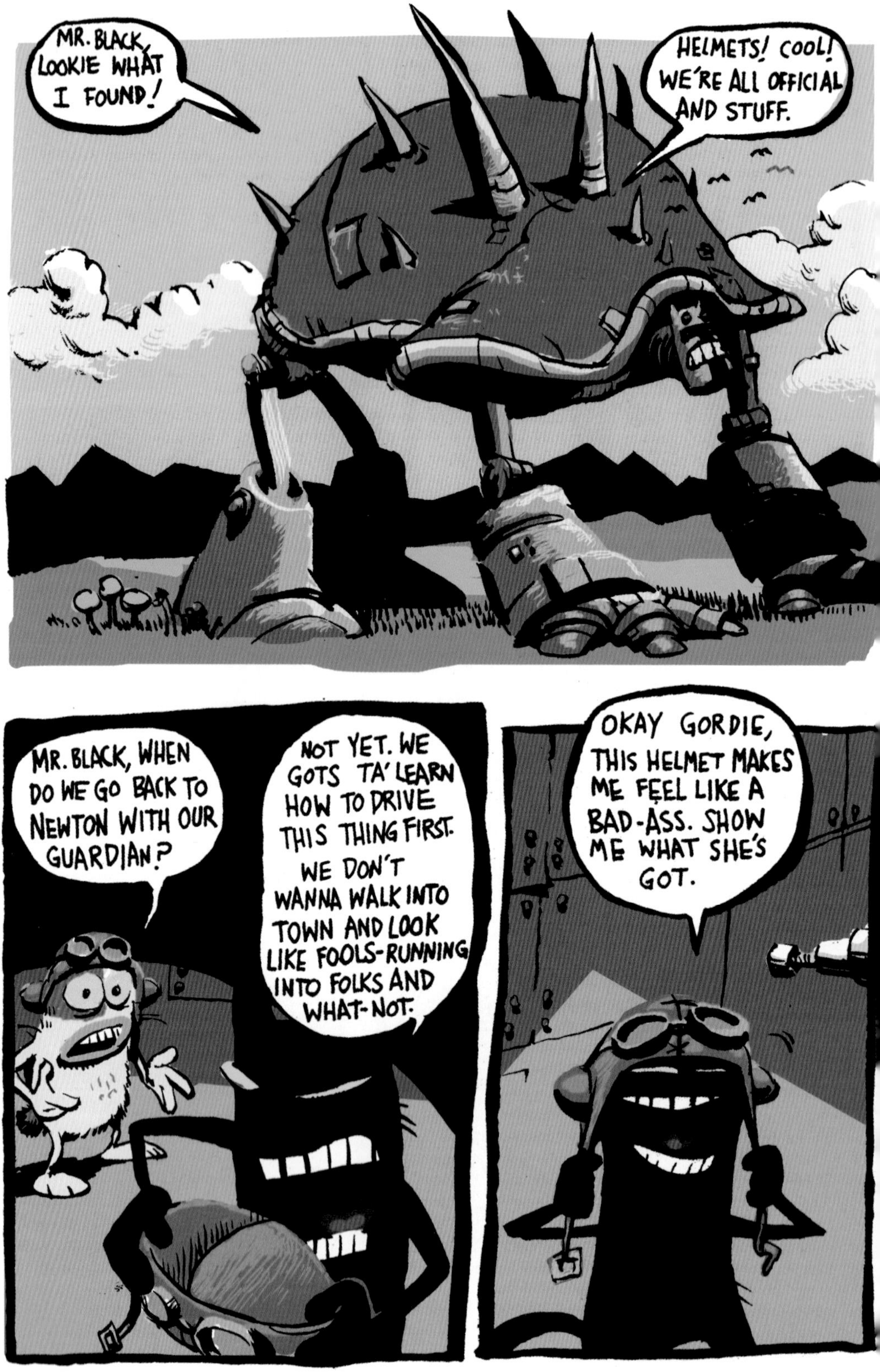
MR. BLACK, LOOKIE WHAT I FOUND!
HELMETS! COOL! WE'RE ALL OFFICIAL AND STUFF.
MR. BLACK, WHEN DO WE GO BACK TO NEWTON WITH OUR GUARDIAN?
NOT YET. WE GOTS TA' LEARN HOW TO DRIVE THIS THING FIRST.
WE DON'T WANNA WALK INTO TOWN AND LOOK LIKE FOOLS-RUNNING INTO FOLKS AND WHAT-NOT.
OKAY GORDIE, THIS HELMET MAKES ME FEEL LIKE A BAD-ASS. SHOW ME WHAT SHE'S GOT.

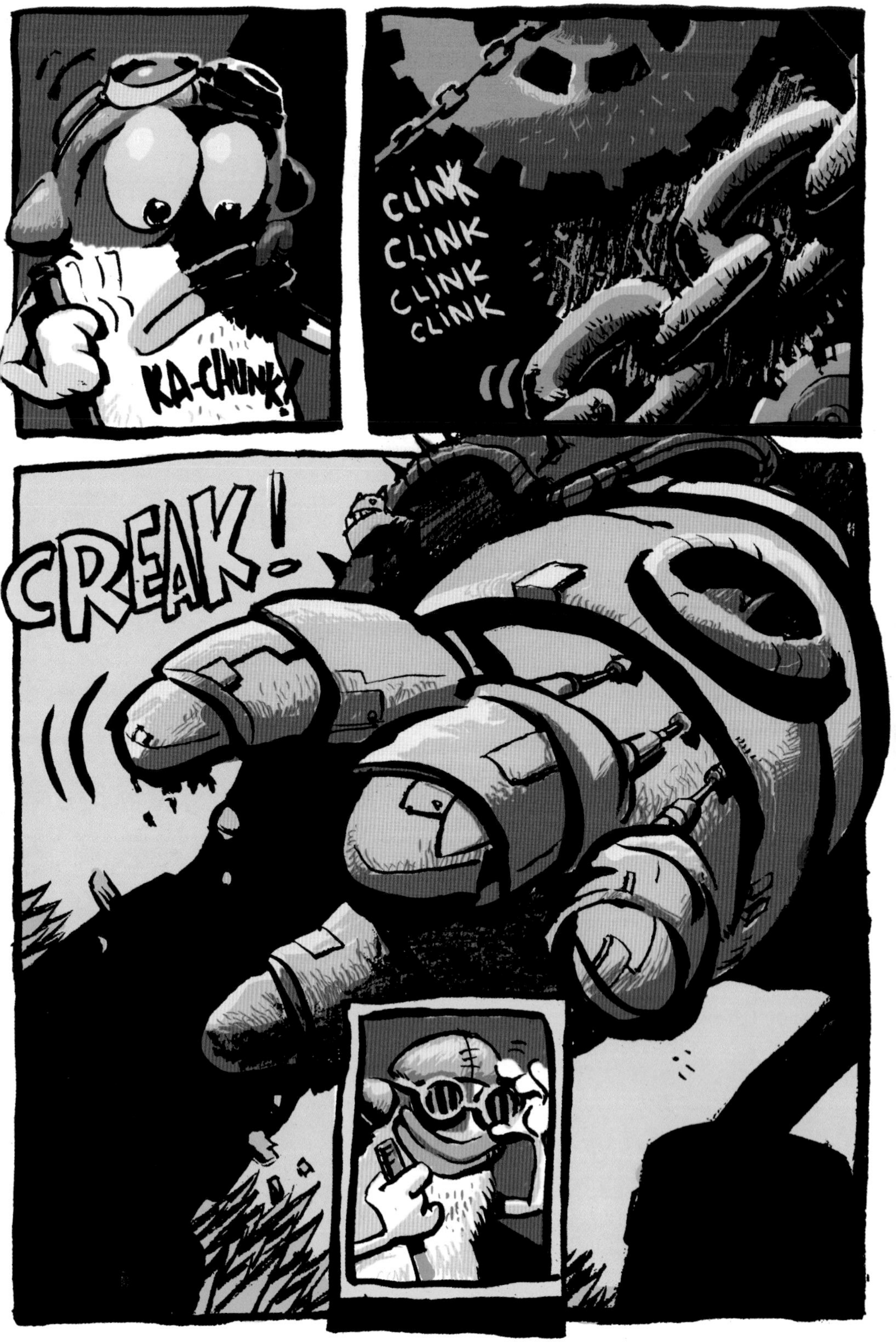
KA-CHUNK!
CLINK
CLINK
CLINK
CLINK
CREAK!

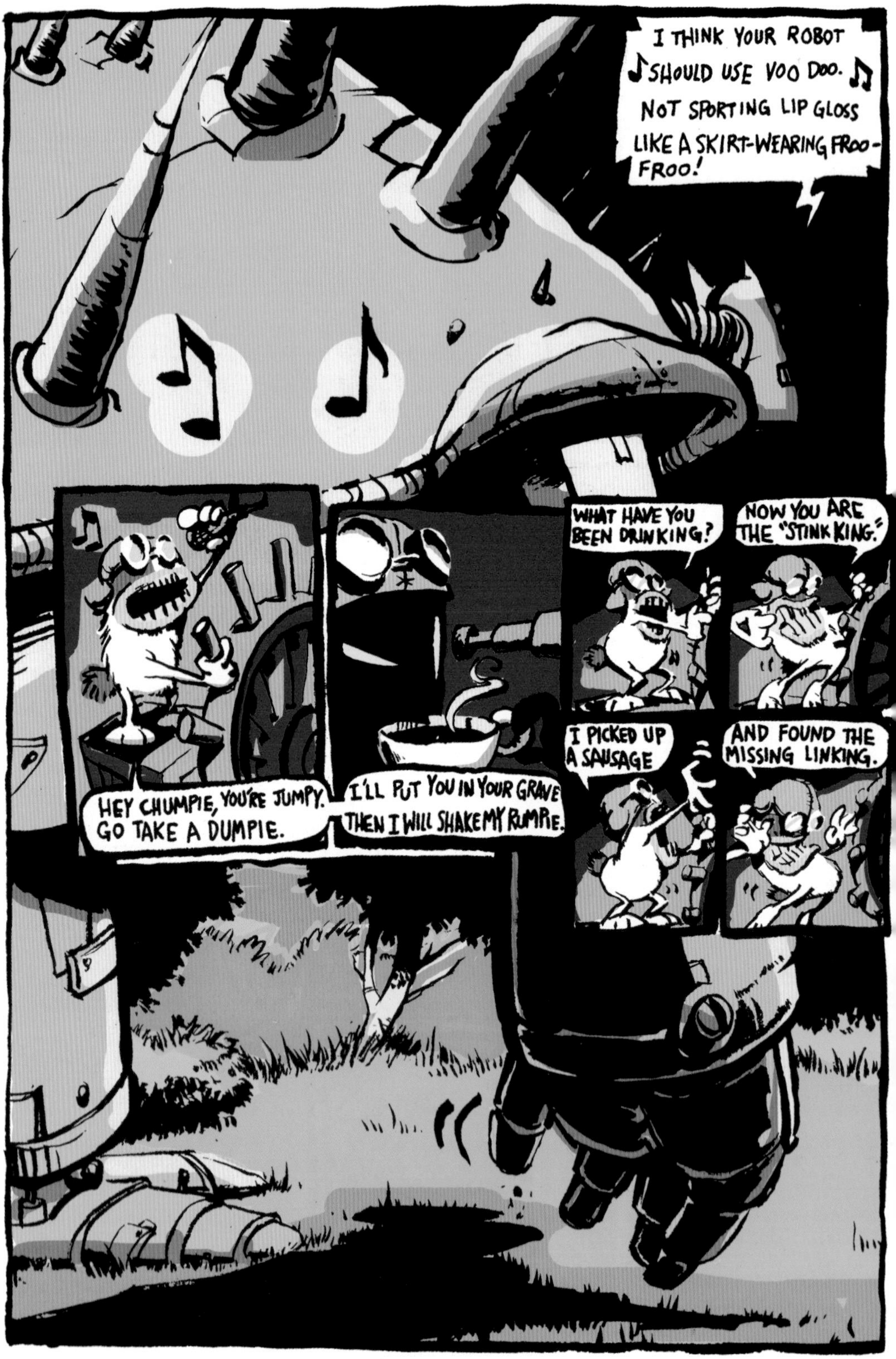
I THINK YOUR ROBOT SHOULD USE VOO DOO. NOT SPORTING LIP GLOSS LIKE A SKIRT-WEARING FROO-FROO!
HEY CHUMPIE, YOU'RE JUMPY. GO TAKE A DUMPIE.
I'LL PUT YOU IN YOUR GRAVE THEN I WILL SHAKE MY RUMPIE.
WHAT HAVE YOU BEEN DRINKING?
NOW YOU ARE THE "STINK KING."
I PICKED UP A SAUSAGE
AND FOUND THE MISSING LINKING.

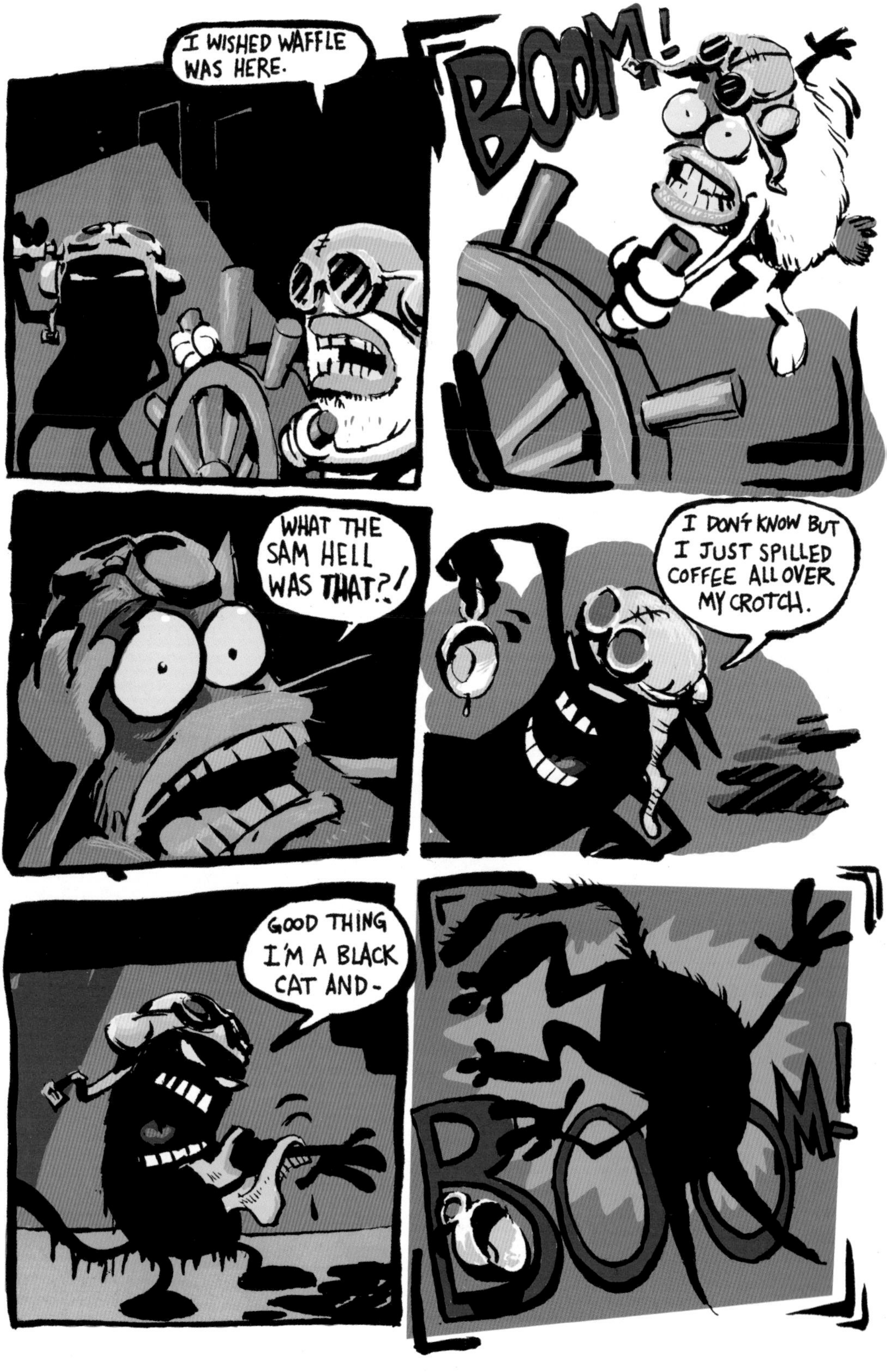
I WISHED WAFFLE WAS HERE.
BOOM!
WHAT THE SAM HELL WAS THAT?!
I DON'T KNOW BUT I JUST SPILLED COFFEE ALL OVER MY CROTCH.
GOOD THING I'M A BLACK CAT AND-
BOOOM!

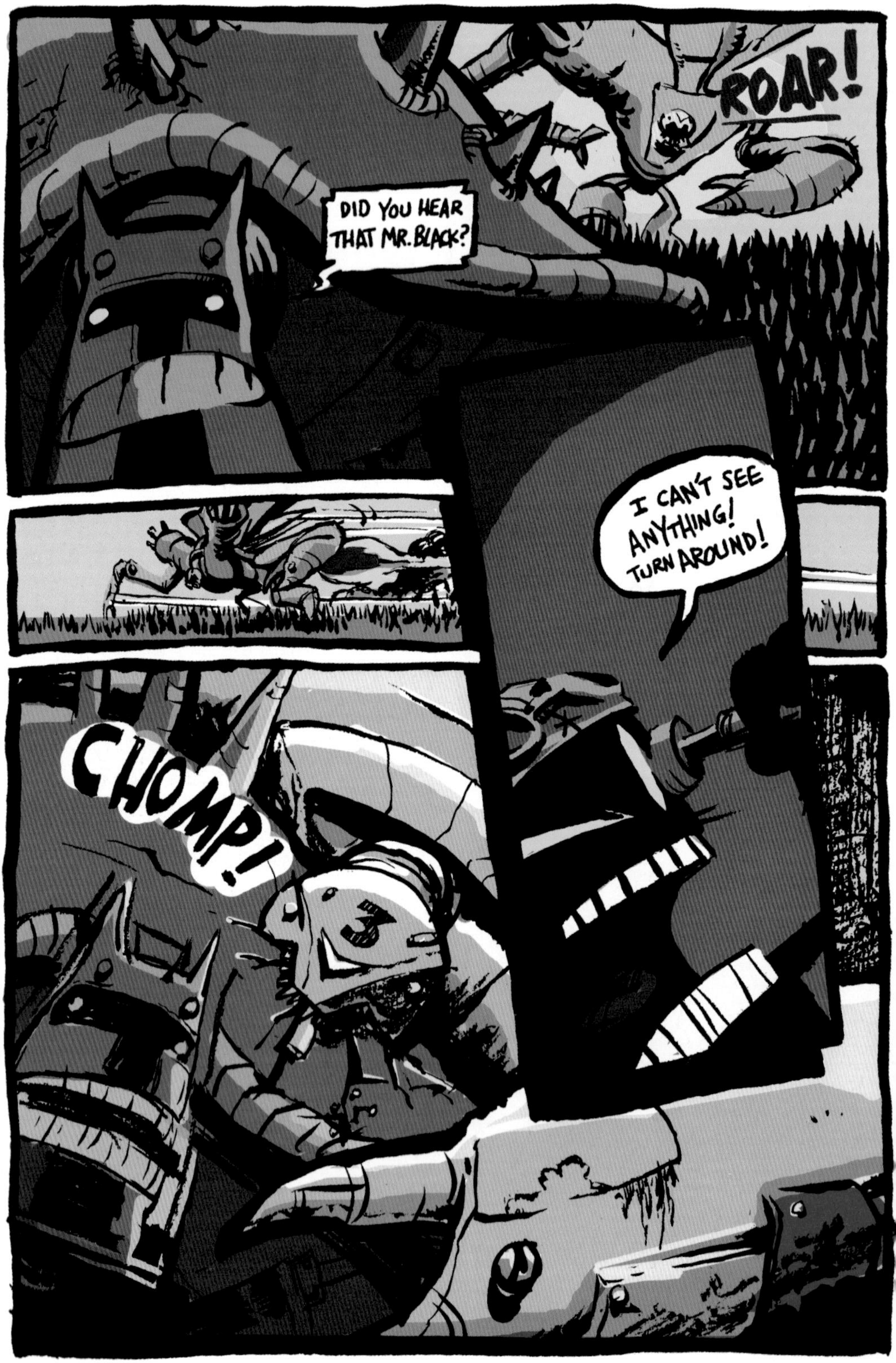
ROAR!
DID YOU HEAR THAT MR. BLACK?
I CAN'T SEE ANYTHING! TURN AROUND!
CHOMP!

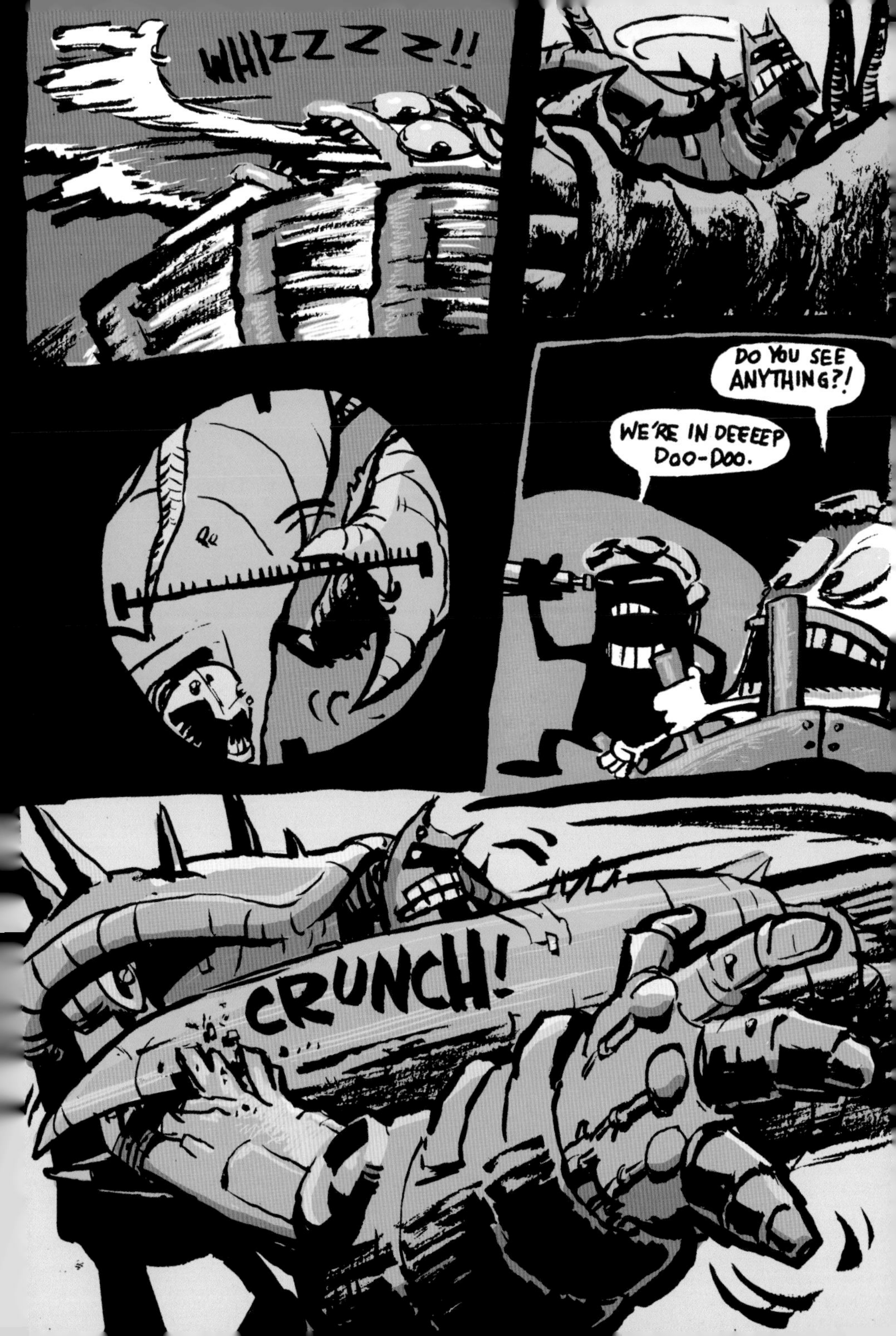
WHIZZZZZ!!
DO YOU SEE ANYTHING?!
WE'RE IN DEEEEP DOO-DOO.
CRUNCH!

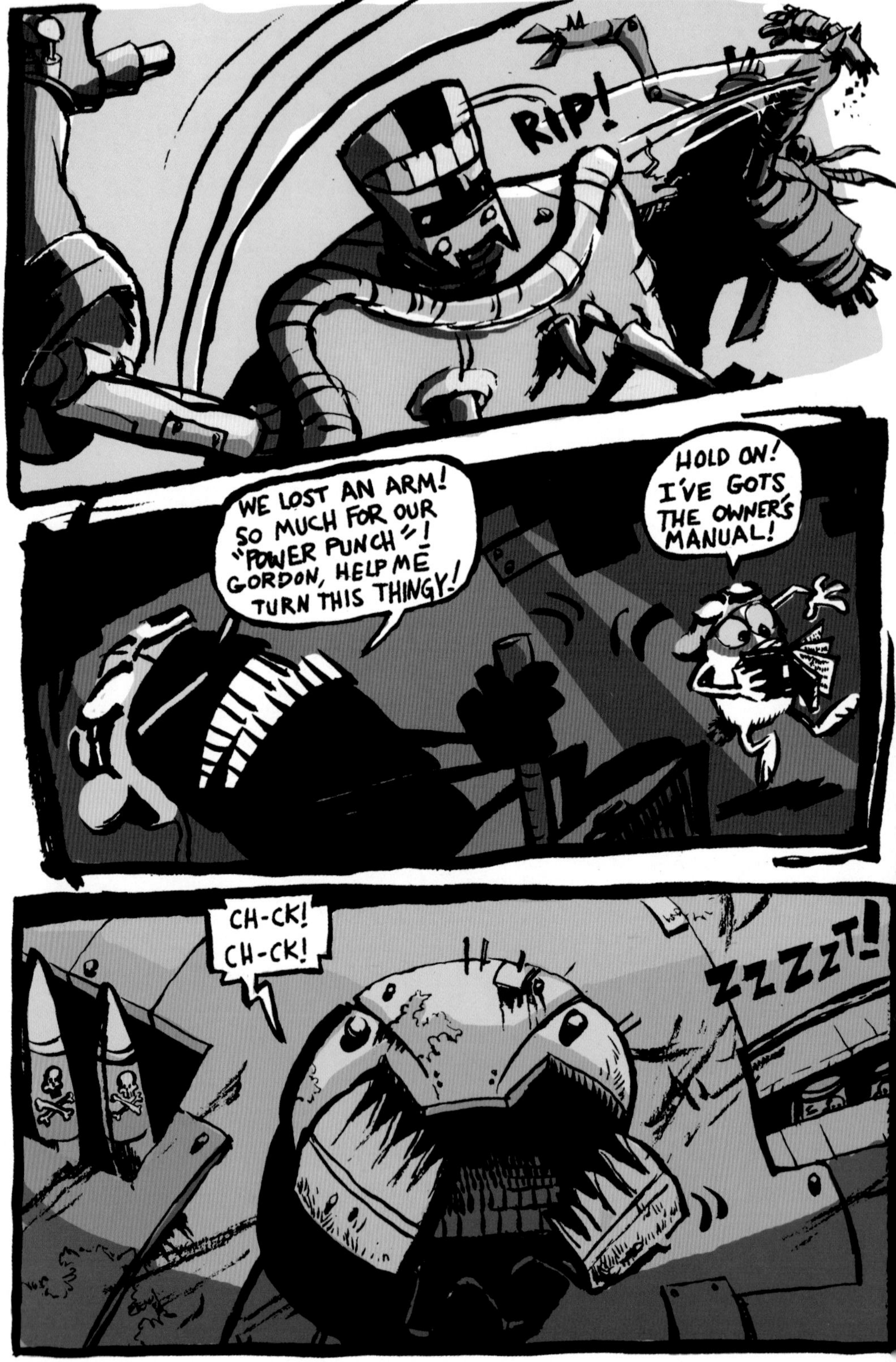
RIP!
WE LOST AN ARM! SO MUCH FOR OUR "POWER PUNCH"! GORDON, HELP ME TURN THIS THINGY!
HOLD ON! I'VE GOTS THE OWNER'S MANUAL!
CH-CK! CH-CK!
ZZZZT!

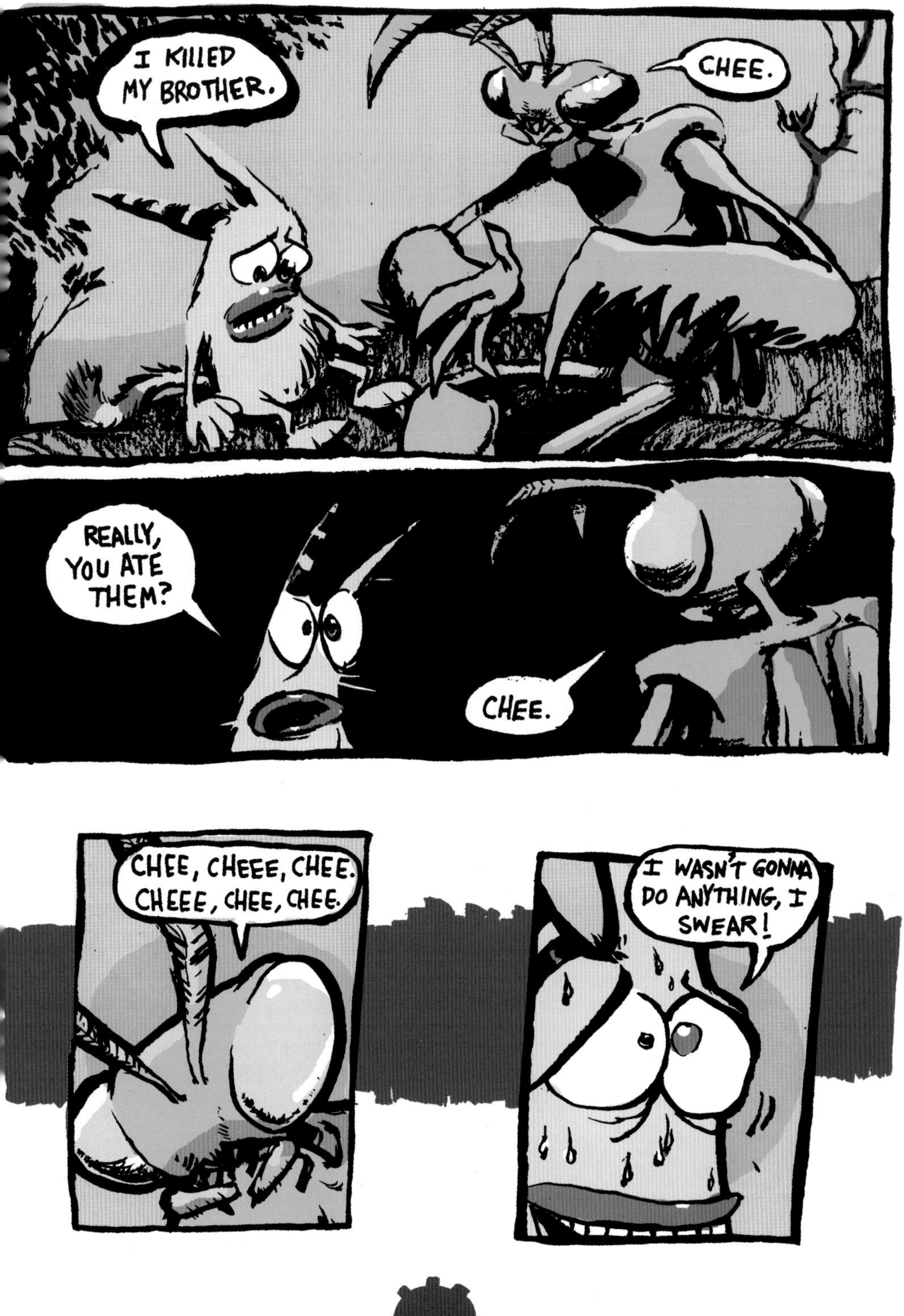
I KILLED MY BROTHER.
CHEE.
REALLY, YOU ATE THEM?
CHEE.
CHEE, CHEEE, CHEE. CHEEE, CHEE, CHEE.
I WASN'T GONNA DO ANYTHING, I SWEAR!

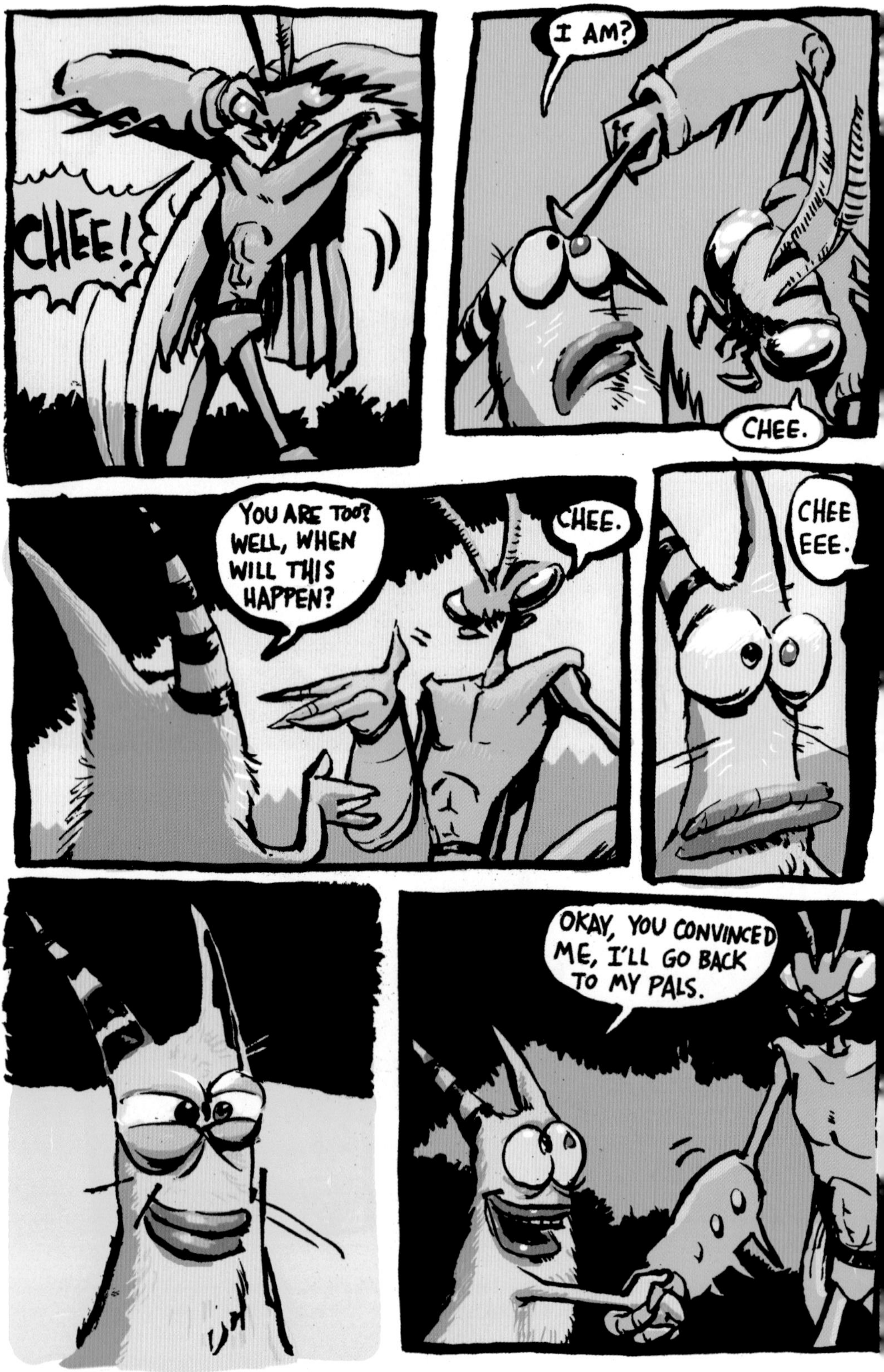
CHEE!
I AM?
CHEE.
YOU ARE TOO? WELL, WHEN WILL THIS HAPPEN?
CHEE.
CHEE EEE.
OKAY, YOU CONVINCED ME, I'LL GO BACK TO MY PALS.

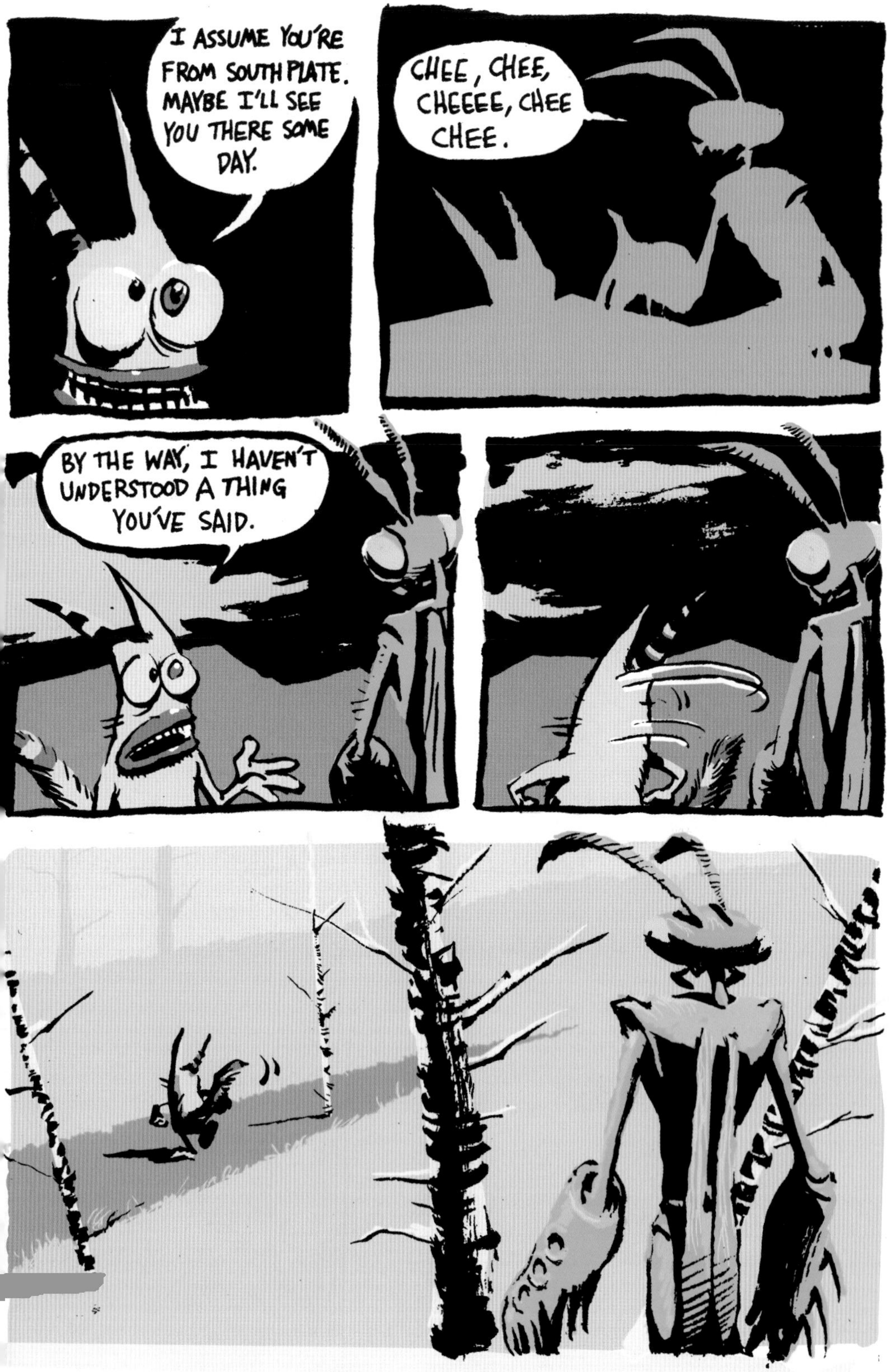
I ASSUME YOU'RE FROM SOUTH PLATE. MAYBE I'LL SEE YOU THERE SOME DAY.
CHEE, CHEE, CHEEEE, CHEE CHEE.
BY THE WAY, I HAVEN'T UNDERSTOOD A THING YOU'VE SAID.

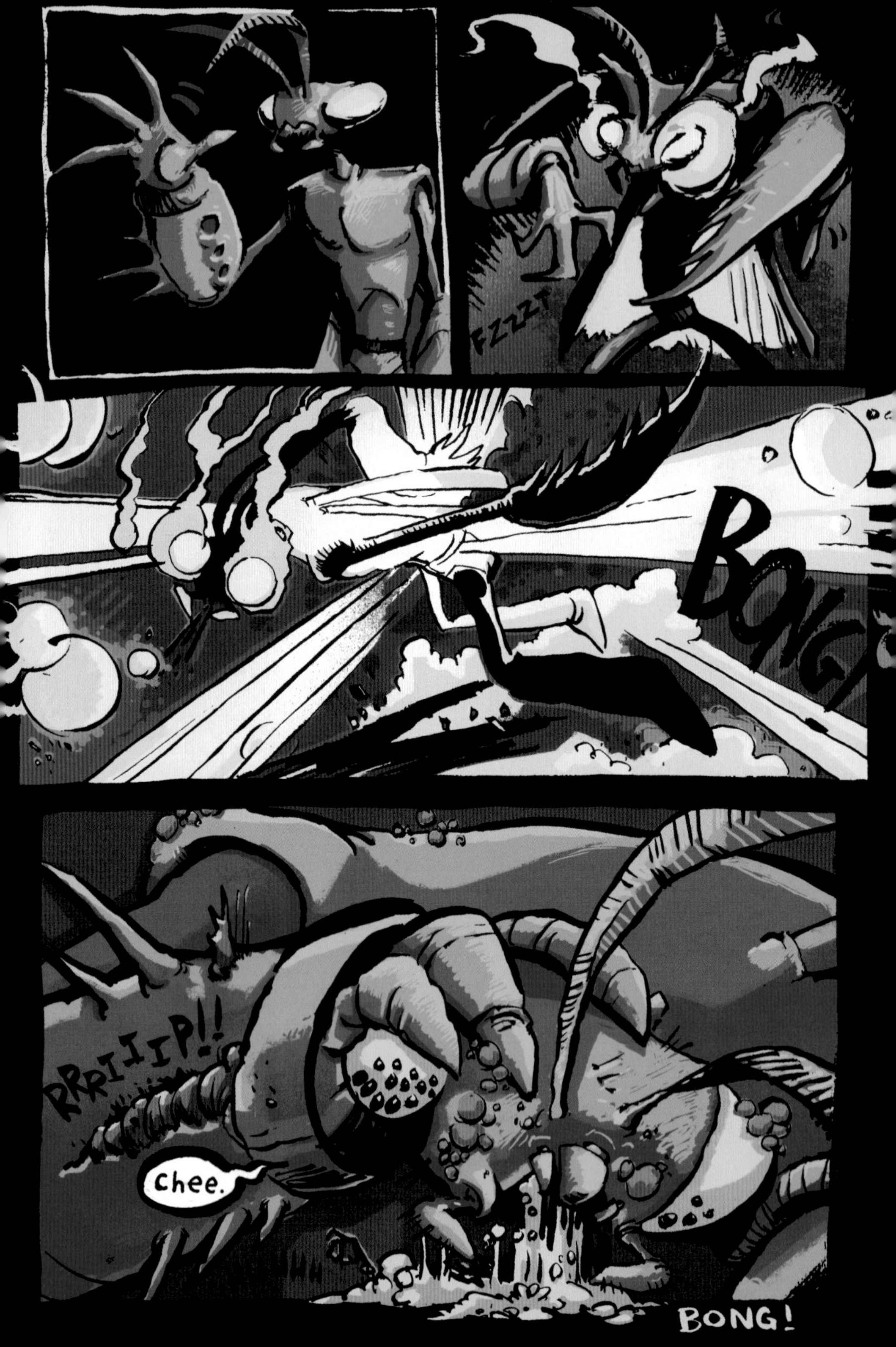
FZZZT
BONG
RRRIIIP!!
chee.
BONG!

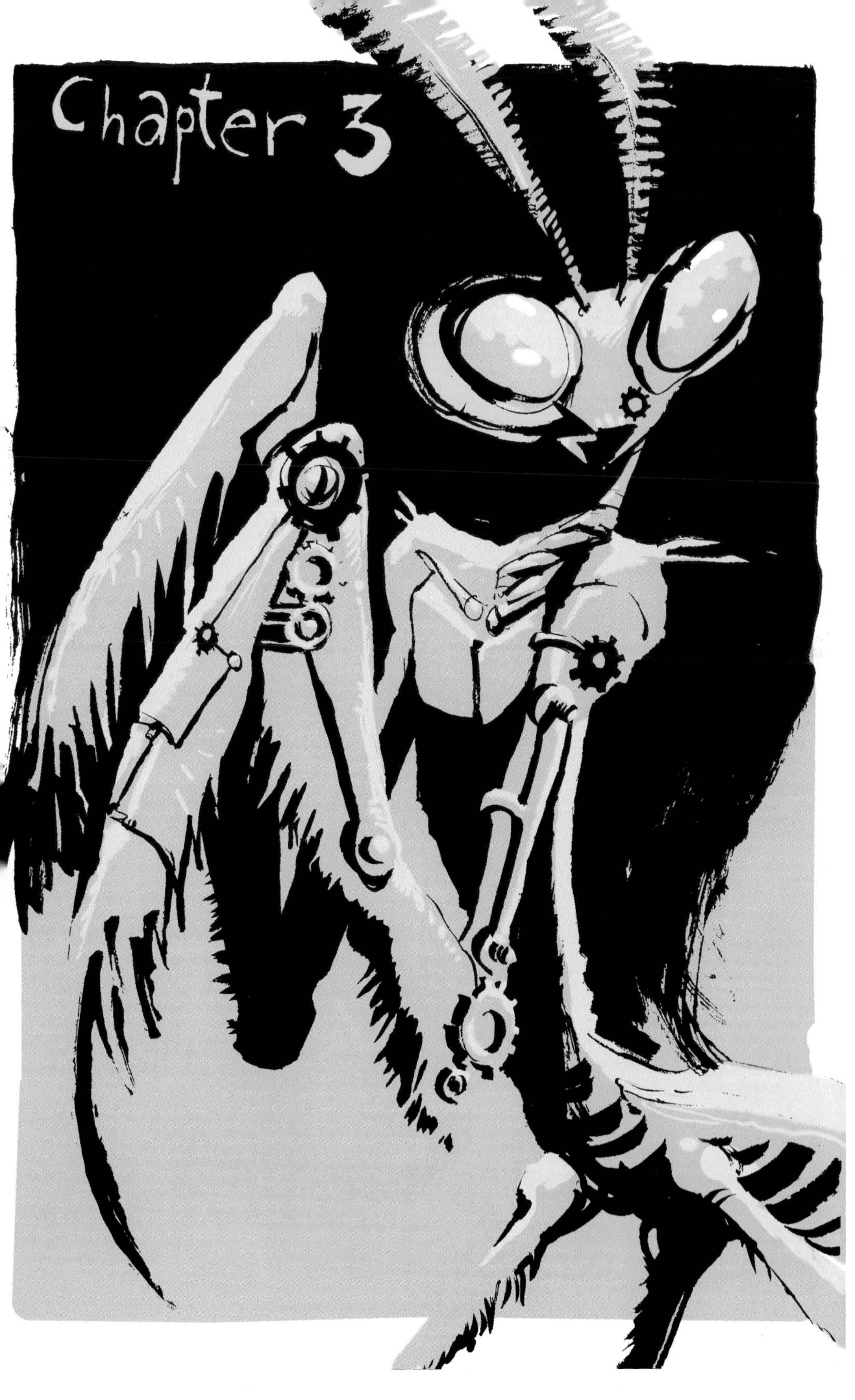
Chapter 3

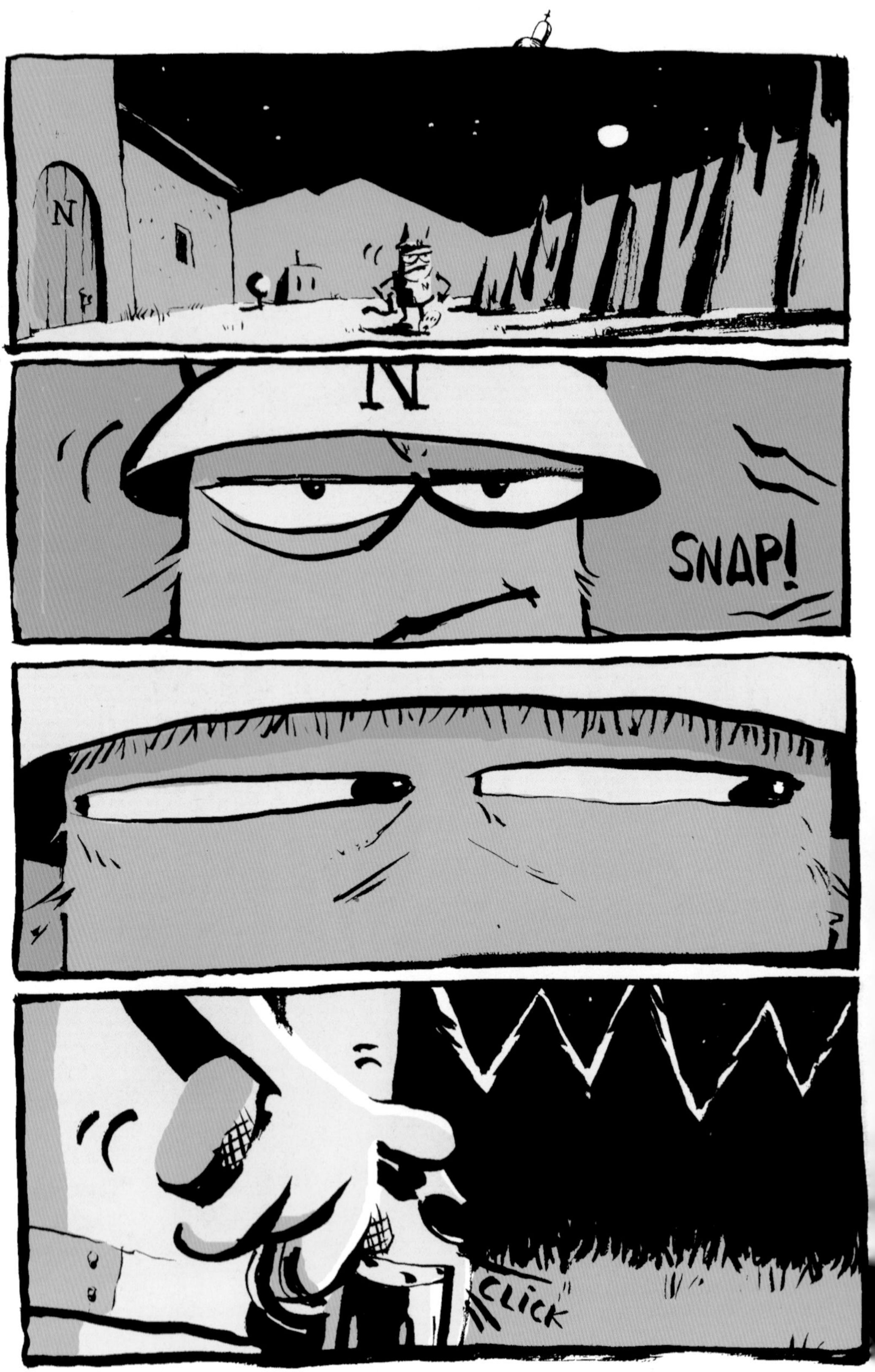
SNAP!
CLICK

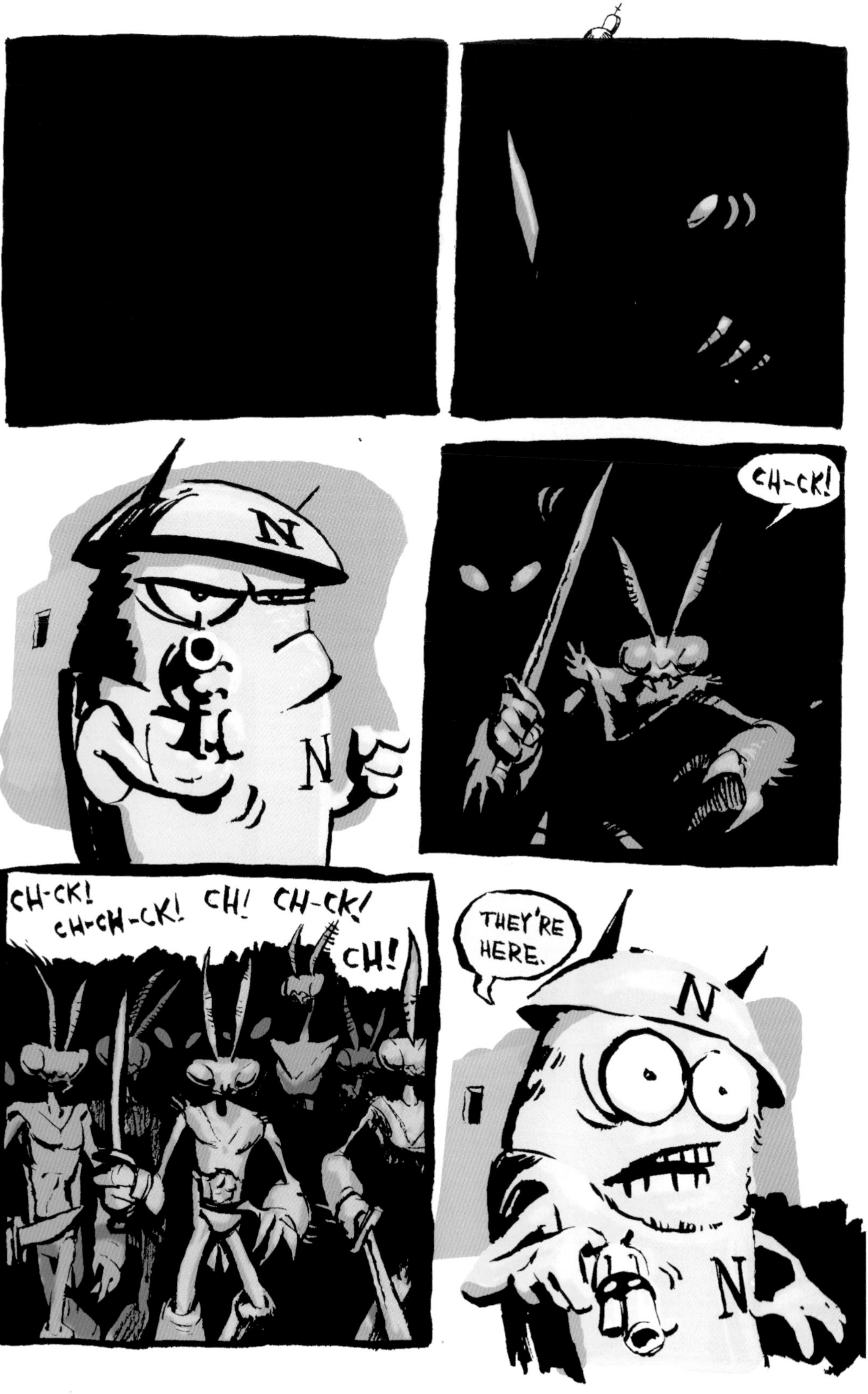
CH-CK!
CH-CK! CH-CH-CK! CH! CH-CK! CH!
THEY'RE HERE.

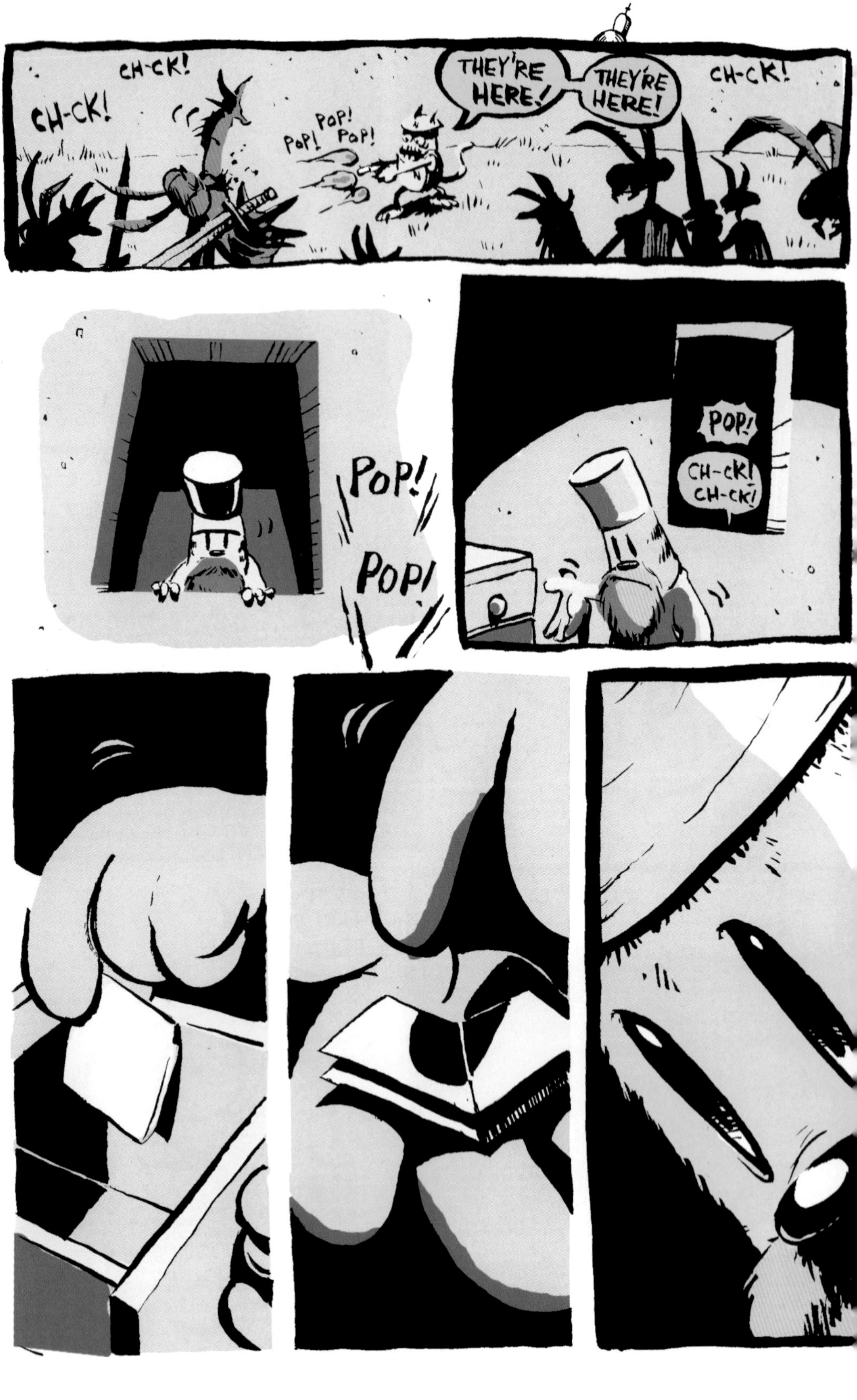
CH-CK!
CH-CK!
POP!
POP!
POP!
THEY'RE HERE!
THEY'RE HERE!
CH-CK!
POP!
POP!
POP!
CH-CK! CH-CK!

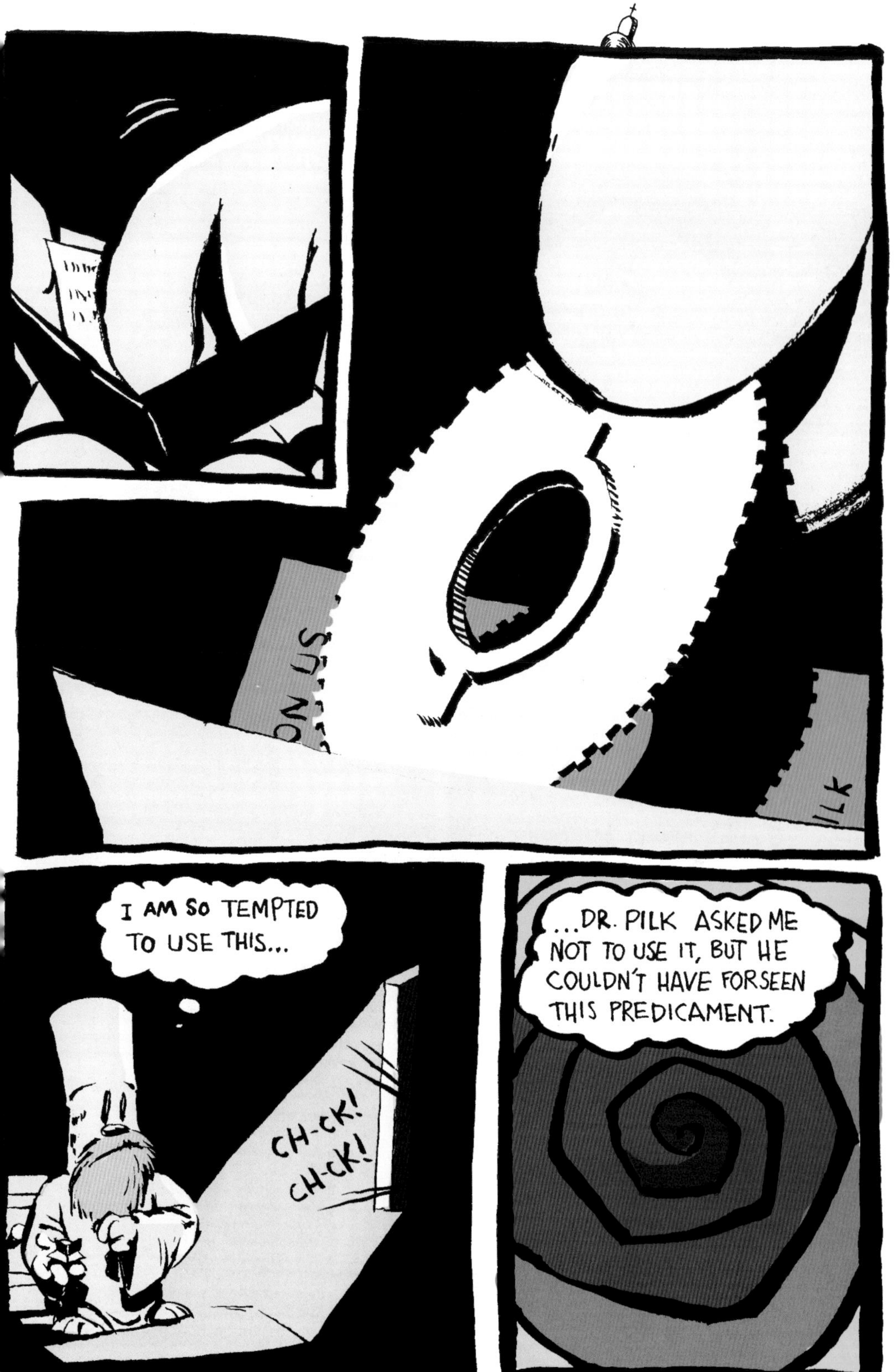
I AM SO TEMPTED TO USE THIS...
CH-CK! CH-CK!
...DR. PILK ASKED ME NOT TO USE IT, BUT HE COULDN'T HAVE FORSEEN THIS PREDICAMENT.

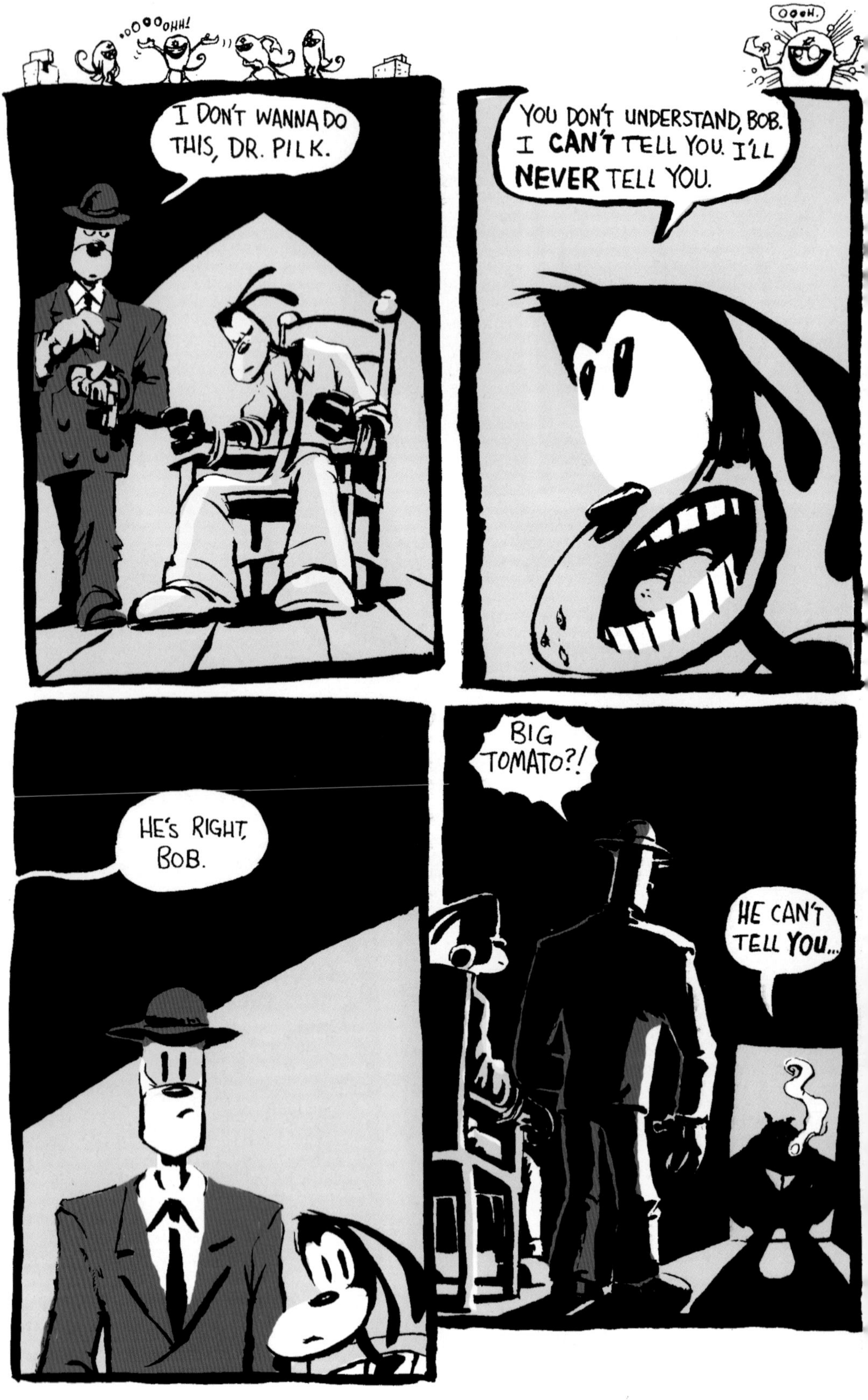
ooOOOOHH!
OOOH.
I DON'T WANNA DO THIS, DR. PILK.
YOU DON'T UNDERSTAND, BOB. I CAN'T TELL YOU. I'LL NEVER TELL YOU.
HE'S RIGHT, BOB.
BIG TOMATO?!
HE CAN'T TELL YOU...

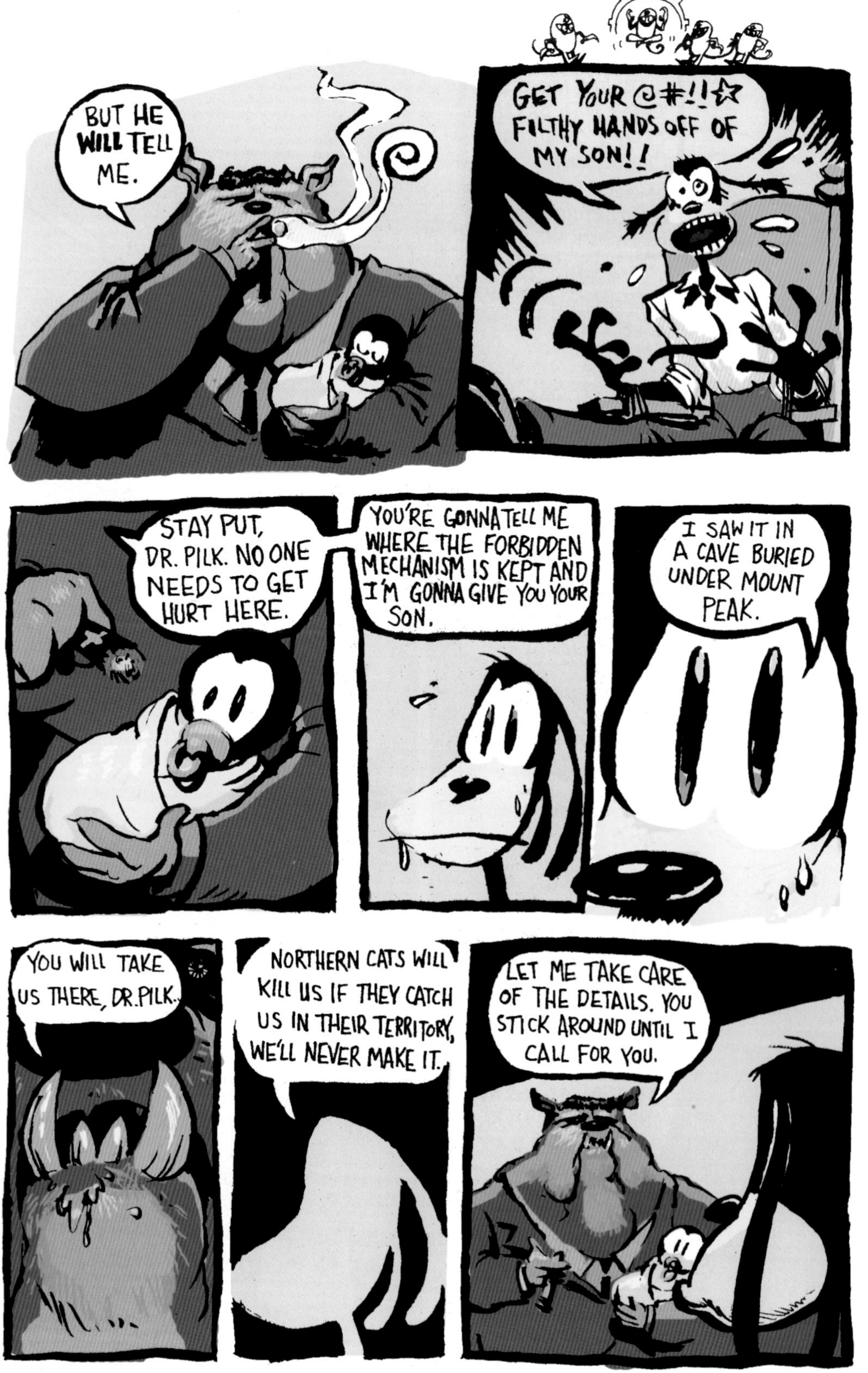
BUT HE **WILL** TELL ME.
GET YOUR @#!!☆ FILTHY HANDS OFF OF MY SON!!
STAY PUT, DR. PILK. NO ONE NEEDS TO GET HURT HERE.
YOU'RE GONNA TELL ME WHERE THE FORBIDDEN MECHANISM IS KEPT AND I'M GONNA GIVE YOU YOUR SON.
I SAW IT IN A CAVE BURIED UNDER MOUNT PEAK.
YOU WILL TAKE US THERE, DR. PILK.
NORTHERN CATS WILL KILL US IF THEY CATCH US IN THEIR TERRITORY, WE'LL NEVER MAKE IT.
LET ME TAKE CARE OF THE DETAILS. YOU STICK AROUND UNTIL I CALL FOR YOU.

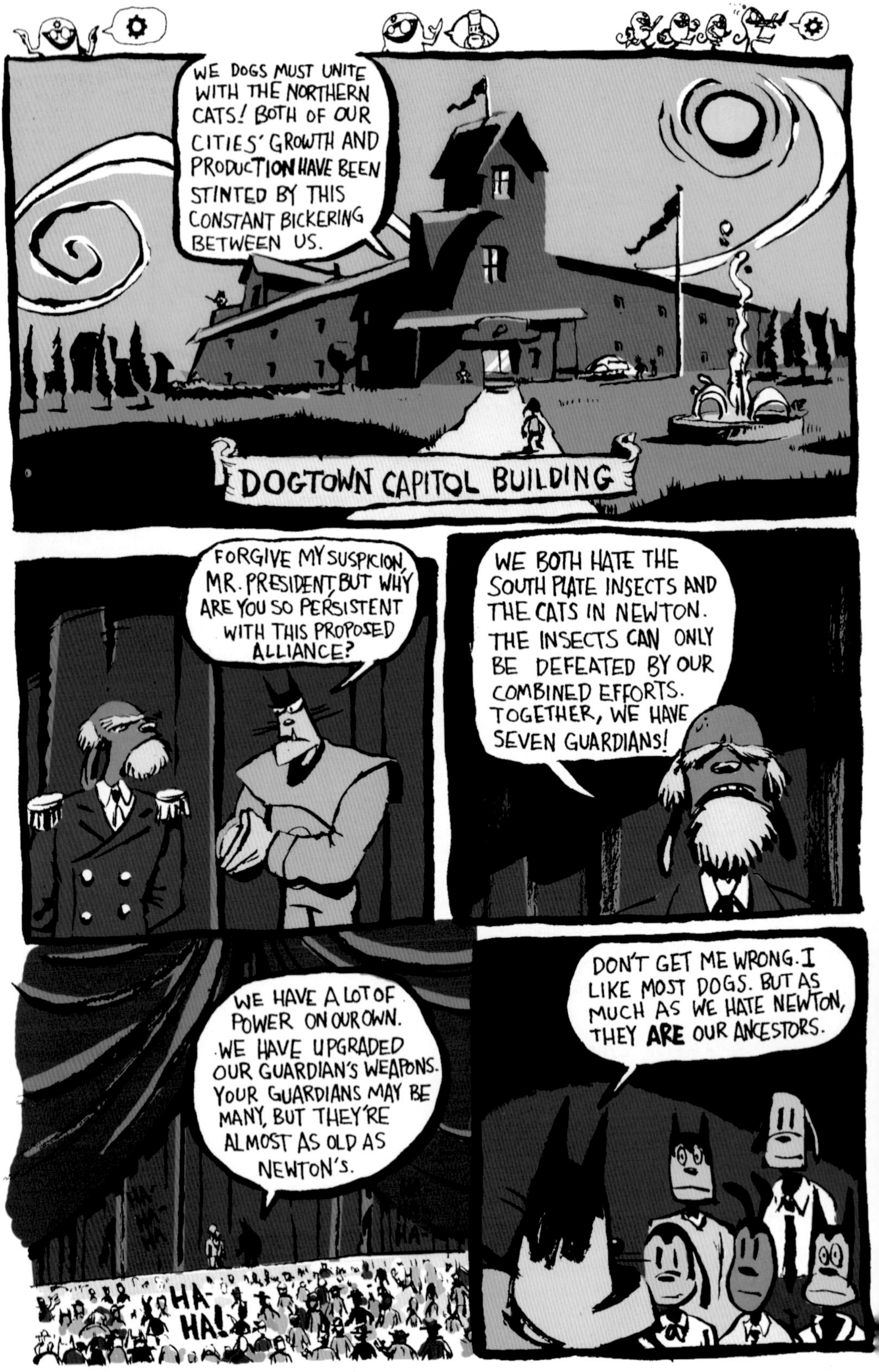
WE DOGS MUST UNITE WITH THE NORTHERN CATS! BOTH OF OUR CITIES' GROWTH AND PRODUCTION HAVE BEEN STINTED BY THIS CONSTANT BICKERING BETWEEN US.
DOGTOWN CAPITOL BUILDING
FORGIVE MY SUSPICION, MR. PRESIDENT, BUT WHY ARE YOU SO PERSISTENT WITH THIS PROPOSED ALLIANCE?
WE BOTH HATE THE SOUTH PLATE INSECTS AND THE CATS IN NEWTON. THE INSECTS CAN ONLY BE DEFEATED BY OUR COMBINED EFFORTS. TOGETHER, WE HAVE SEVEN GUARDIANS!
WE HAVE A LOT OF POWER ON OUR OWN. WE HAVE UPGRADED OUR GUARDIAN'S WEAPONS. YOUR GUARDIANS MAY BE MANY, BUT THEY'RE ALMOST AS OLD AS NEWTON'S.
HA-HA!
DON'T GET ME WRONG. I LIKE MOST DOGS. BUT AS MUCH AS WE HATE NEWTON, THEY ARE OUR ANCESTORS.

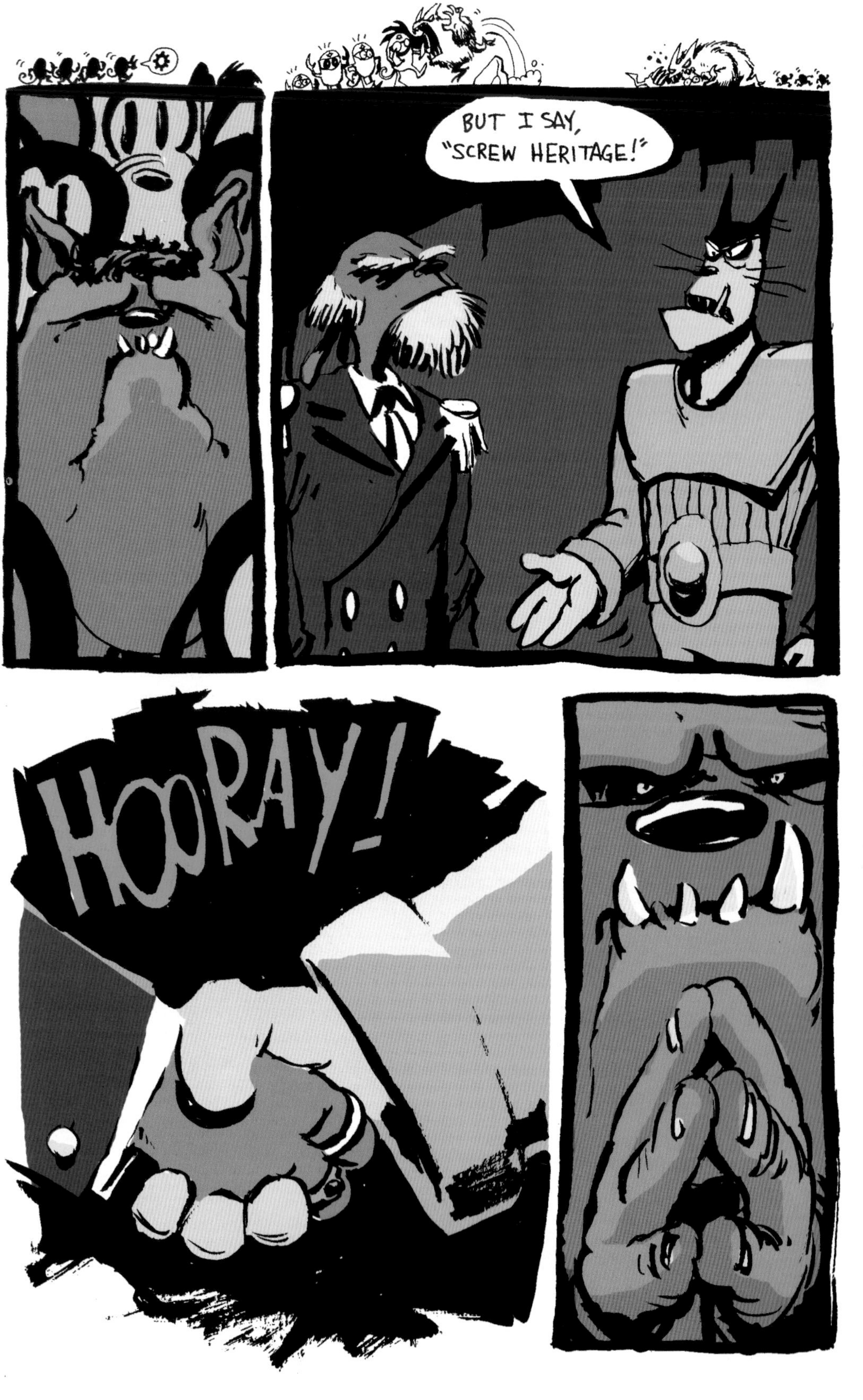
BUT I SAY, "SCREW HERITAGE!"
HOORAY!

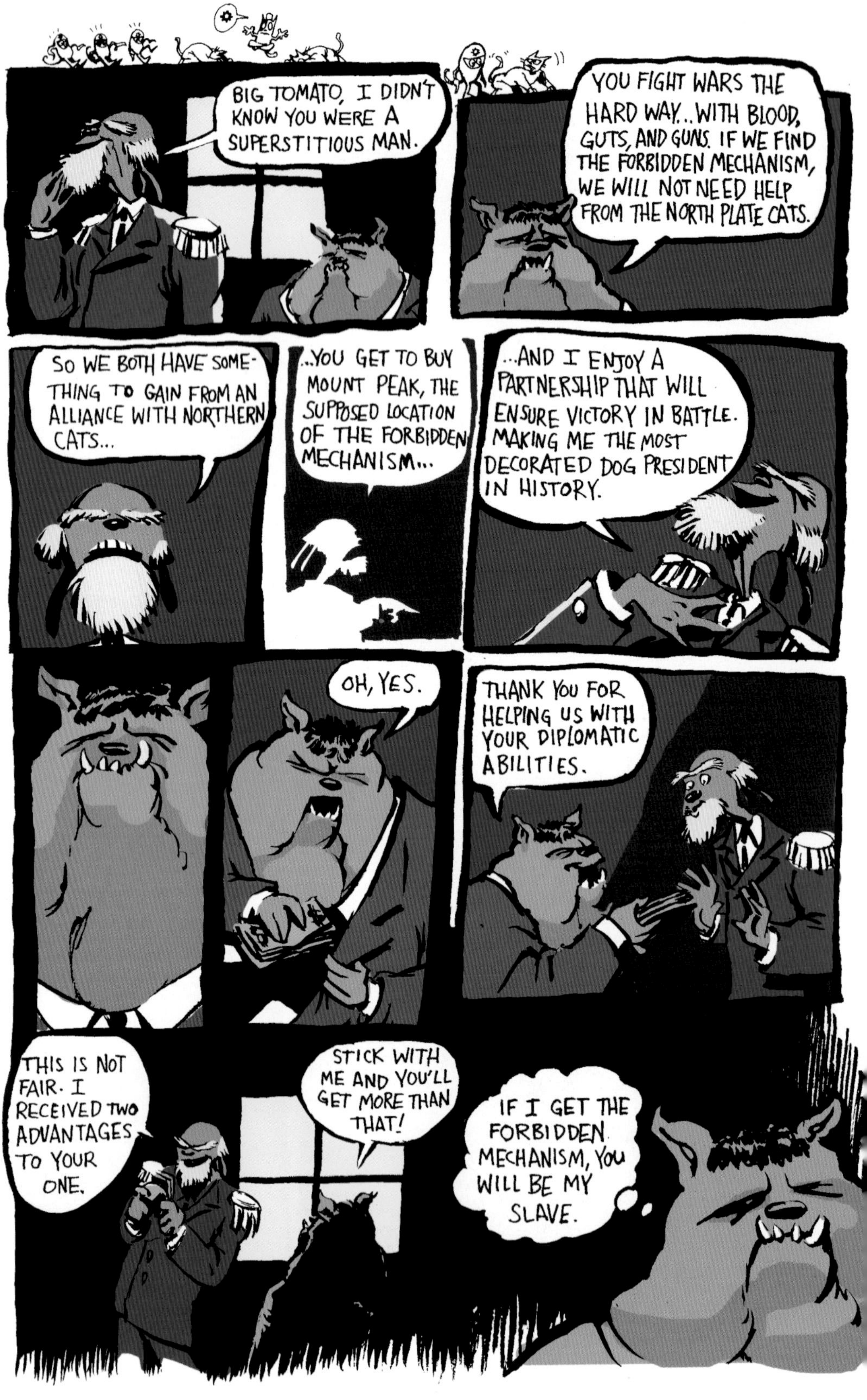
BIG TOMATO, I DIDN'T KNOW YOU WERE A SUPERSTITIOUS MAN.
YOU FIGHT WARS THE HARD WAY... WITH BLOOD, GUTS, AND GUNS. IF WE FIND THE FORBIDDEN MECHANISM, WE WILL NOT NEED HELP FROM THE NORTH PLATE CATS.
SO WE BOTH HAVE SOMETHING TO GAIN FROM AN ALLIANCE WITH NORTHERN CATS...
...YOU GET TO BUY MOUNT PEAK, THE SUPPOSED LOCATION OF THE FORBIDDEN MECHANISM...
...AND I ENJOY A PARTNERSHIP THAT WILL ENSURE VICTORY IN BATTLE. MAKING ME THE MOST DECORATED DOG PRESIDENT IN HISTORY.
OH, YES.
THANK YOU FOR HELPING US WITH YOUR DIPLOMATIC ABILITIES.
THIS IS NOT FAIR. I RECEIVED TWO ADVANTAGES TO YOUR ONE.
STICK WITH ME AND YOU'LL GET MORE THAN THAT!
IF I GET THE FORBIDDEN MECHANISM, YOU WILL BE MY SLAVE.

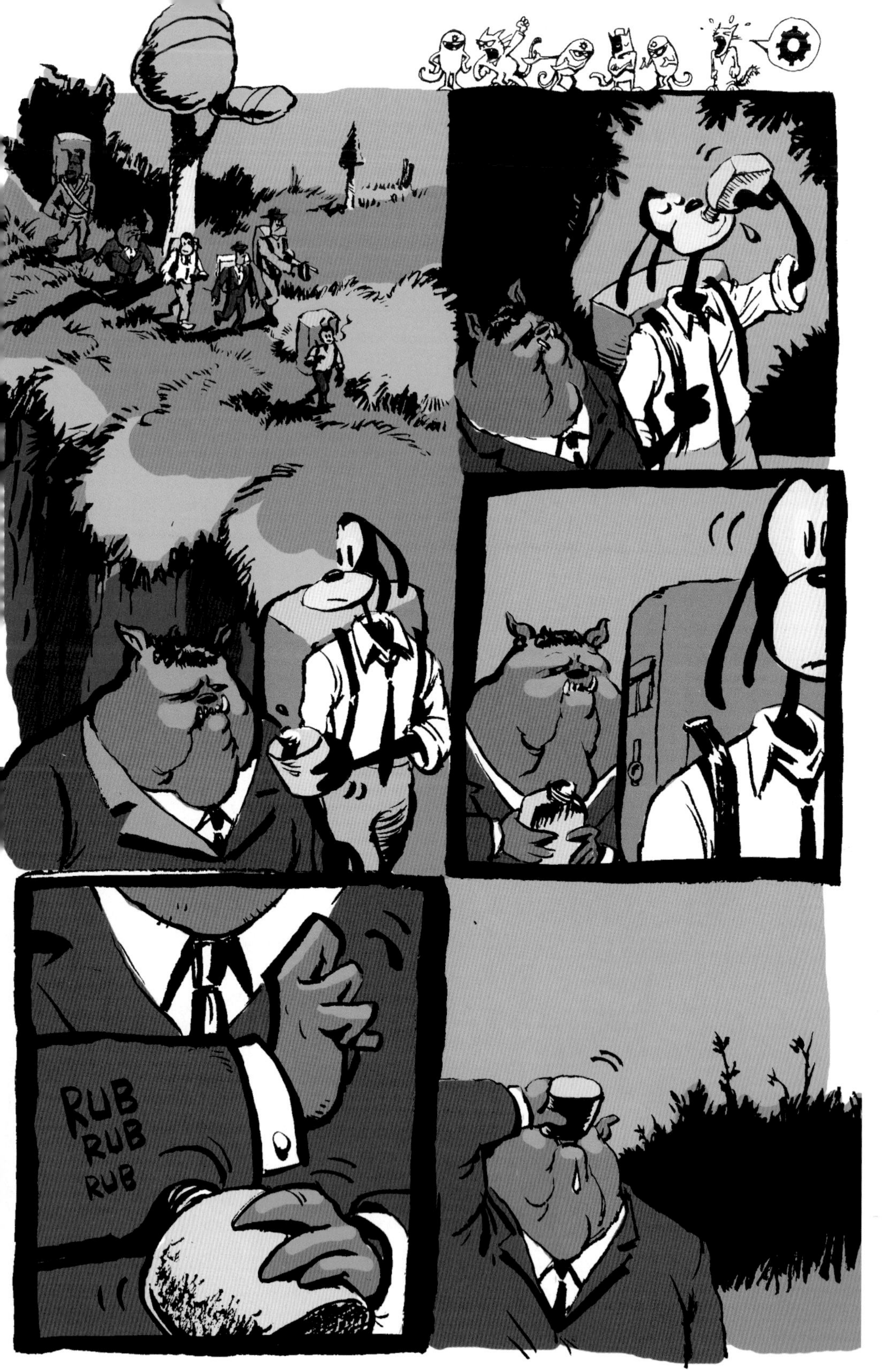
RUB
RUB
RUB

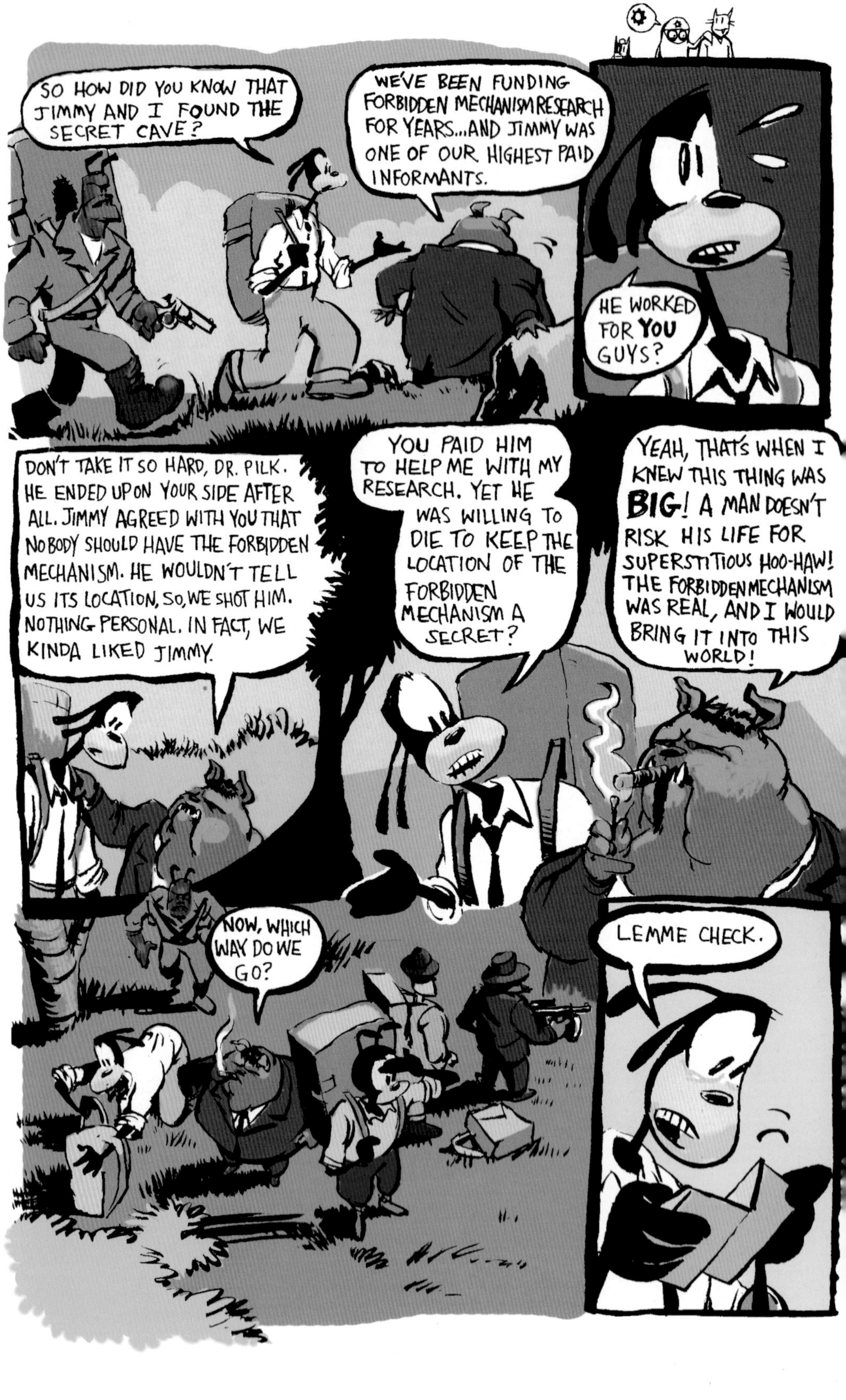
SO HOW DID YOU KNOW THAT JIMMY AND I FOUND THE SECRET CAVE?
WE'VE BEEN FUNDING FORBIDDEN MECHANISM RESEARCH FOR YEARS... AND JIMMY WAS ONE OF OUR HIGHEST PAID INFORMANTS.
HE WORKED FOR **YOU** GUYS?
DON'T TAKE IT SO HARD, DR. PILK. HE ENDED UP ON YOUR SIDE AFTER ALL. JIMMY AGREED WITH YOU THAT NOBODY SHOULD HAVE THE FORBIDDEN MECHANISM. HE WOULDN'T TELL US ITS LOCATION, SO, WE SHOT HIM. NOTHING PERSONAL. IN FACT, WE KINDA LIKED JIMMY.
YOU PAID HIM TO HELP ME WITH MY RESEARCH. YET HE WAS WILLING TO DIE TO KEEP THE LOCATION OF THE FORBIDDEN MECHANISM A SECRET?
YEAH, THAT'S WHEN I KNEW THIS THING WAS **BIG**! A MAN DOESN'T RISK HIS LIFE FOR SUPERSTITIOUS HOO-HAW! THE FORBIDDEN MECHANISM WAS REAL, AND I WOULD BRING IT INTO THIS WORLD!
NOW, WHICH WAY DO WE GO?
LEMME CHECK.

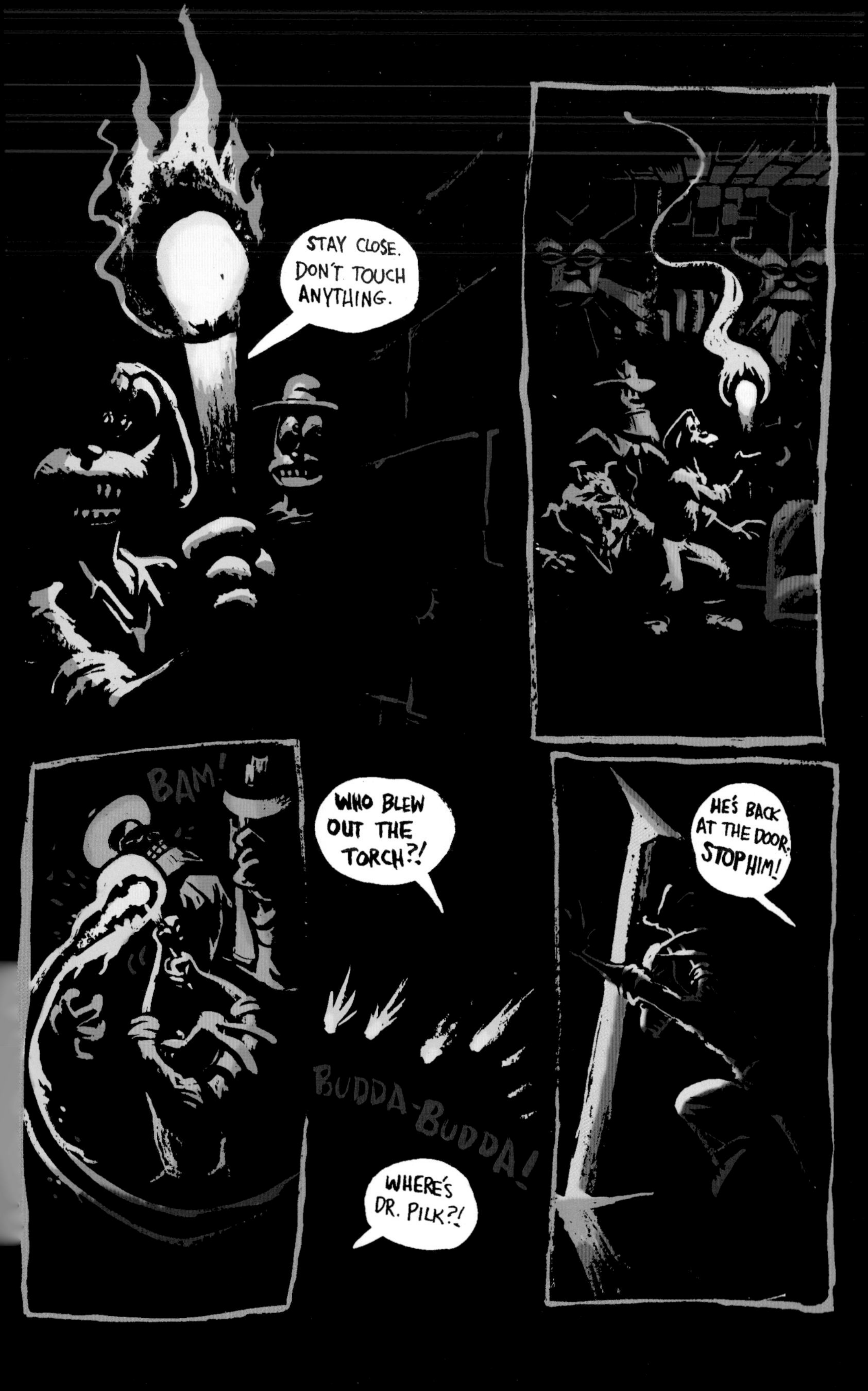
STAY CLOSE. DON'T TOUCH ANYTHING.
BAM!
WHO BLEW OUT THE TORCH?!
BUDDA-BUDDA!
WHERE'S DR. PILK?!
HE'S BACK AT THE DOOR: STOP HIM!

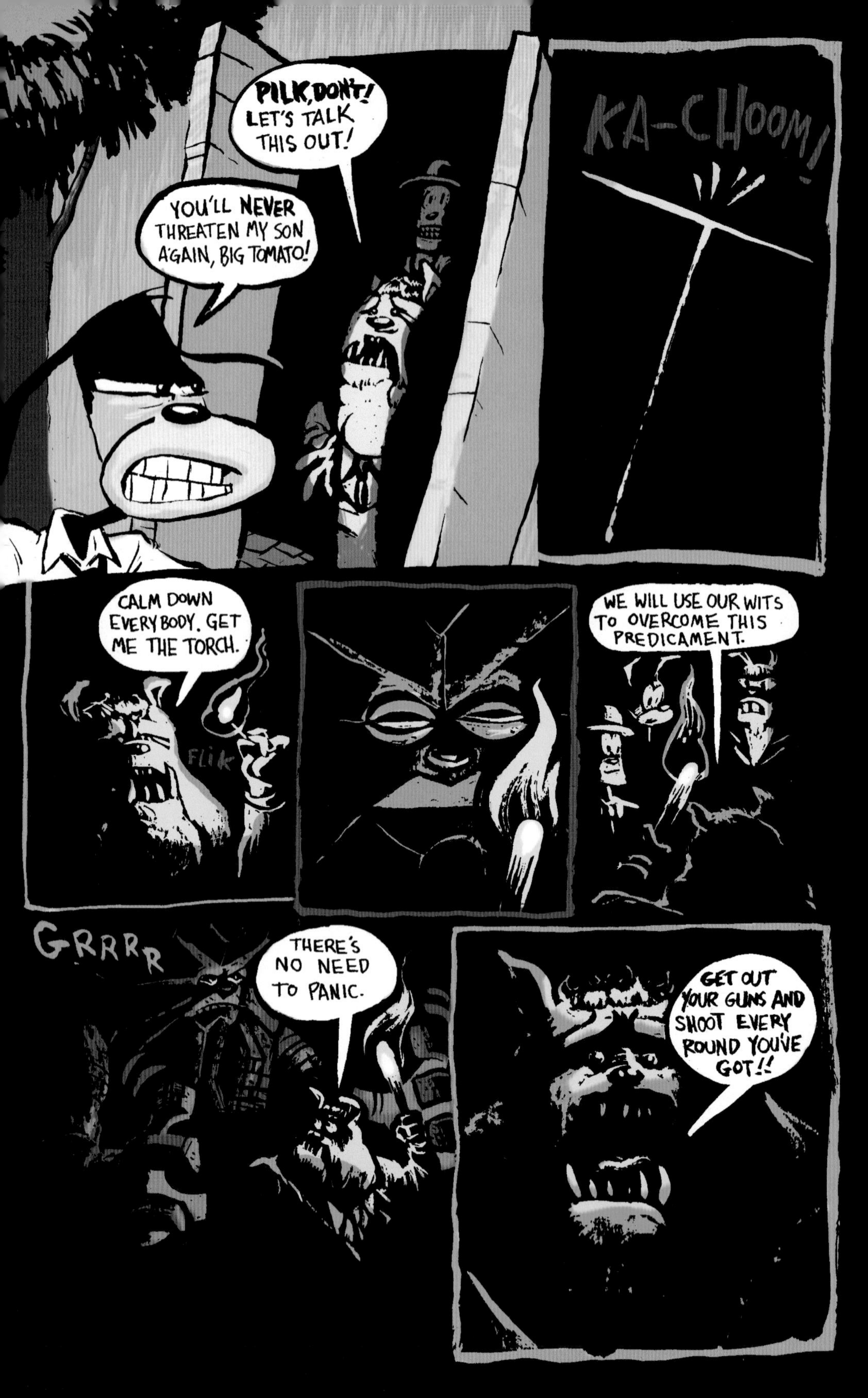
PILK, DON'T! LET'S TALK THIS OUT!
YOU'LL NEVER THREATEN MY SON AGAIN, BIG TOMATO!
KA-CHOOM!
CALM DOWN EVERYBODY. GET ME THE TORCH.
FLIK
WE WILL USE OUR WITS TO OVERCOME THIS PREDICAMENT.
GRRRR
THERE'S NO NEED TO PANIC.
GET OUT YOUR GUNS AND SHOOT EVERY ROUND YOU'VE GOT!!

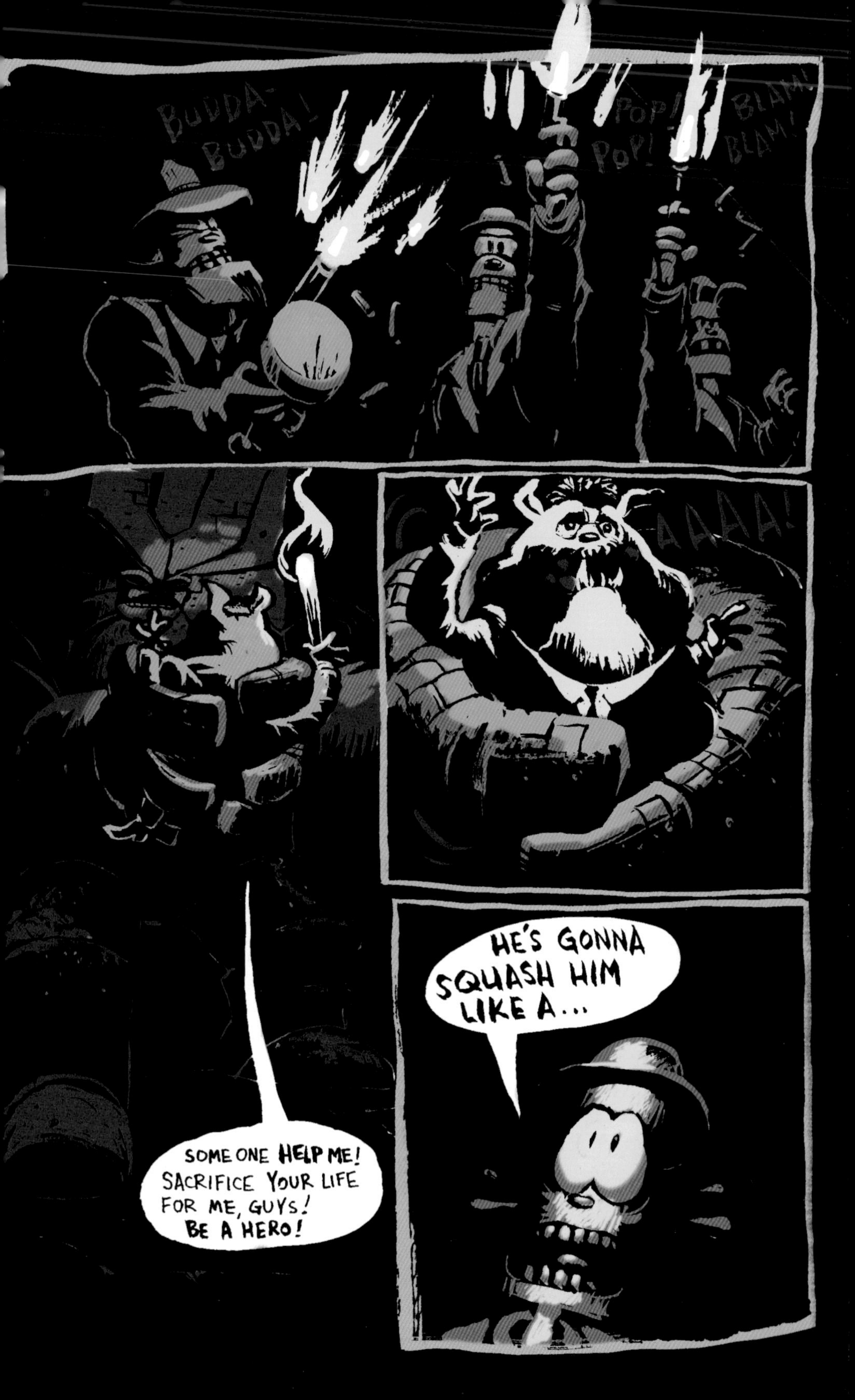
BUDDA-BUDDA!
POP! POP!
BLAM! BLAM!
AAAA!
SOME ONE HELP ME! SACRIFICE YOUR LIFE FOR ME, GUYS! BE A HERO!
HE'S GONNA SQUASH HIM LIKE A...

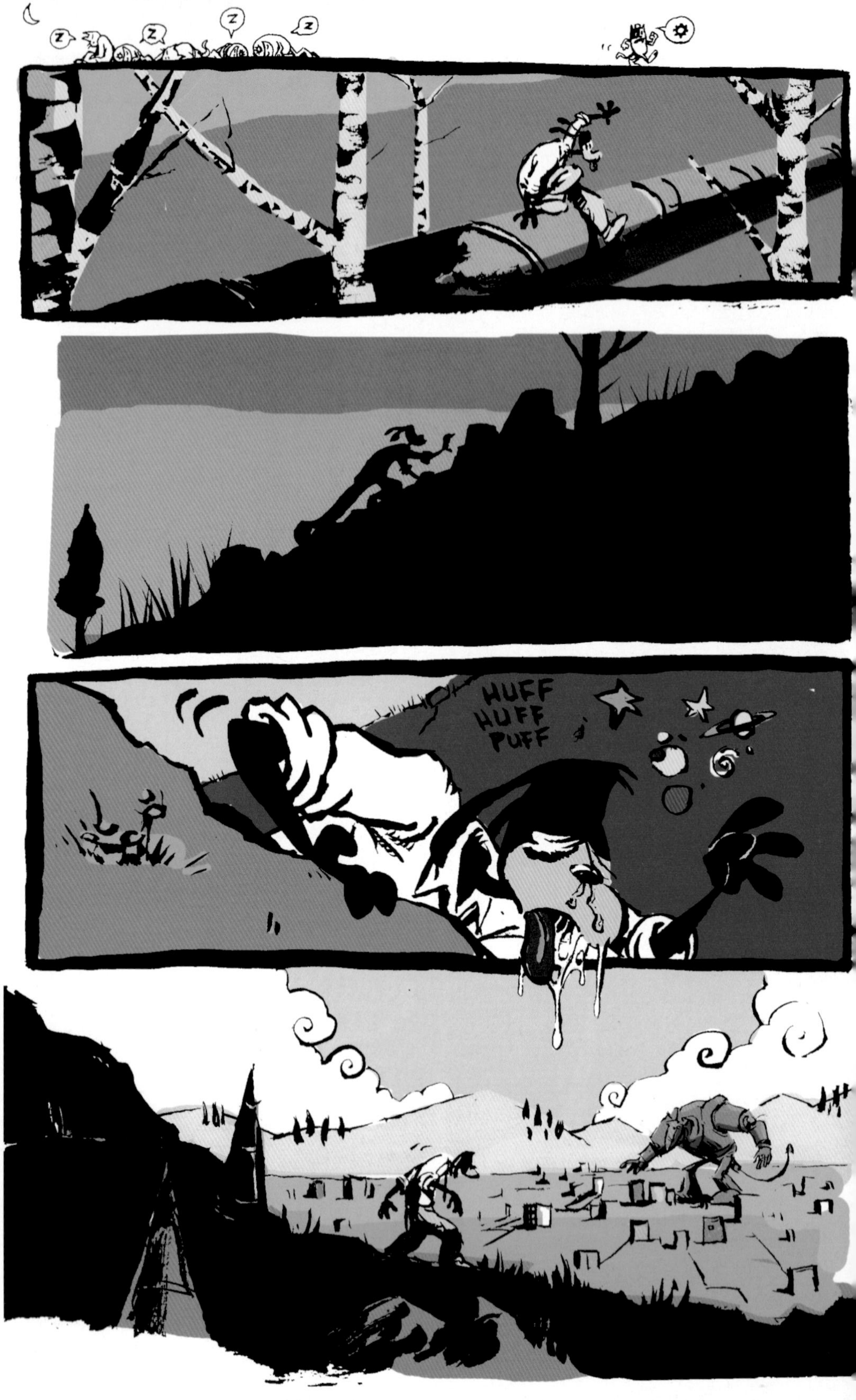
Z
Z
Z
Z
HUFF
HUFF
PUFF

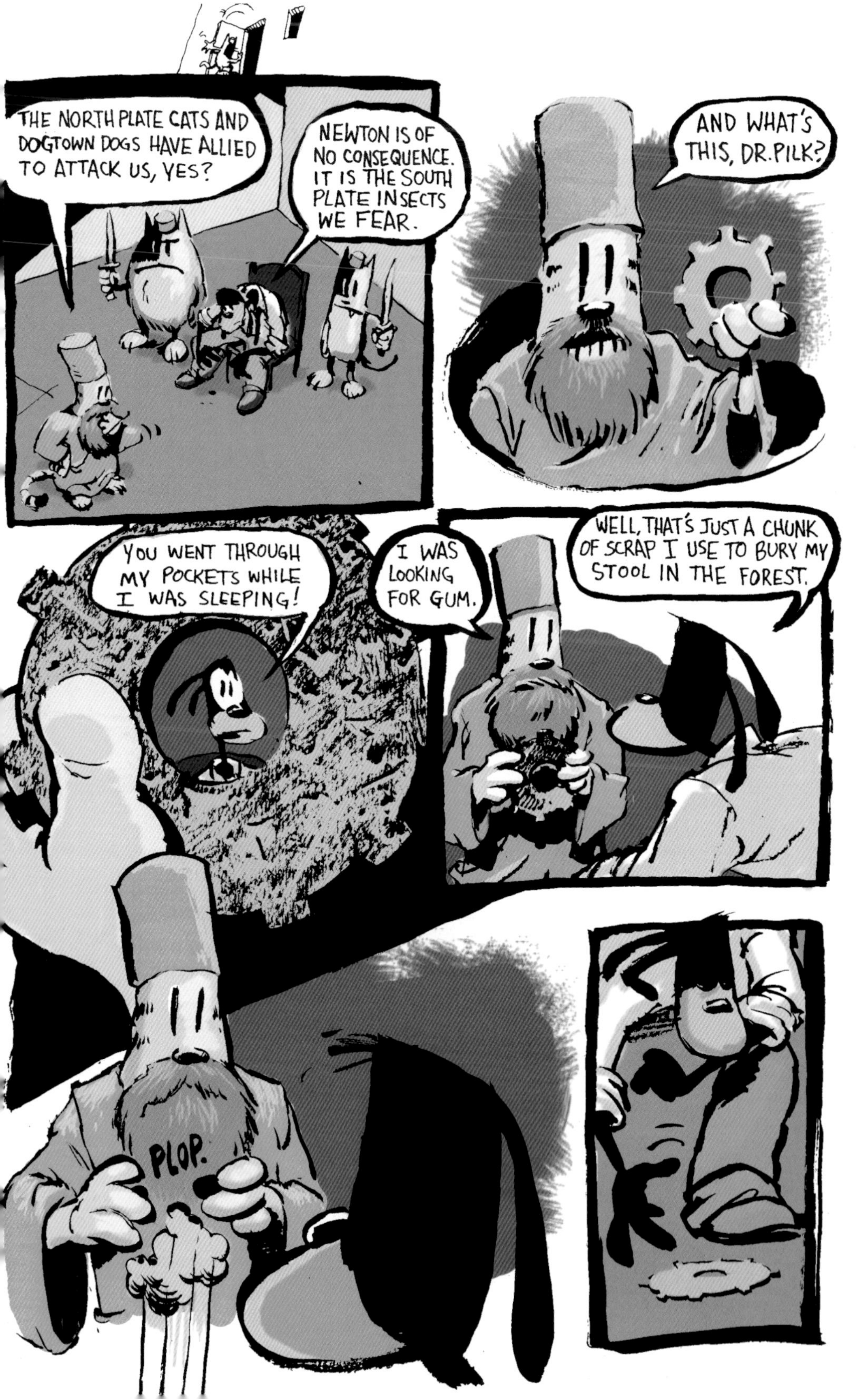
THE NORTH PLATE CATS AND DOGTOWN DOGS HAVE ALLIED TO ATTACK US, YES?
NEWTON IS OF NO CONSEQUENCE. IT IS THE SOUTH PLATE INSECTS WE FEAR.
AND WHAT'S THIS, DR. PILK?
YOU WENT THROUGH MY POCKETS WHILE I WAS SLEEPING!
I WAS LOOKING FOR GUM.
WELL, THAT'S JUST A CHUNK OF SCRAP I USE TO BURY MY STOOL IN THE FOREST.
PLOP.

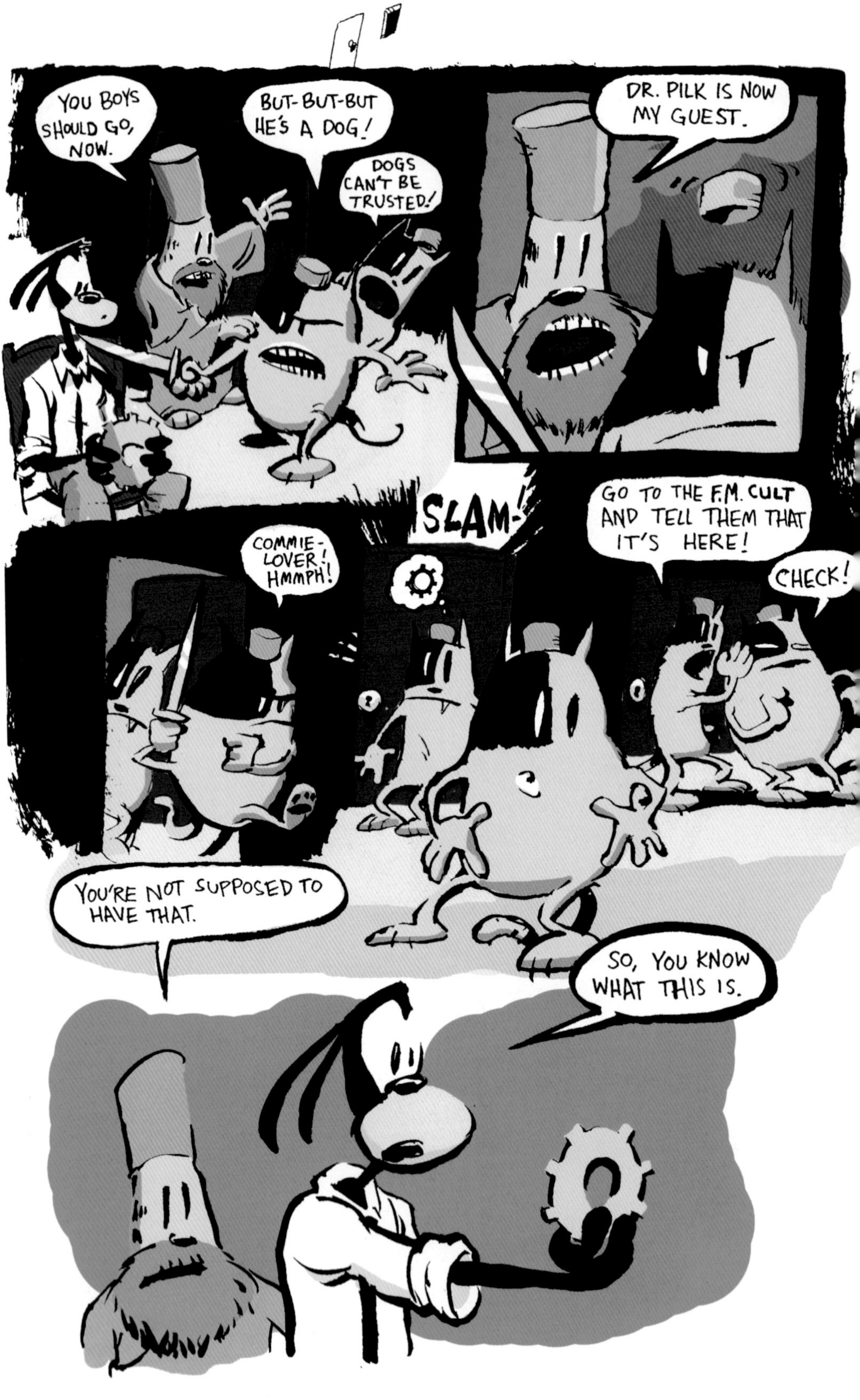
YOU BOYS SHOULD GO, NOW.
BUT-BUT-BUT HE'S A DOG!
DOGS CAN'T BE TRUSTED!
DR. PILK IS NOW MY GUEST.
SLAM!
COMMIE-LOVER! HMMPH!
GO TO THE F.M. CULT AND TELL THEM THAT IT'S HERE!
CHECK!
YOU'RE NOT SUPPOSED TO HAVE THAT.
SO, YOU KNOW WHAT THIS IS.

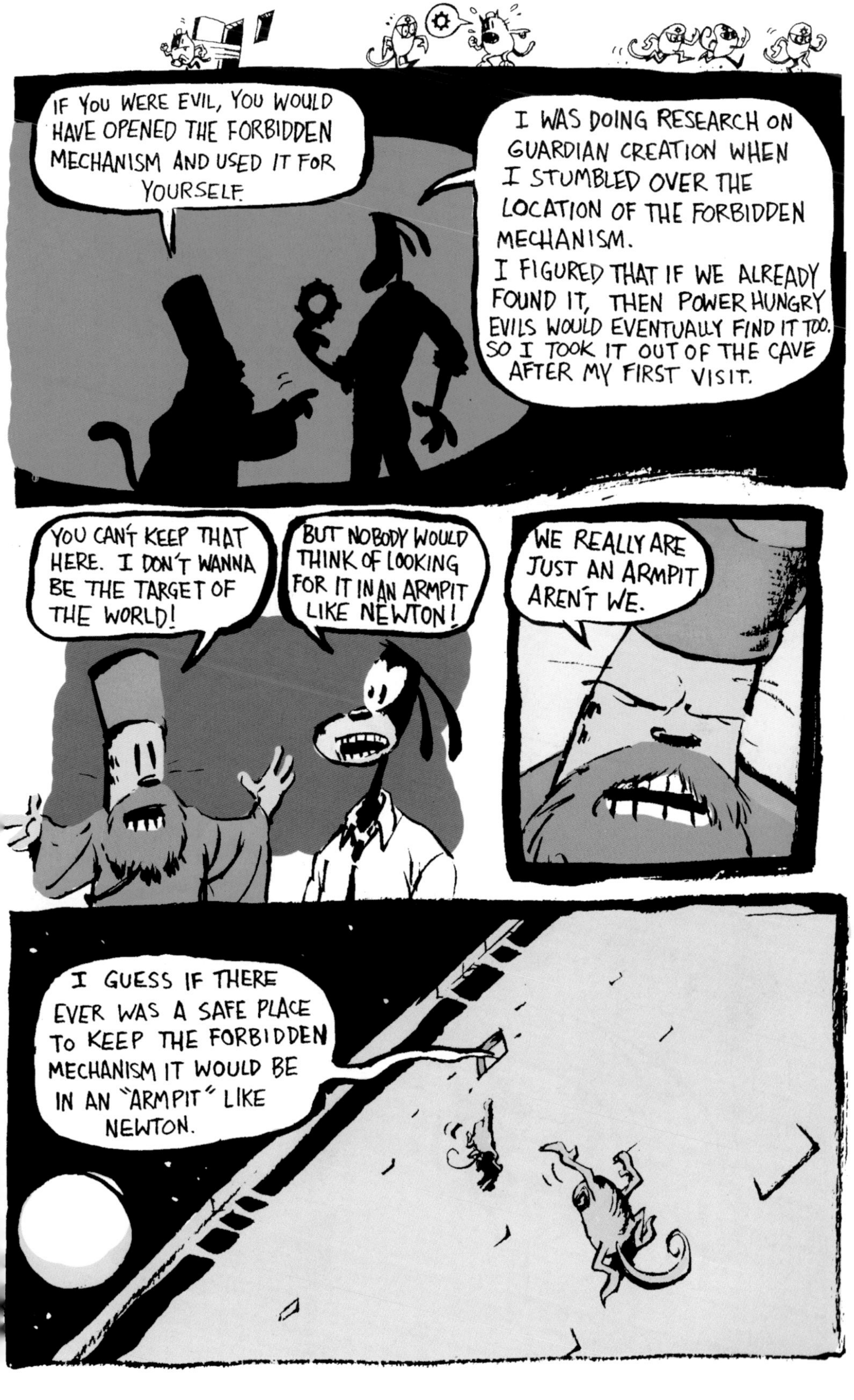
IF YOU WERE EVIL, YOU WOULD HAVE OPENED THE FORBIDDEN MECHANISM AND USED IT FOR YOURSELF.
I WAS DOING RESEARCH ON GUARDIAN CREATION WHEN I STUMBLED OVER THE LOCATION OF THE FORBIDDEN MECHANISM.
I FIGURED THAT IF WE ALREADY FOUND IT, THEN POWER HUNGRY EVILS WOULD EVENTUALLY FIND IT TOO. SO I TOOK IT OUT OF THE CAVE AFTER MY FIRST VISIT.
YOU CAN'T KEEP THAT HERE. I DON'T WANNA BE THE TARGET OF THE WORLD!
BUT NOBODY WOULD THINK OF LOOKING FOR IT IN AN ARMPIT LIKE NEWTON!
WE REALLY ARE JUST AN ARMPIT AREN'T WE.
I GUESS IF THERE EVER WAS A SAFE PLACE TO KEEP THE FORBIDDEN MECHANISM IT WOULD BE IN AN "ARMPIT" LIKE NEWTON.

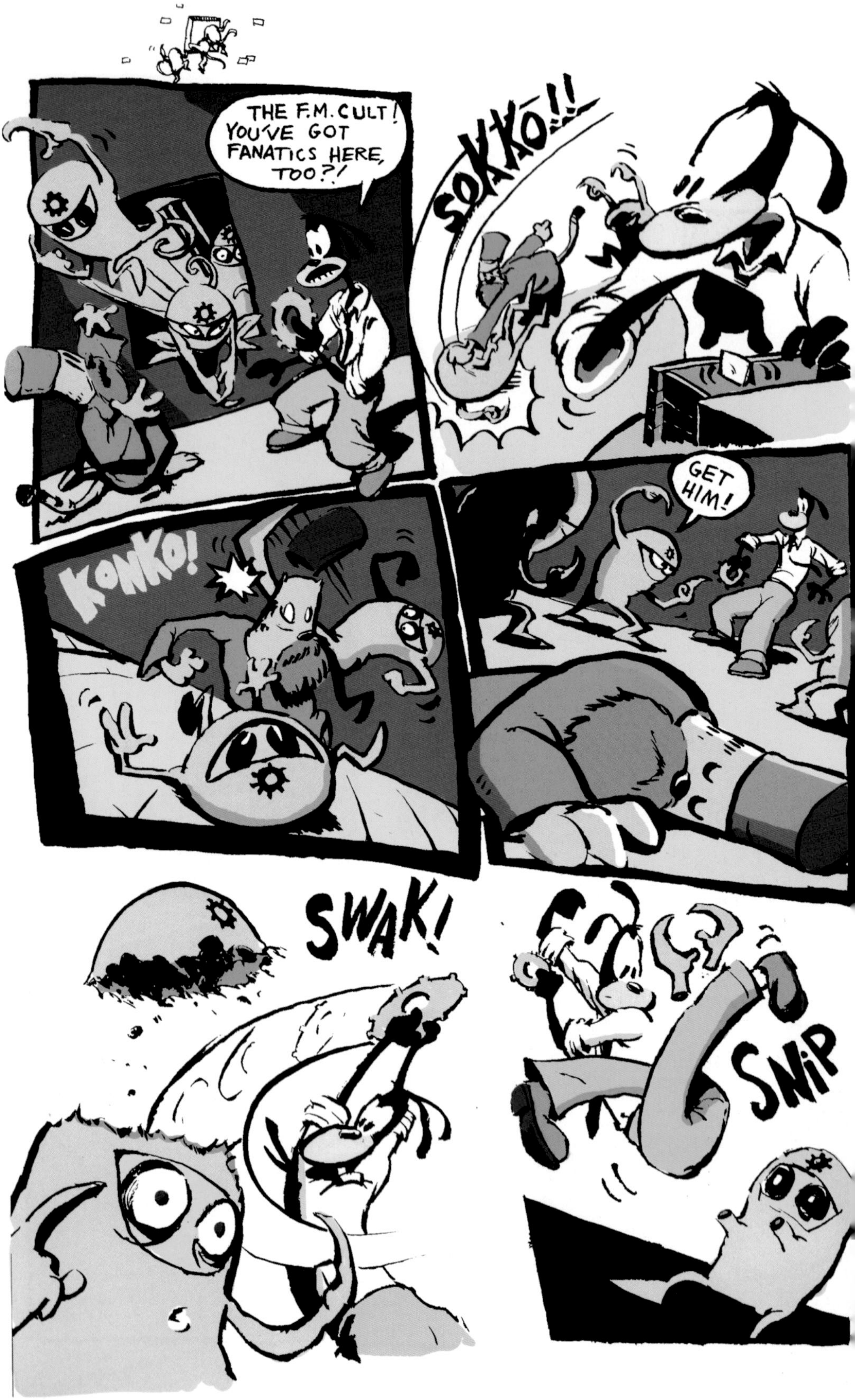
THE F.M. CULT! YOU'VE GOT FANATICS HERE, TOO?!
SOKKO!!
KONKO!
GET HIM!
SWAK!
SNIP

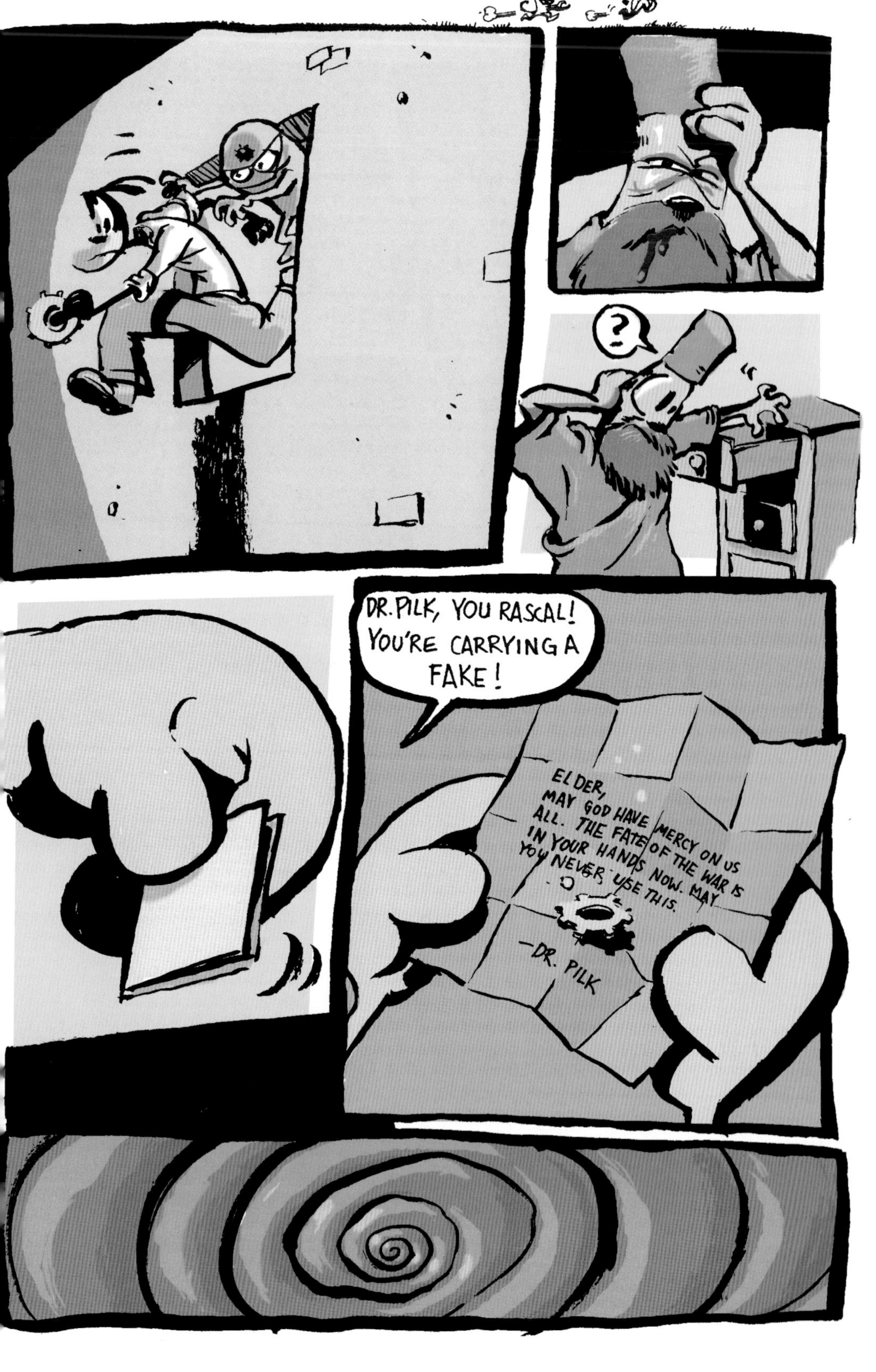
?
DR. PILK, YOU RASCAL! YOU'RE CARRYING A FAKE!
ELDER,
MAY GOD HAVE MERCY ON US ALL. THE FATE OF THE WAR IS IN YOUR HANDS NOW. MAY YOU NEVER USE THIS.
—DR. PILK

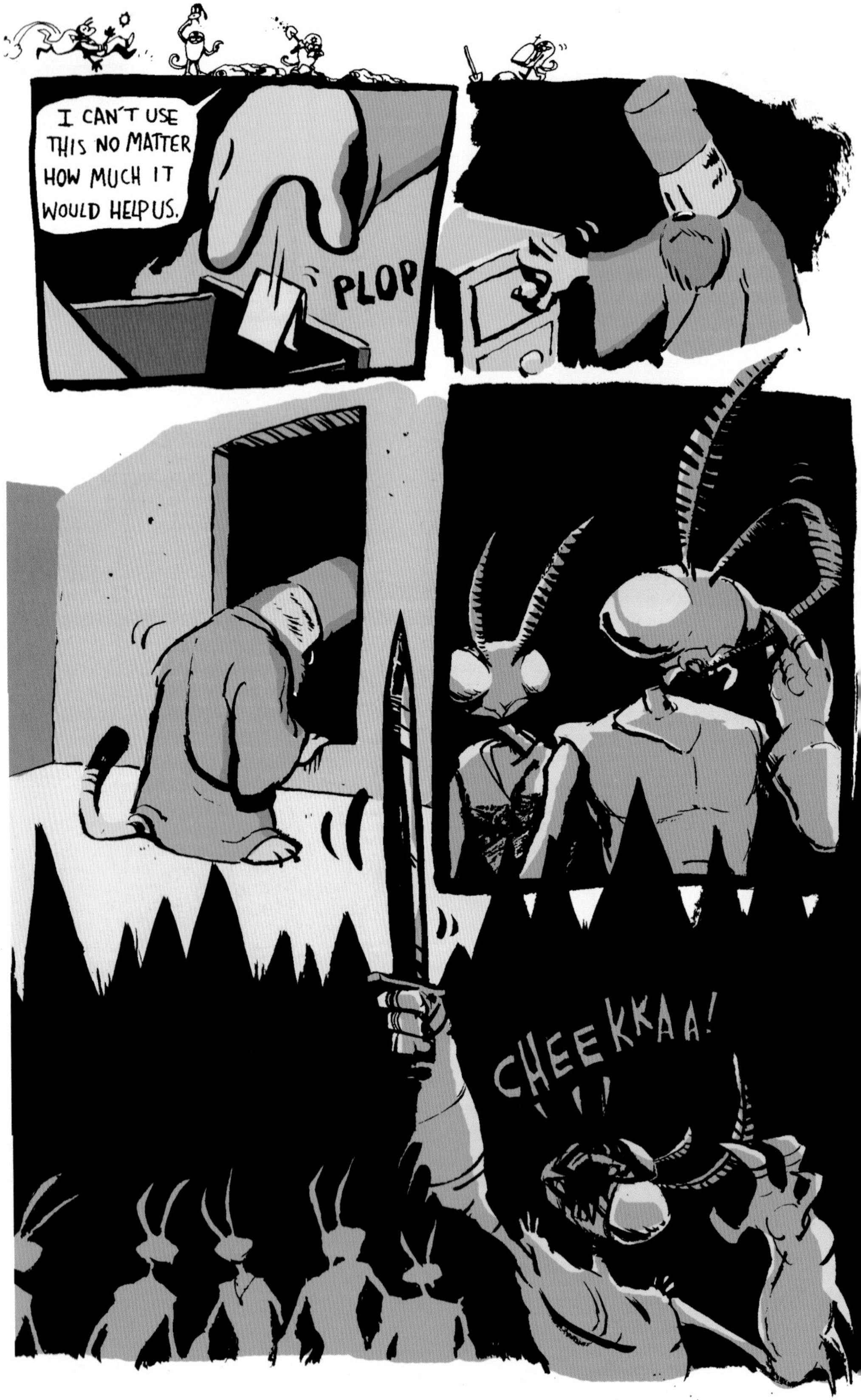
I CAN'T USE THIS NO MATTER HOW MUCH IT WOULD HELP US.
PLOP
CHEEKKAA!

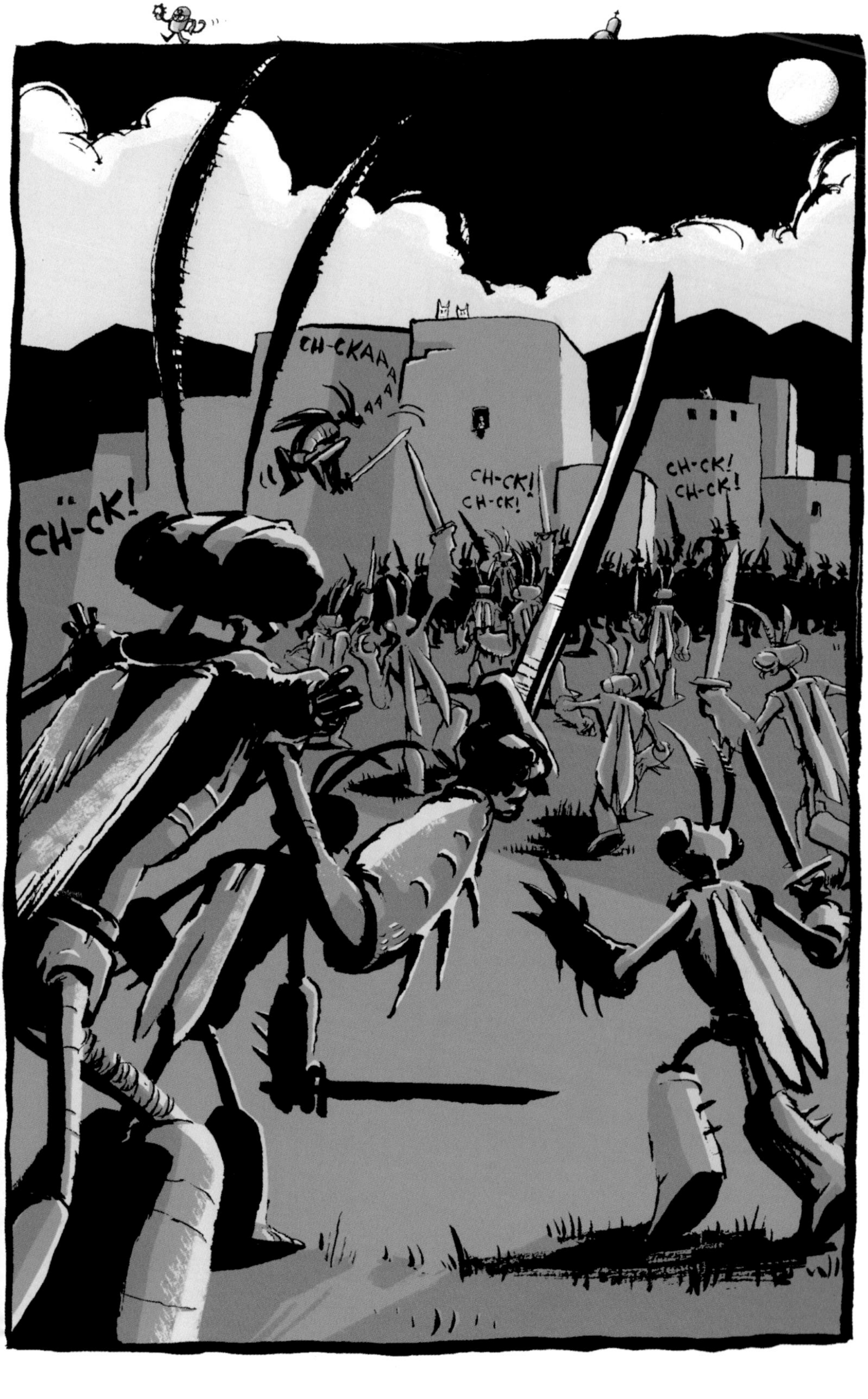
CH-CKAAAAAA
CH-ÏCK!
CH-CK!
CH-CK!
CH-CK!
CH-CK!

chapter 4

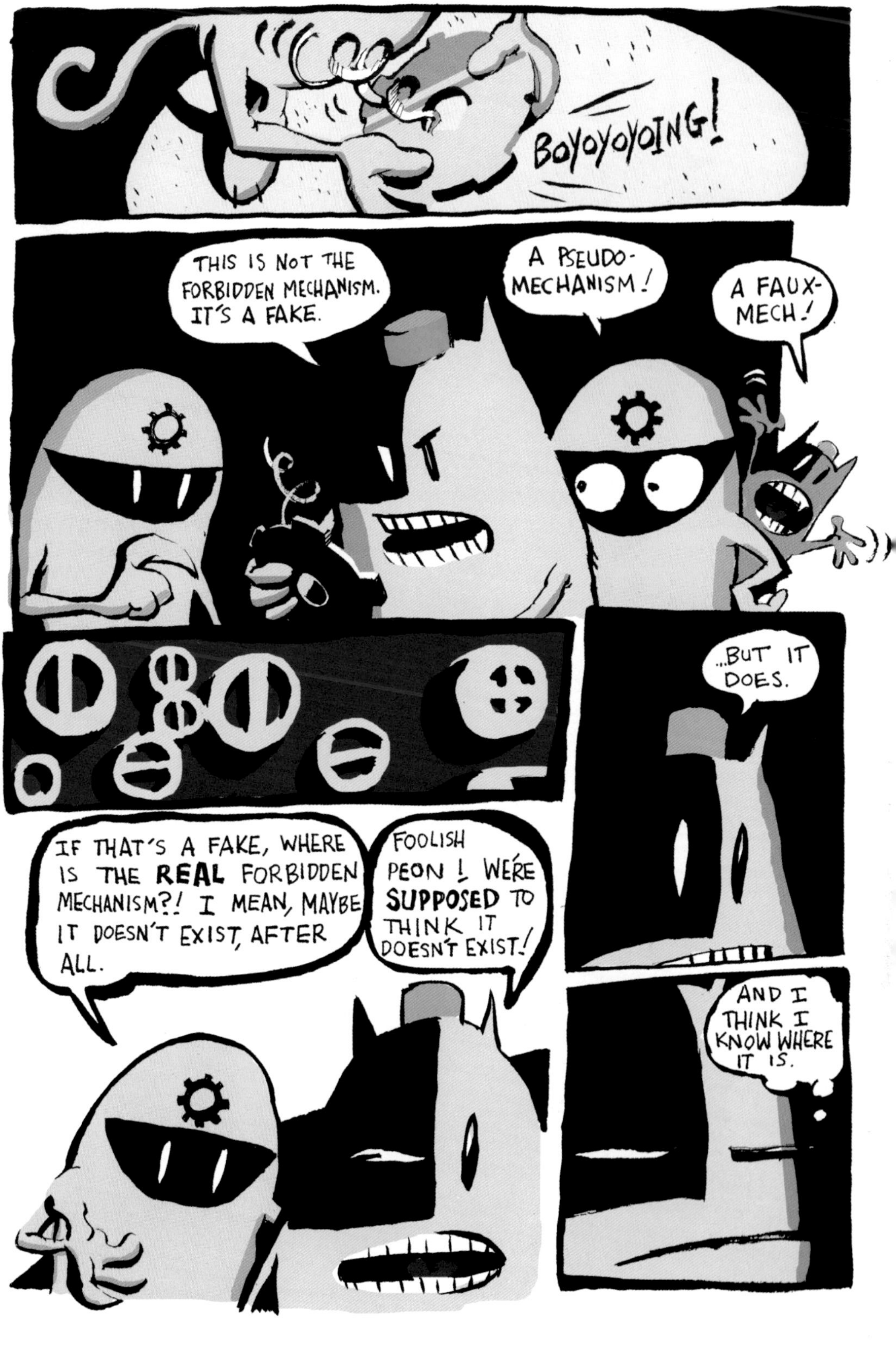
BOYOYOYOYOING!
THIS IS NOT THE FORBIDDEN MECHANISM. IT'S A FAKE.
A PSEUDO-MECHANISM!
A FAUX-MECH!
...BUT IT DOES.
IF THAT'S A FAKE, WHERE IS THE **REAL** FORBIDDEN MECHANISM?! I MEAN, MAYBE IT DOESN'T EXIST, AFTER ALL.
FOOLISH PEON! WE'RE **SUPPOSED** TO THINK IT DOESN'T EXIST!
AND I THINK I KNOW WHERE IT IS.

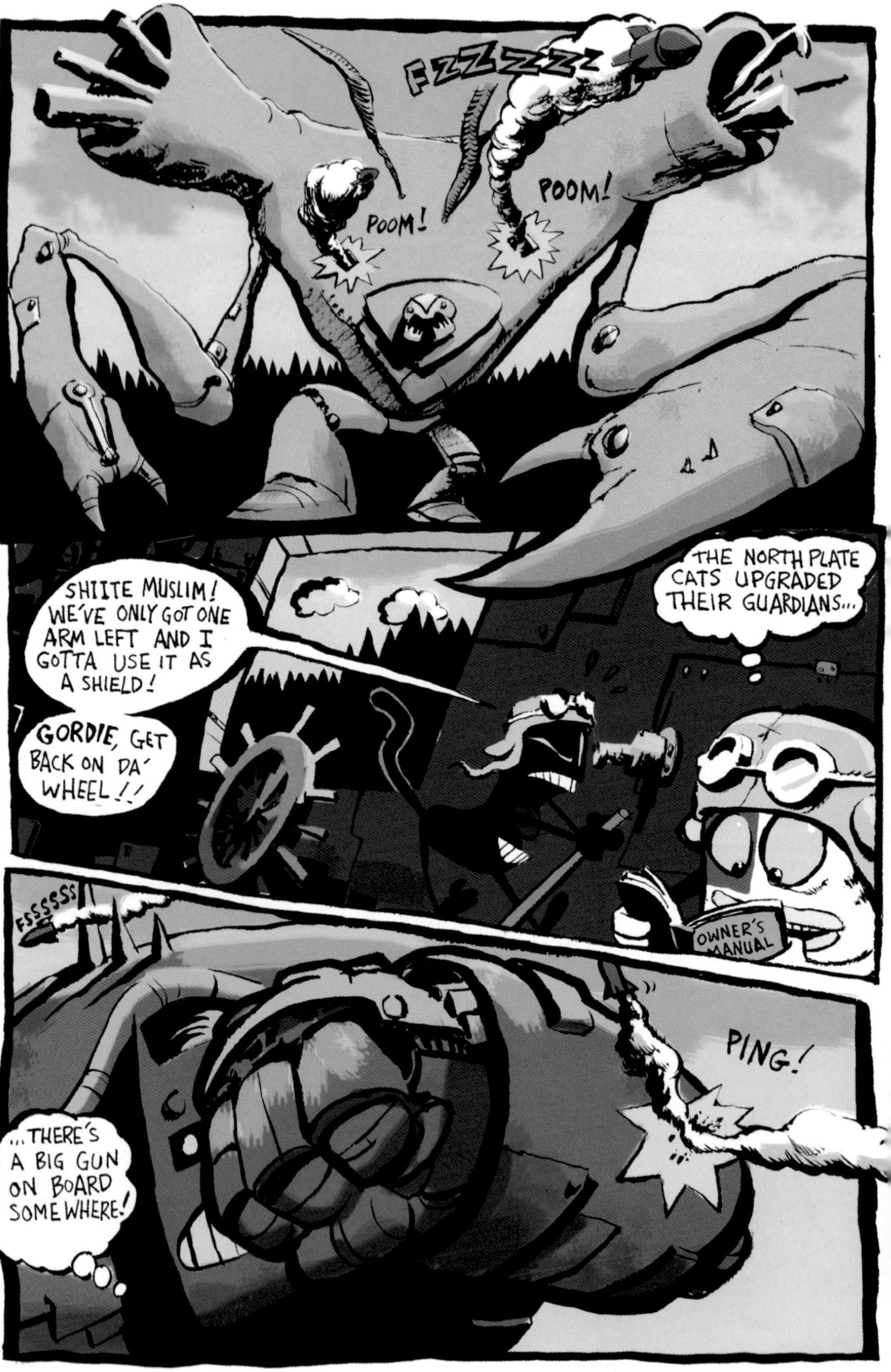
FZZZZZZ
POOM!
POOM!
SHIITE MUSLIM! WE'VE ONLY GOT ONE ARM LEFT AND I GOTTA USE IT AS A SHIELD!
GORDIE, GET BACK ON DA' WHEEL!!
THE NORTH PLATE CATS UPGRADED THEIR GUARDIANS...
OWNER'S MANUAL
FSSSSSS
PING!
...THERE'S A BIG GUN ON BOARD SOMEWHERE!

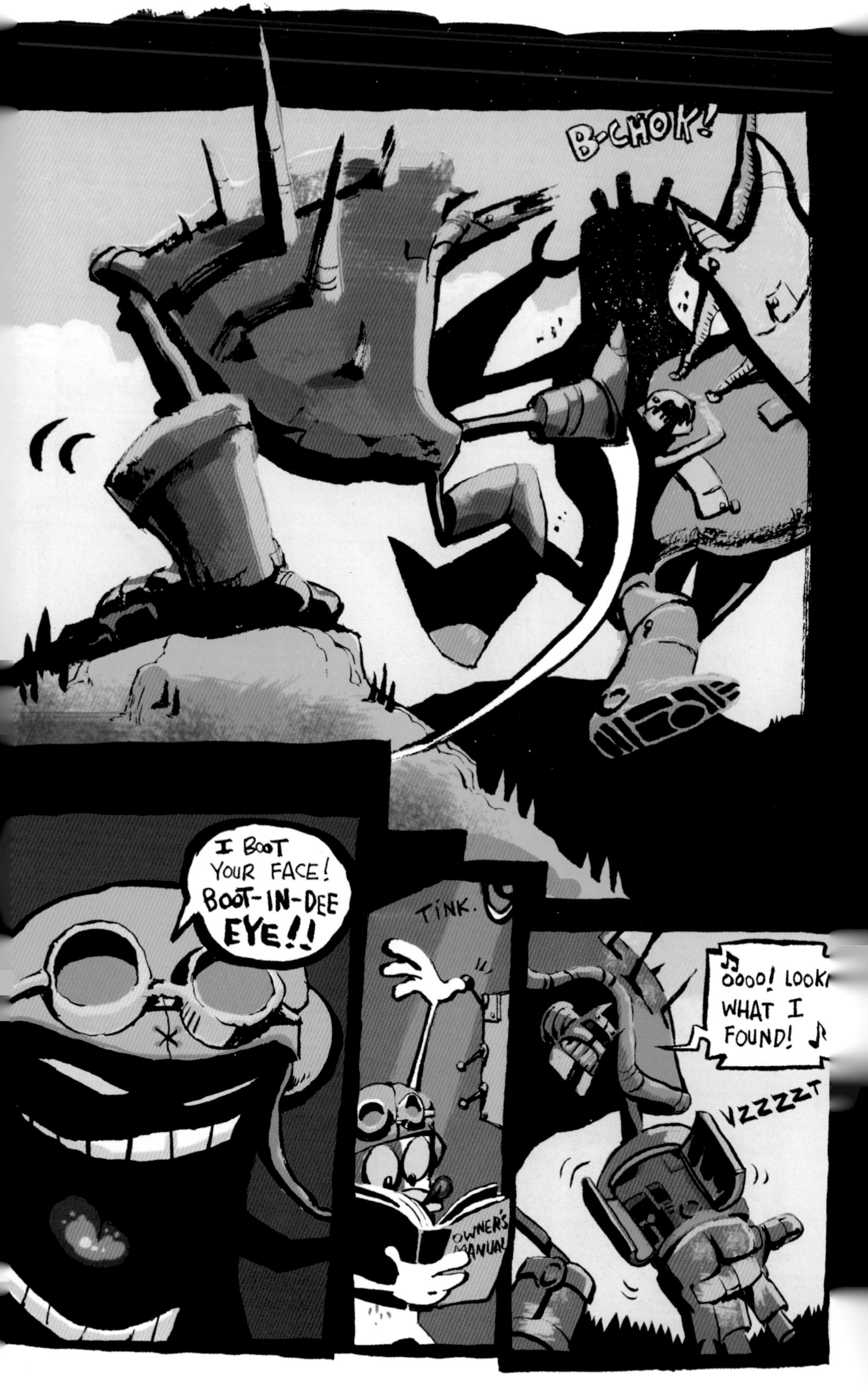
B-CHOK!
I BOOT YOUR FACE! BOOT-IN-DEE EYE!!
TINK.
OWNER'S MANUAL
♫ OOOO! LOOK WHAT I FOUND! ♪
VZZZZT

VZZZT

BZZZT

WHAT'RE YOU WAITIN' FOR GORDIE?! PULL THE TRIGGER!

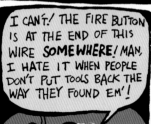

I CAN'T! THE FIRE BUTTON IS AT THE END OF THIS WIRE **SOMEWHERE**! MAN, I HATE IT WHEN PEOPLE DON'T PUT TOOLS BACK THE WAY THEY FOUND 'EM'!

CREAK!

I FOUND IT, MR. BLACK!

CHONK!!

READY... AIM...

EEK-GAD!

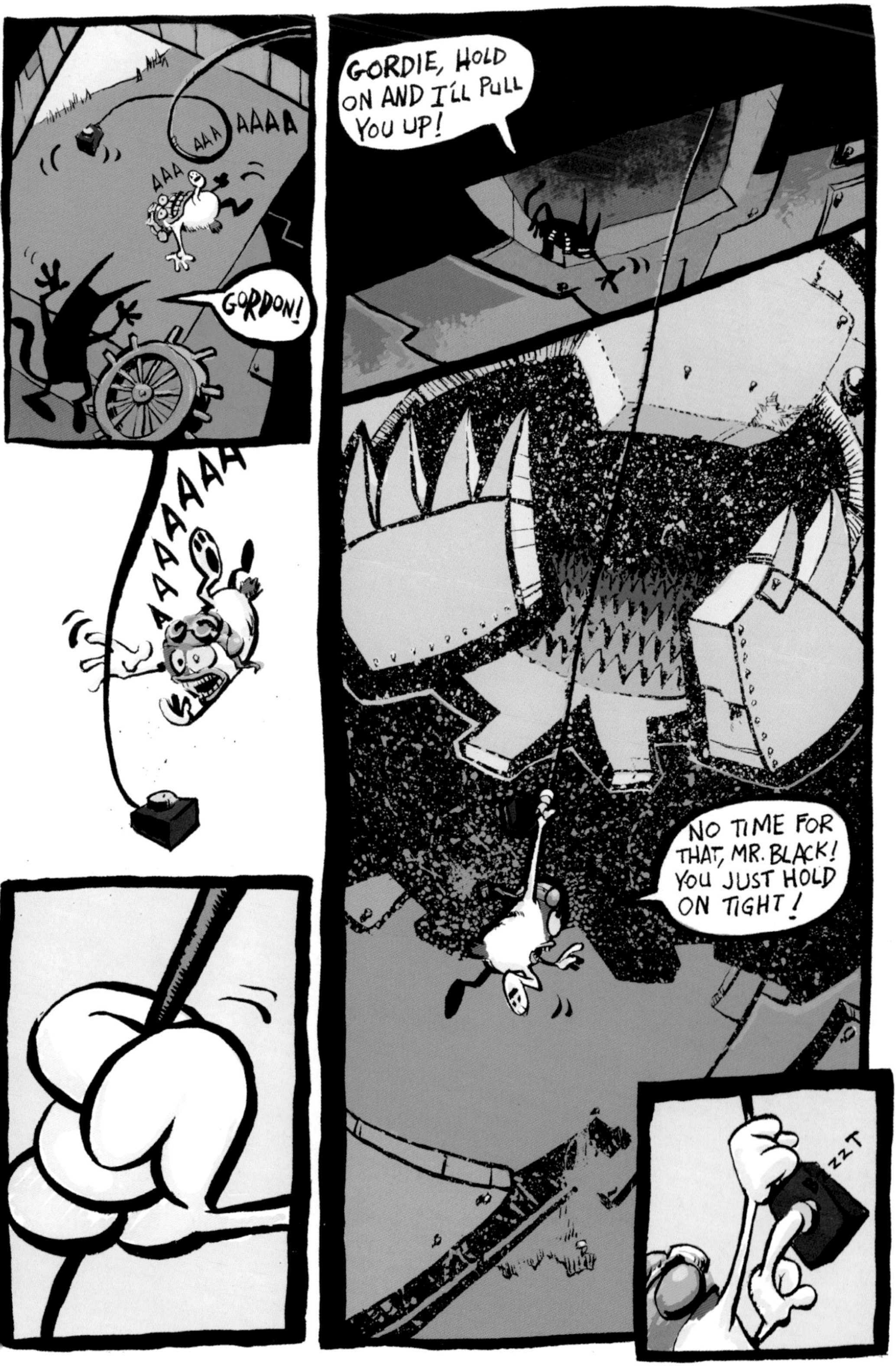
AAAA
AAA
AAA
GORDON!
AAAAAAAAAAA
GORDIE, HOLD ON AND I'LL PULL YOU UP!
NO TIME FOR THAT, MR. BLACK! YOU JUST HOLD ON TIGHT!
ZZZT

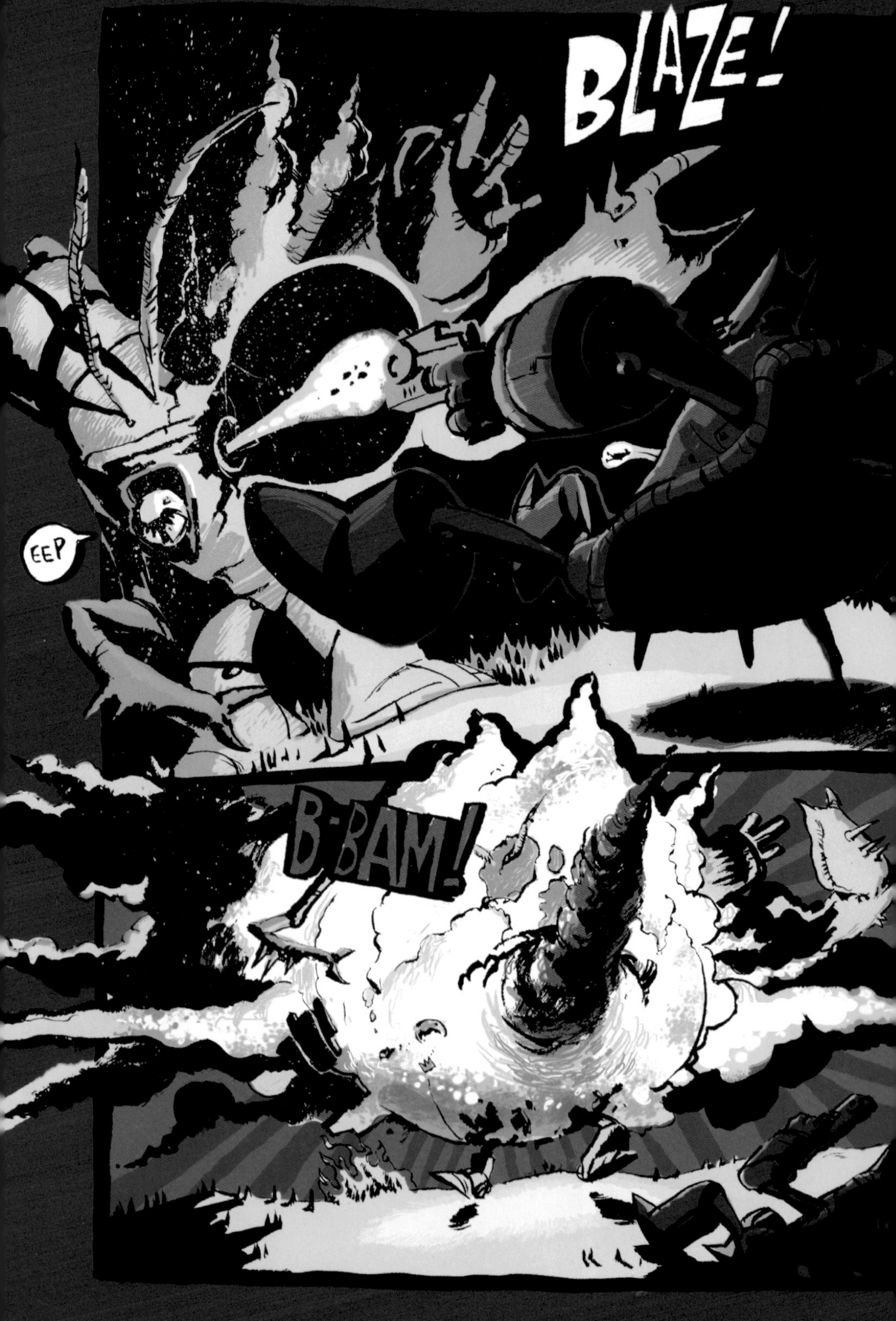
BLAZE!
EEP
B-BAM!

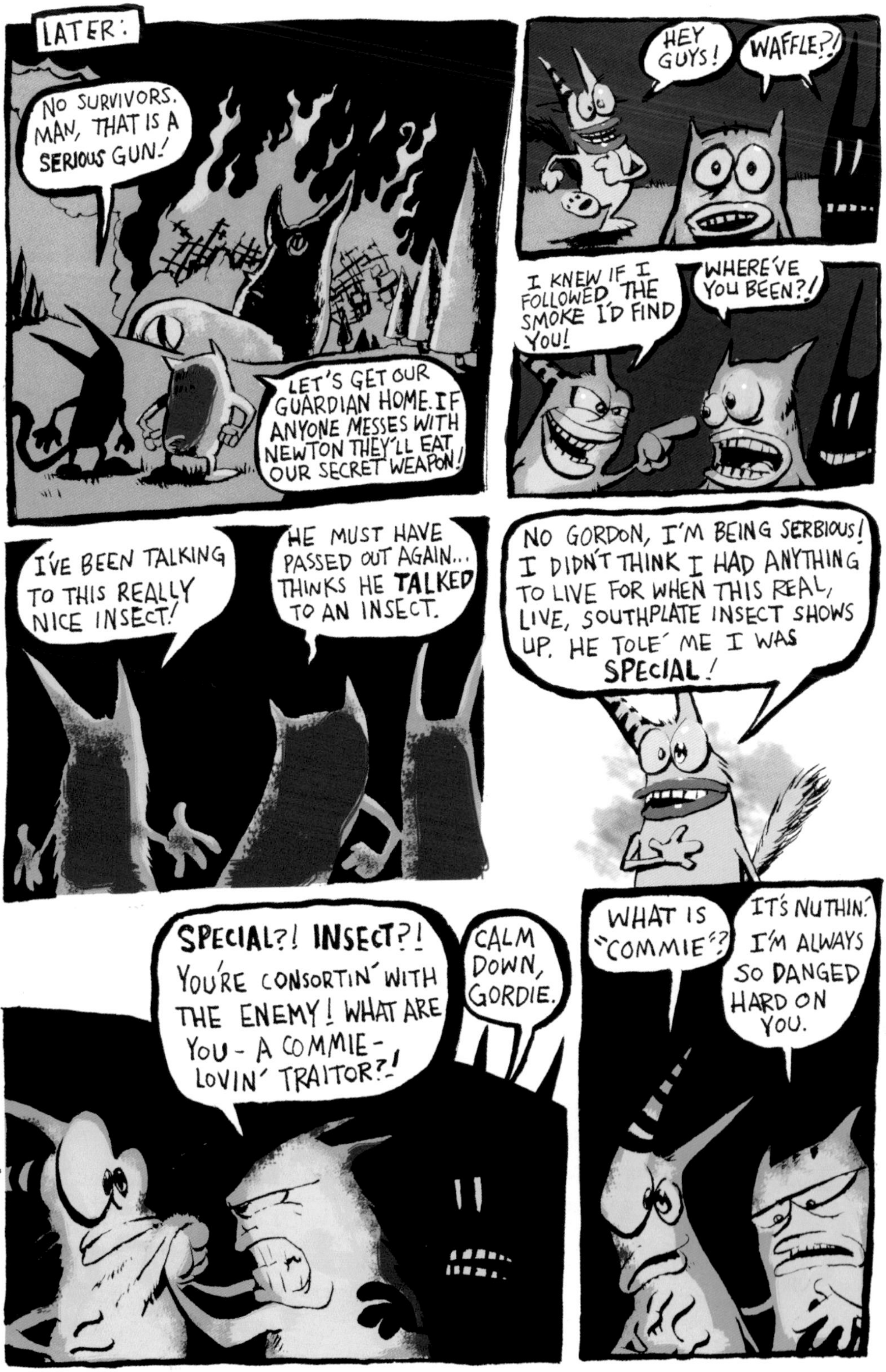
LATER:
NO SURVIVORS. MAN, THAT IS A SERIOUS GUN!
LET'S GET OUR GUARDIAN HOME. IF ANYONE MESSES WITH NEWTON THEY'LL EAT OUR SECRET WEAPON!
HEY GUYS!
WAFFLE?!
I KNEW IF I FOLLOWED THE SMOKE I'D FIND YOU!
WHERE'VE YOU BEEN?!
I'VE BEEN TALKING TO THIS REALLY NICE INSECT!
HE MUST HAVE PASSED OUT AGAIN... THINKS HE TALKED TO AN INSECT.
NO GORDON, I'M BEING SERBIOUS! I DIDN'T THINK I HAD ANYTHING TO LIVE FOR WHEN THIS REAL, LIVE, SOUTHPLATE INSECT SHOWS UP. HE TOLE' ME I WAS SPECIAL!
SPECIAL?! INSECT?! YOU'RE CONSORTIN' WITH THE ENEMY! WHAT ARE YOU - A COMMIE-LOVIN' TRAITOR?!
CALM DOWN, GORDIE.
WHAT IS "COMMIE"?
IT'S NUTHIN'. I'M ALWAYS SO DANGED HARD ON YOU.

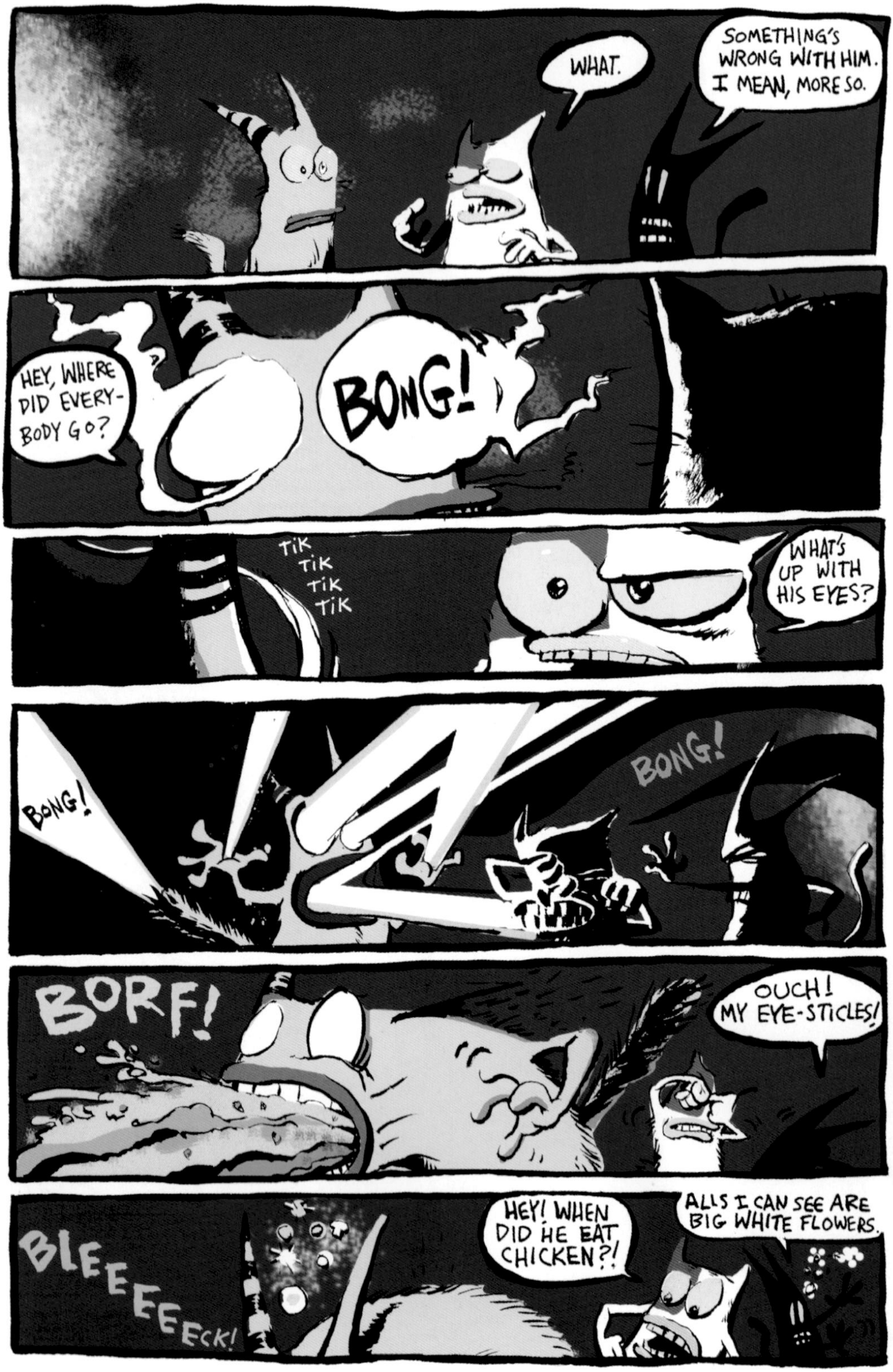
WHAT.
SOMETHING'S WRONG WITH HIM. I MEAN, MORE SO.
HEY, WHERE DID EVERY-BODY GO?
BONG!
TIK TIK TIK TIK
WHAT'S UP WITH HIS EYES?
BONG!
BONG!
BORF!
OUCH! MY EYE-STICLES!
BLEEEEEECK!
HEY! WHEN DID HE EAT CHICKEN?!
ALLS I CAN SEE ARE BIG WHITE FLOWERS.

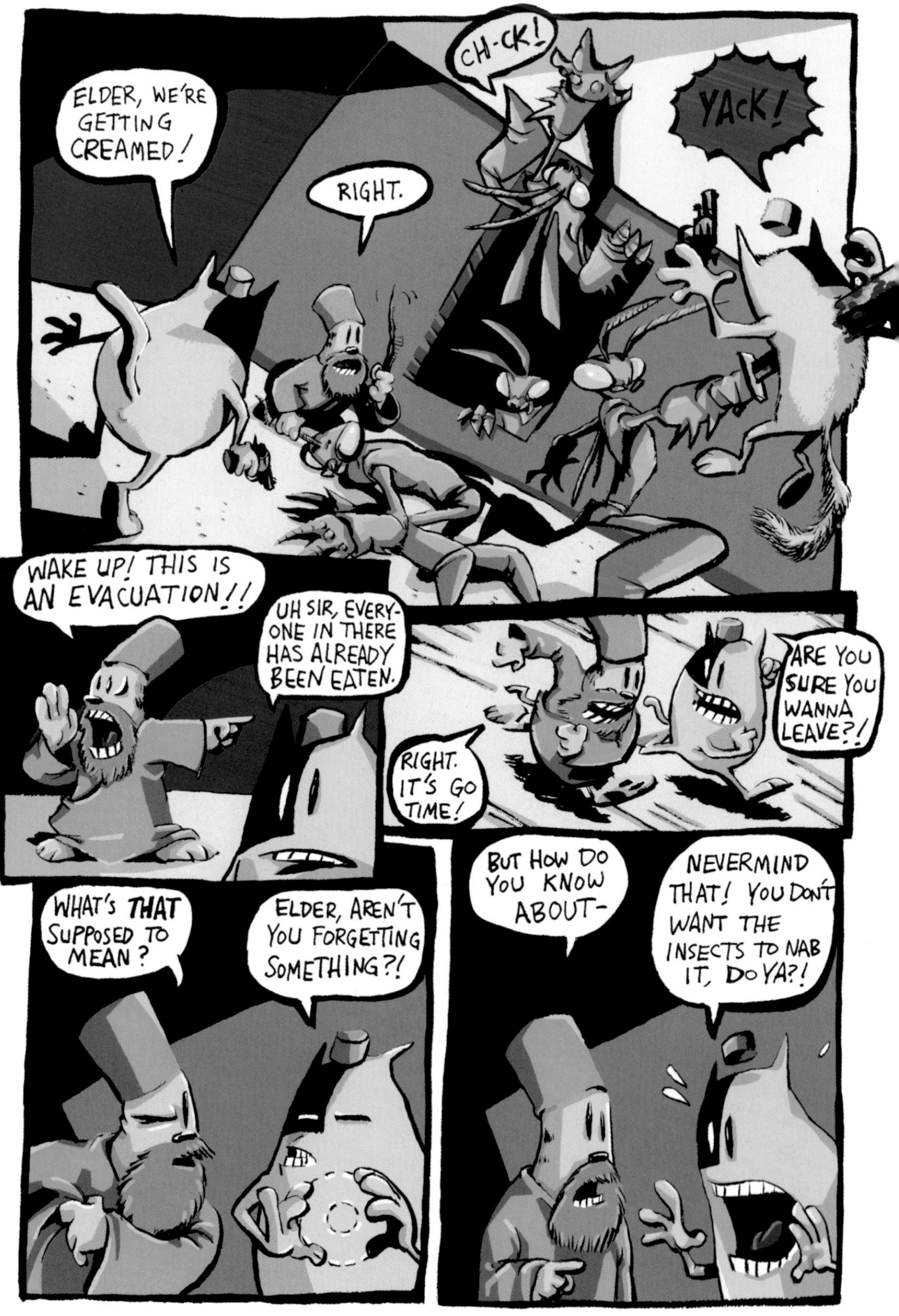
ELDER, WE'RE GETTING CREAMED!
RIGHT.
CH-CK!
YACK!
WAKE UP! THIS IS AN EVACUATION!!
UH SIR, EVERY-ONE IN THERE HAS ALREADY BEEN EATEN.
ARE YOU SURE YOU WANNA LEAVE?!
RIGHT. IT'S GO TIME!
WHAT'S THAT SUPPOSED TO MEAN?
ELDER, AREN'T YOU FORGETTING SOMETHING?!
BUT HOW DO YOU KNOW ABOUT-
NEVERMIND THAT! YOU DON'T WANT THE INSECTS TO NAB IT, DO YA?!

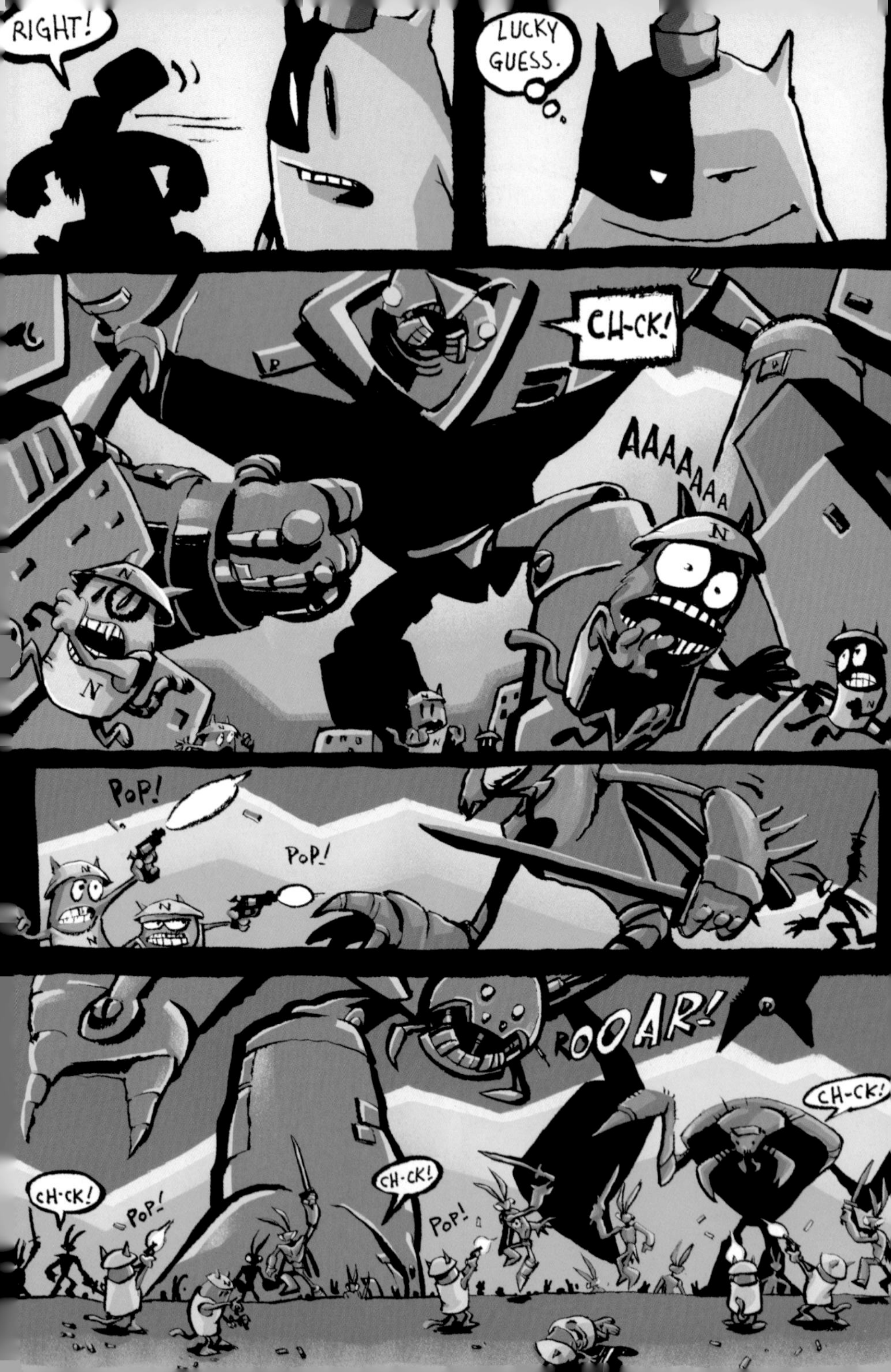
RIGHT!
LUCKY GUESS.
CH-CK!
AAAAAAAA
POP!
POP!
ROOAR!
CH-CK!
CH-CK!
POP!
CH-CK!
POP!

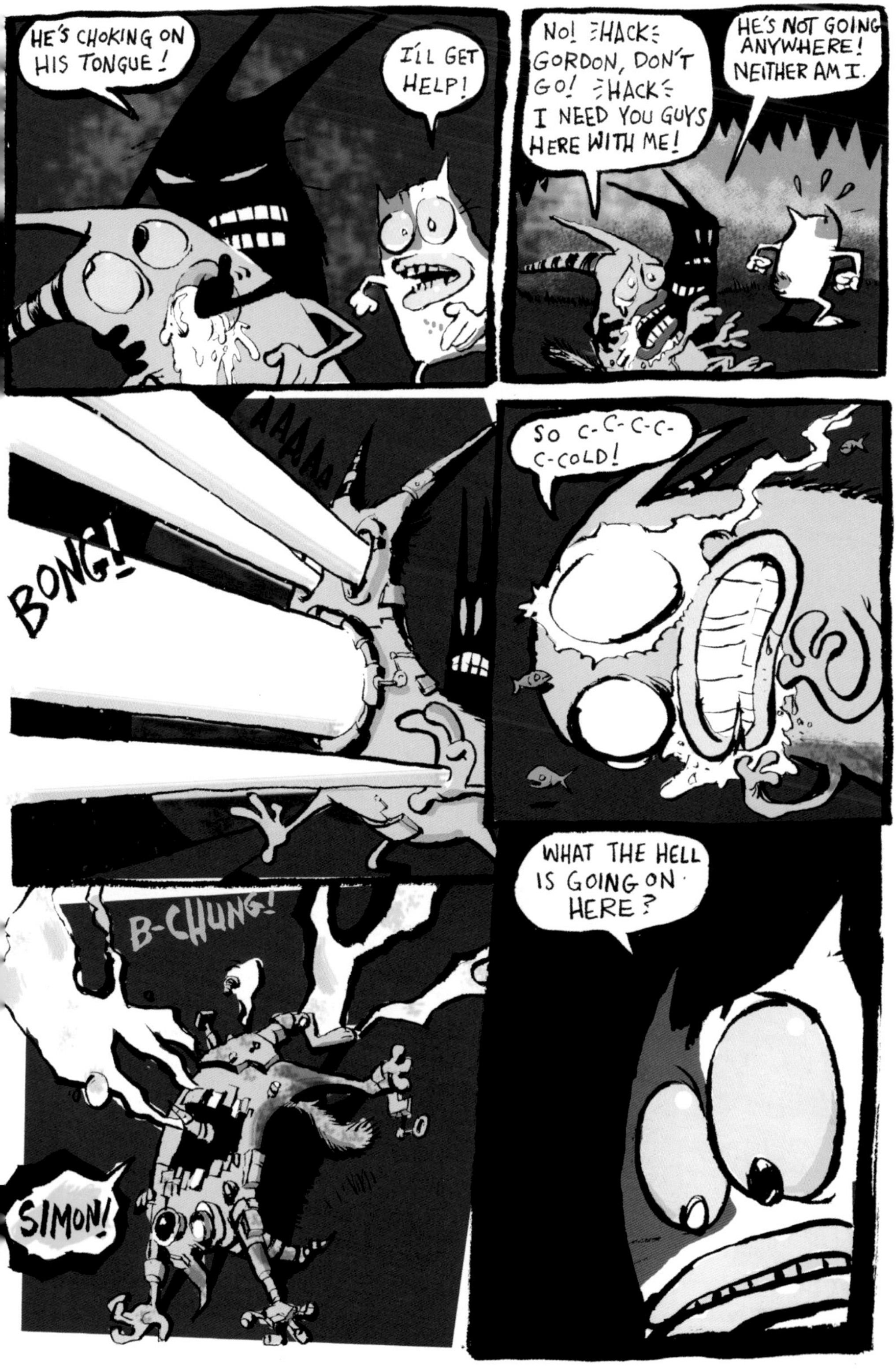
HE'S CHOKING ON HIS TONGUE!
I'LL GET HELP!
NO! HACK GORDON, DON'T GO! HACK I NEED YOU GUYS HERE WITH ME!
HE'S NOT GOING ANYWHERE! NEITHER AM I.
AAAAAA
BONG!
SO C-C-C-C-C-COLD!
B-CHUNG!
SIMON!
WHAT THE HELL IS GOING ON HERE?

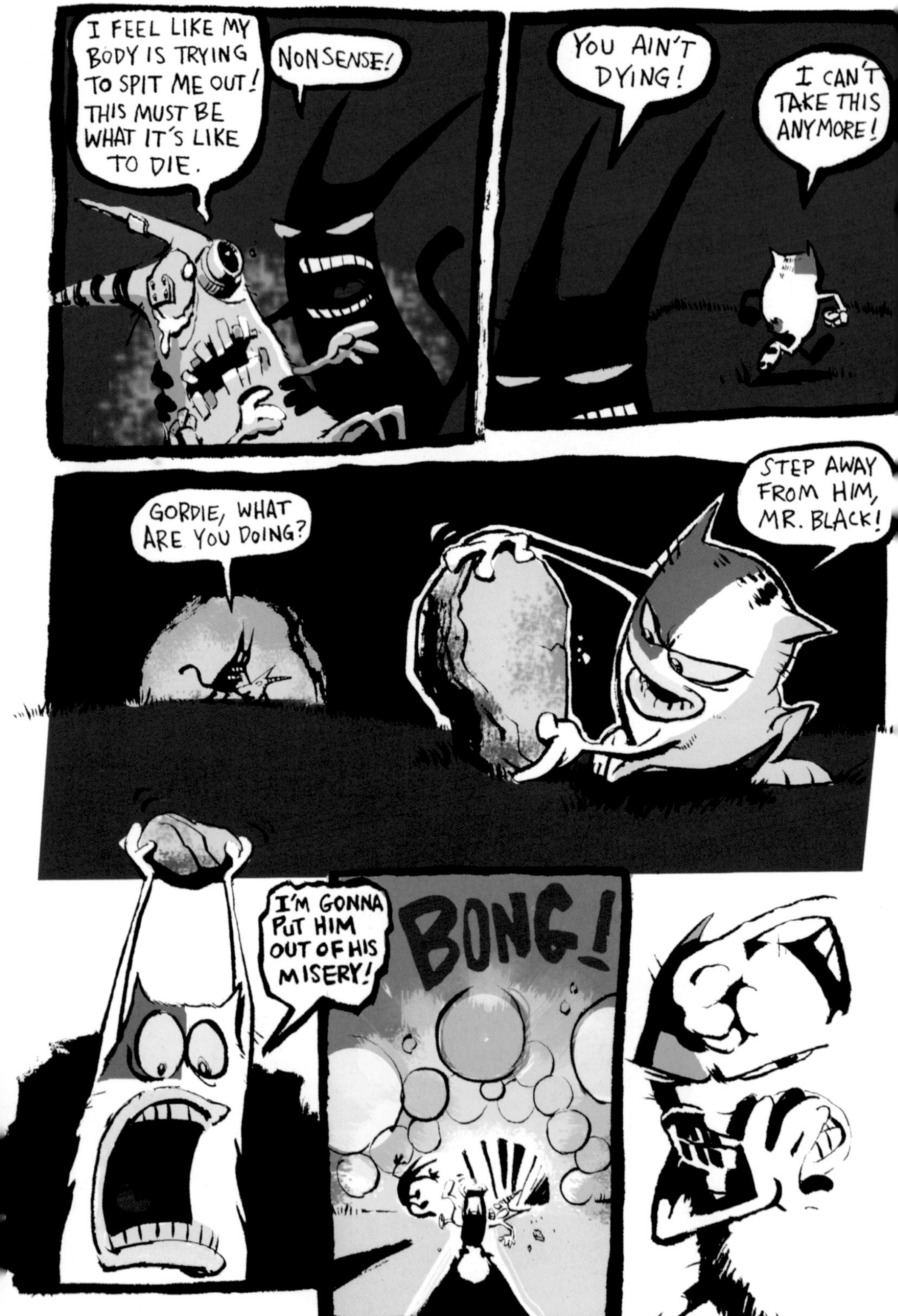
I FEEL LIKE MY BODY IS TRYING TO SPIT ME OUT! THIS MUST BE WHAT IT'S LIKE TO DIE.
NONSENSE!
YOU AIN'T DYING!
I CAN'T TAKE THIS ANYMORE!
GORDIE, WHAT ARE YOU DOING?
STEP AWAY FROM HIM, MR. BLACK!
I'M GONNA PUT HIM OUT OF HIS MISERY!
BONG!

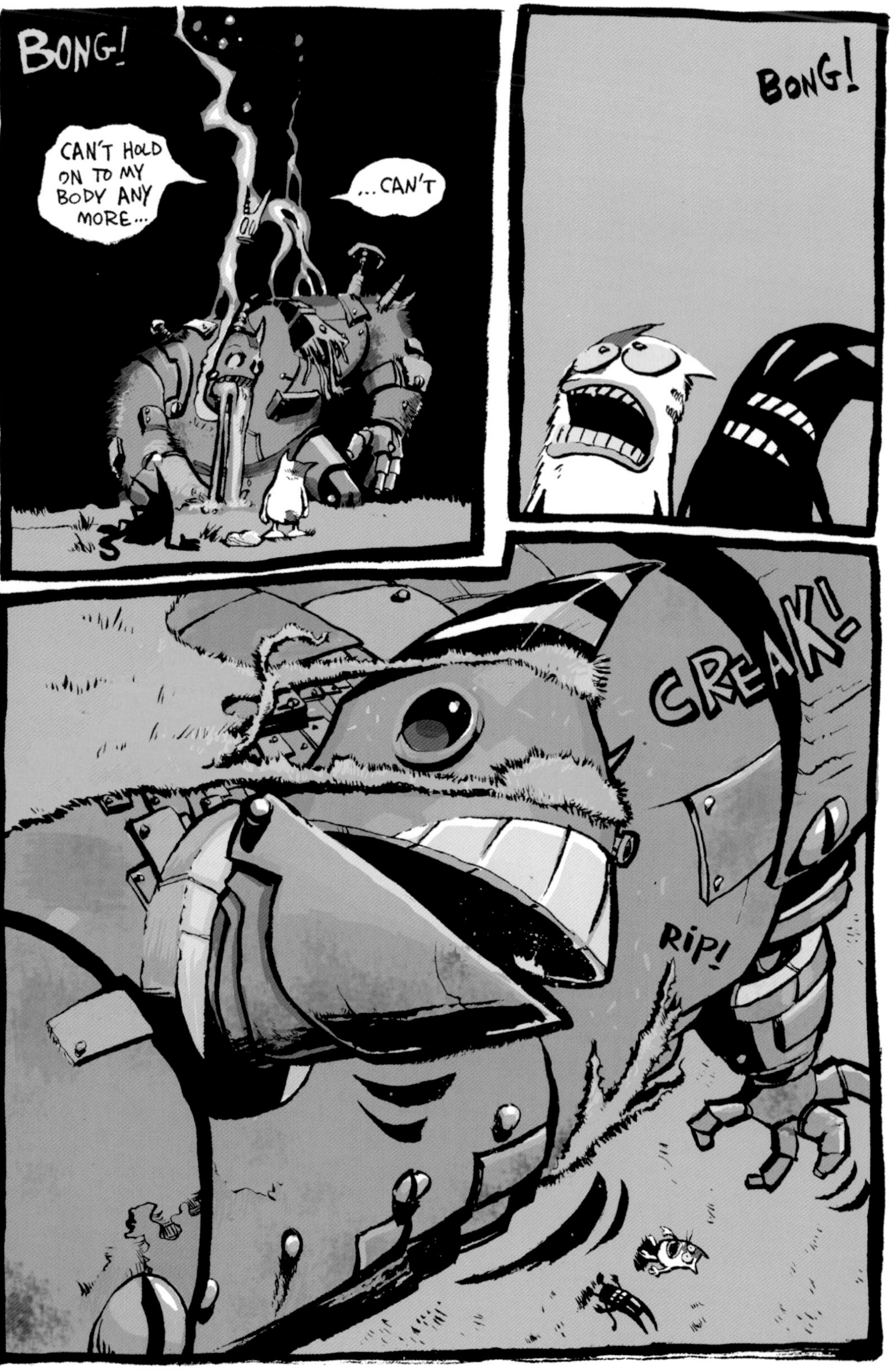
BONG!
CAN'T HOLD ON TO MY BODY ANY MORE...
...CAN'T
BONG!
CREAK!
RIP!

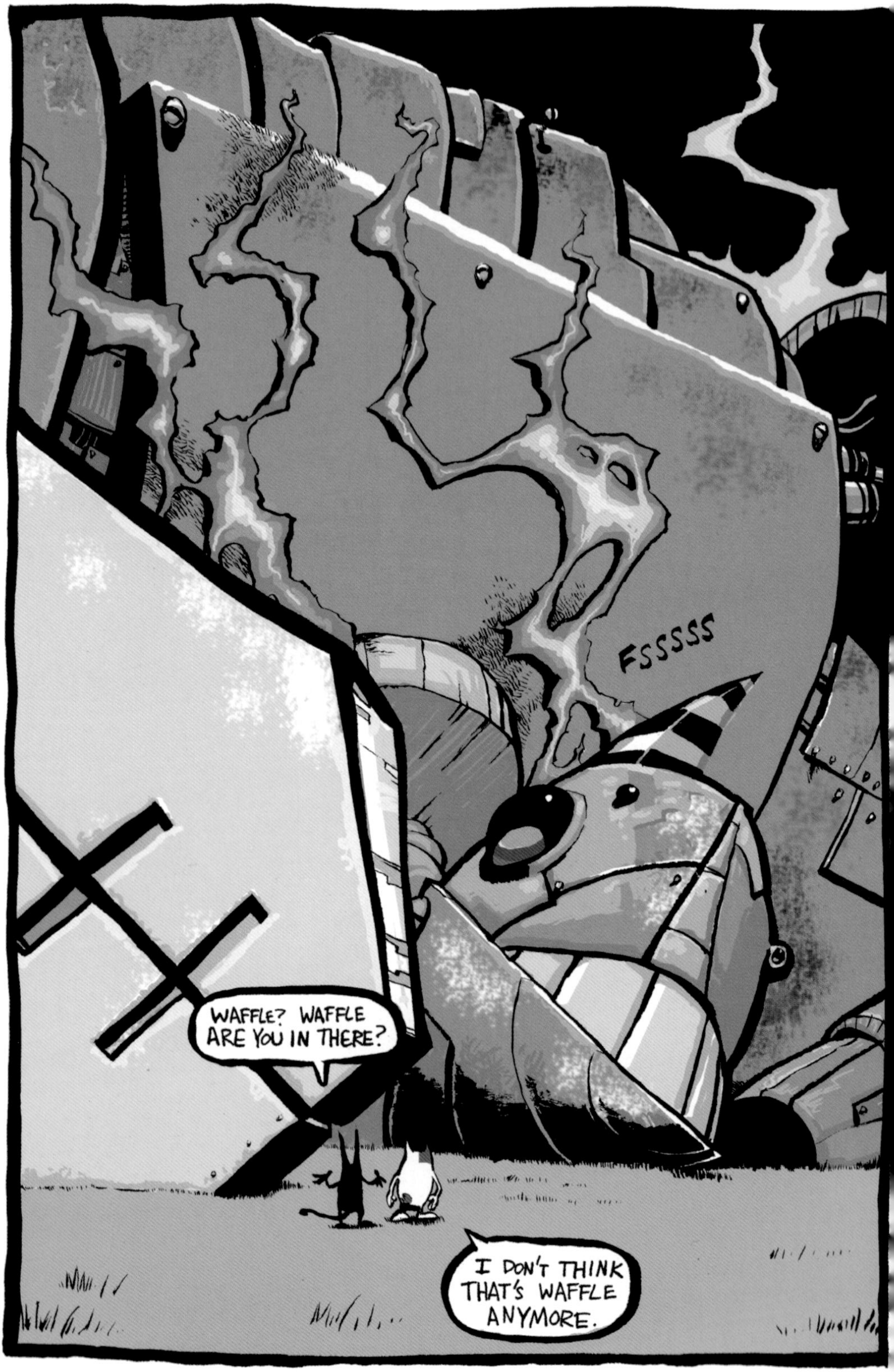
FSSSSS
WAFFLE? WAFFLE ARE YOU IN THERE?
I DON'T THINK THAT'S WAFFLE ANYMORE.

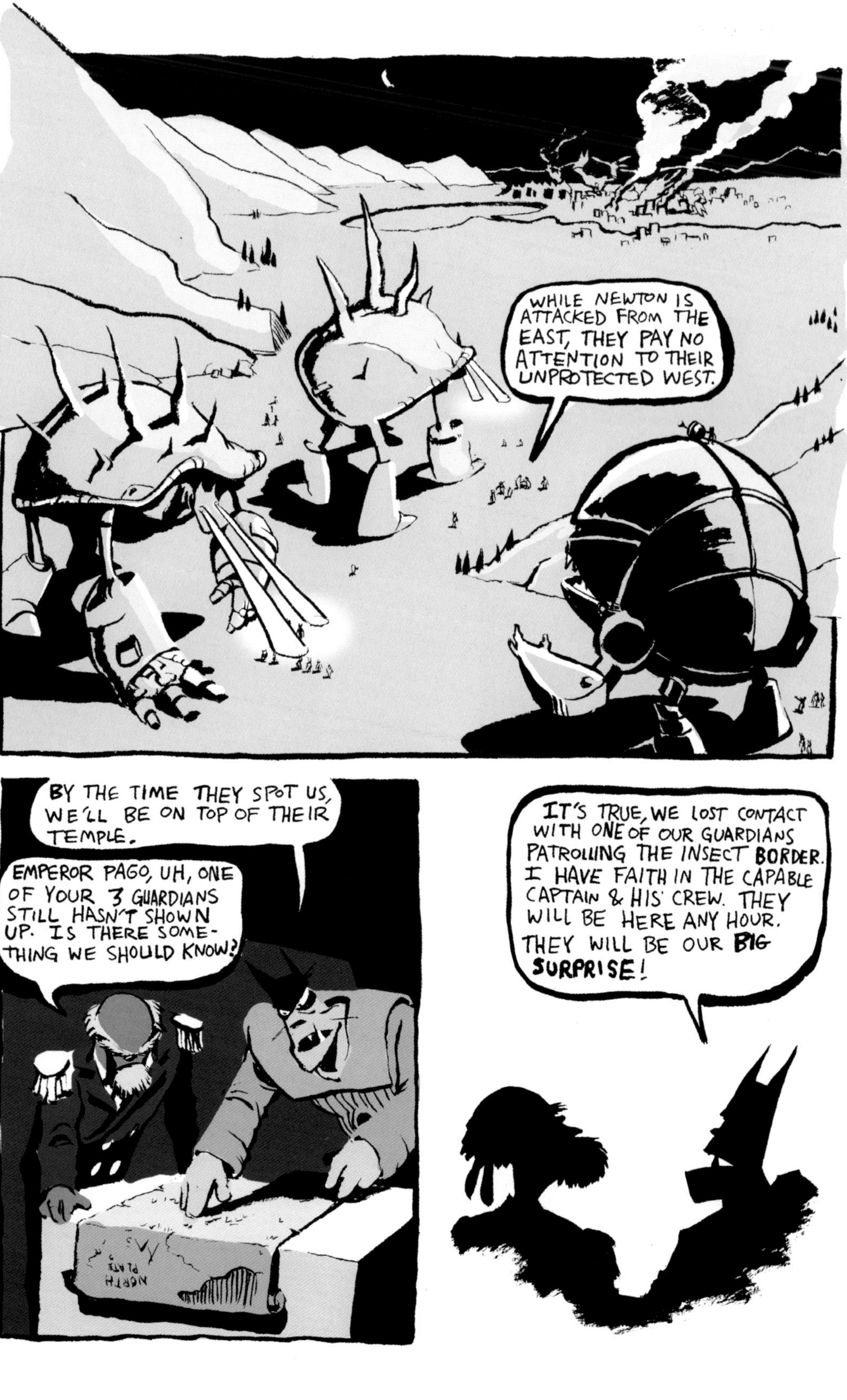
WHILE NEWTON IS ATTACKED FROM THE EAST, THEY PAY NO ATTENTION TO THEIR UNPROTECTED WEST.
BY THE TIME THEY SPOT US, WE'LL BE ON TOP OF THEIR TEMPLE.
EMPEROR PAGO, UH, ONE OF YOUR 3 GUARDIANS STILL HASN'T SHOWN UP. IS THERE SOME-THING WE SHOULD KNOW?
IT'S TRUE, WE LOST CONTACT WITH ONE OF OUR GUARDIANS PATROLLING THE INSECT BORDER. I HAVE FAITH IN THE CAPABLE CAPTAIN & HIS' CREW. THEY WILL BE HERE ANY HOUR. THEY WILL BE OUR BIG SURPRISE!

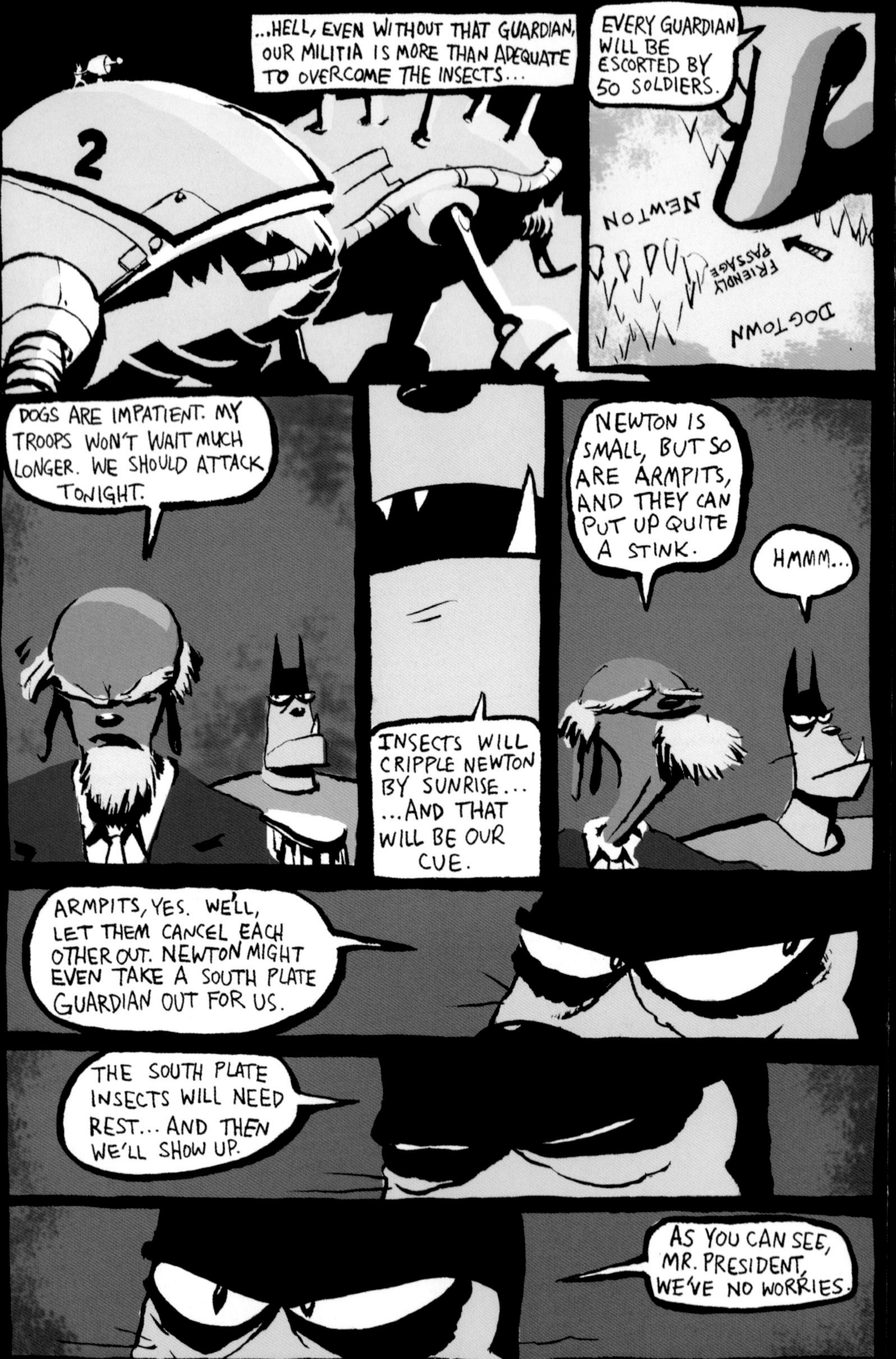

...HELL, EVEN WITHOUT THAT GUARDIAN, OUR MILITIA IS MORE THAN ADEQUATE TO OVERCOME THE INSECTS...
2
EVERY GUARDIAN WILL BE ESCORTED BY 50 SOLDIERS.
NEWTON
FRIENDLY PASSAGE
DOGTOWN
DOGS ARE IMPATIENT. MY TROOPS WON'T WAIT MUCH LONGER. WE SHOULD ATTACK TONIGHT.
INSECTS WILL CRIPPLE NEWTON BY SUNRISE... ...AND THAT WILL BE OUR CUE.
NEWTON IS SMALL, BUT SO ARE ARMPITS, AND THEY CAN PUT UP QUITE A STINK.
HMMM...
ARMPITS, YES. WE'LL, LET THEM CANCEL EACH OTHER OUT. NEWTON MIGHT EVEN TAKE A SOUTH PLATE GUARDIAN OUT FOR US.
THE SOUTH PLATE INSECTS WILL NEED REST... AND THEN WE'LL SHOW UP.
AS YOU CAN SEE, MR. PRESIDENT, WE'VE NO WORRIES.

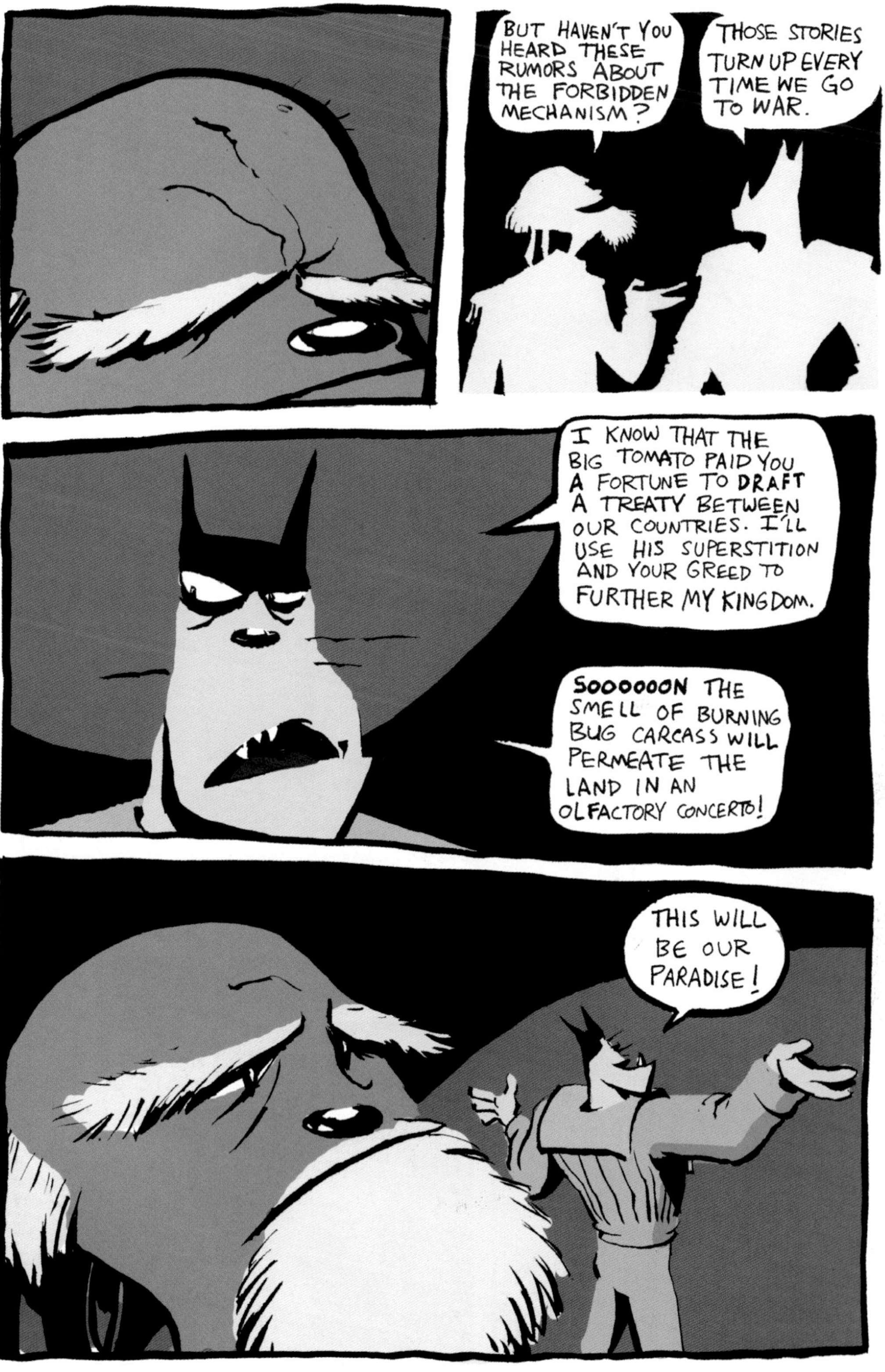
BUT HAVEN'T YOU HEARD THESE RUMORS ABOUT THE FORBIDDEN MECHANISM?
THOSE STORIES TURN UP EVERY TIME WE GO TO WAR.
I KNOW THAT THE BIG TOMATO PAID YOU A FORTUNE TO DRAFT A TREATY BETWEEN OUR COUNTRIES. I'LL USE HIS SUPERSTITION AND YOUR GREED TO FURTHER MY KINGDOM.
SOOOOOON THE SMELL OF BURNING BUG CARCASS WILL PERMEATE THE LAND IN AN OLFACTORY CONCERTO!
THIS WILL BE OUR PARADISE!

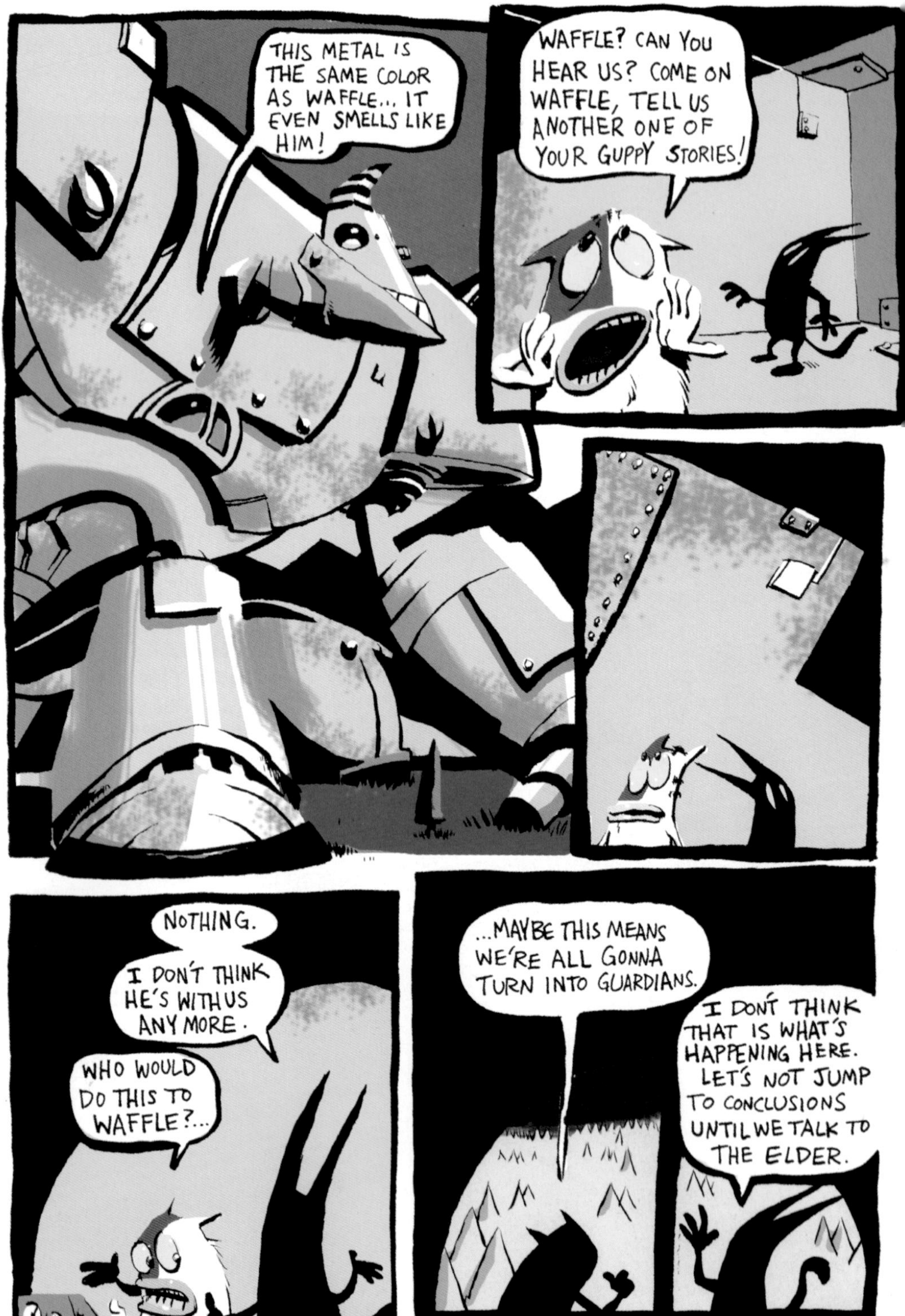
THIS METAL IS THE SAME COLOR AS WAFFLE... IT EVEN SMELLS LIKE HIM!
WAFFLE? CAN YOU HEAR US? COME ON WAFFLE, TELL US ANOTHER ONE OF YOUR GUPPY STORIES!
NOTHING.
I DON'T THINK HE'S WITH US ANY MORE.
WHO WOULD DO THIS TO WAFFLE?...
...MAYBE THIS MEANS WE'RE ALL GONNA TURN INTO GUARDIANS.
I DON'T THINK THAT IS WHAT'S HAPPENING HERE. LET'S NOT JUMP TO CONCLUSIONS UNTIL WE TALK TO THE ELDER.

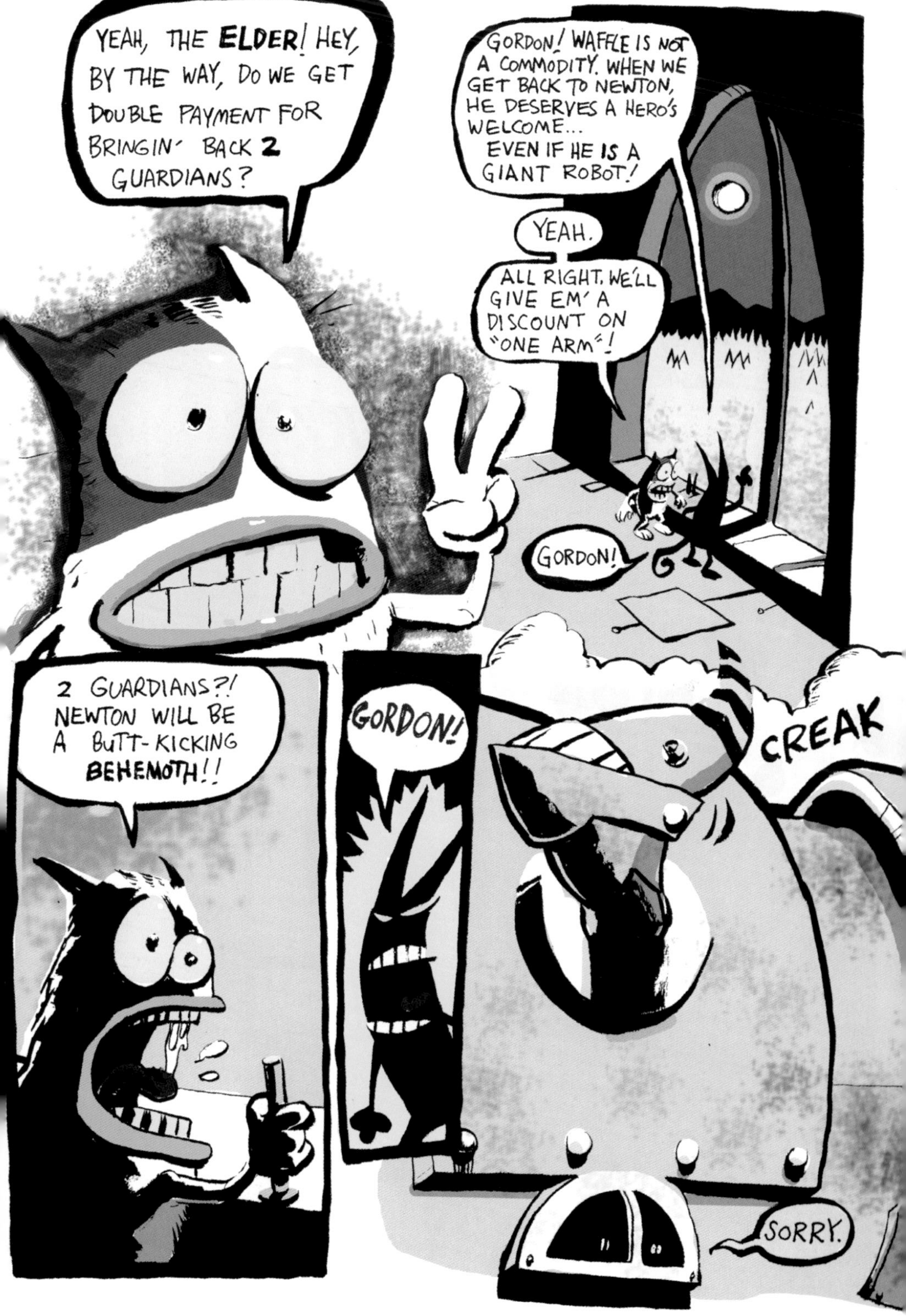
YEAH, THE **ELDER**! HEY, BY THE WAY, DO WE GET DOUBLE PAYMENT FOR BRINGIN' BACK **2** GUARDIANS?
GORDON! WAFFLE IS NOT A COMMODITY. WHEN WE GET BACK TO NEWTON, HE DESERVES A HERO'S WELCOME... EVEN IF HE **IS** A GIANT ROBOT!
YEAH.
ALL RIGHT. WE'LL GIVE EM' A DISCOUNT ON "ONE ARM"!
GORDON!
2 GUARDIANS?! NEWTON WILL BE A BUTT-KICKING **BEHEMOTH**!!
GORDON!
CREAK
SORRY.

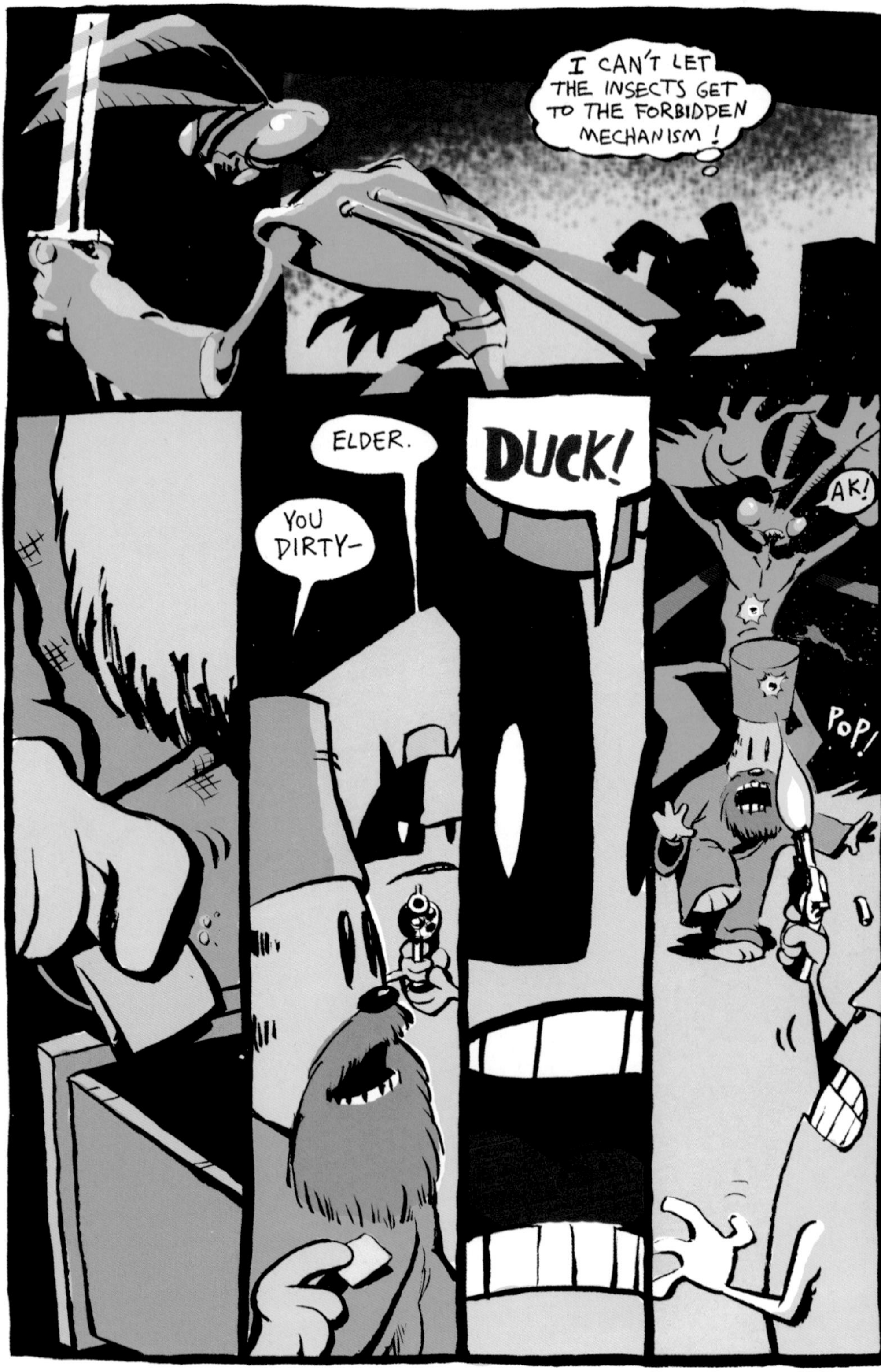
I CAN'T LET THE INSECTS GET TO THE FORBIDDEN MECHANISM!
ELDER.
YOU DIRTY-
DUCK!
AK!
POP!

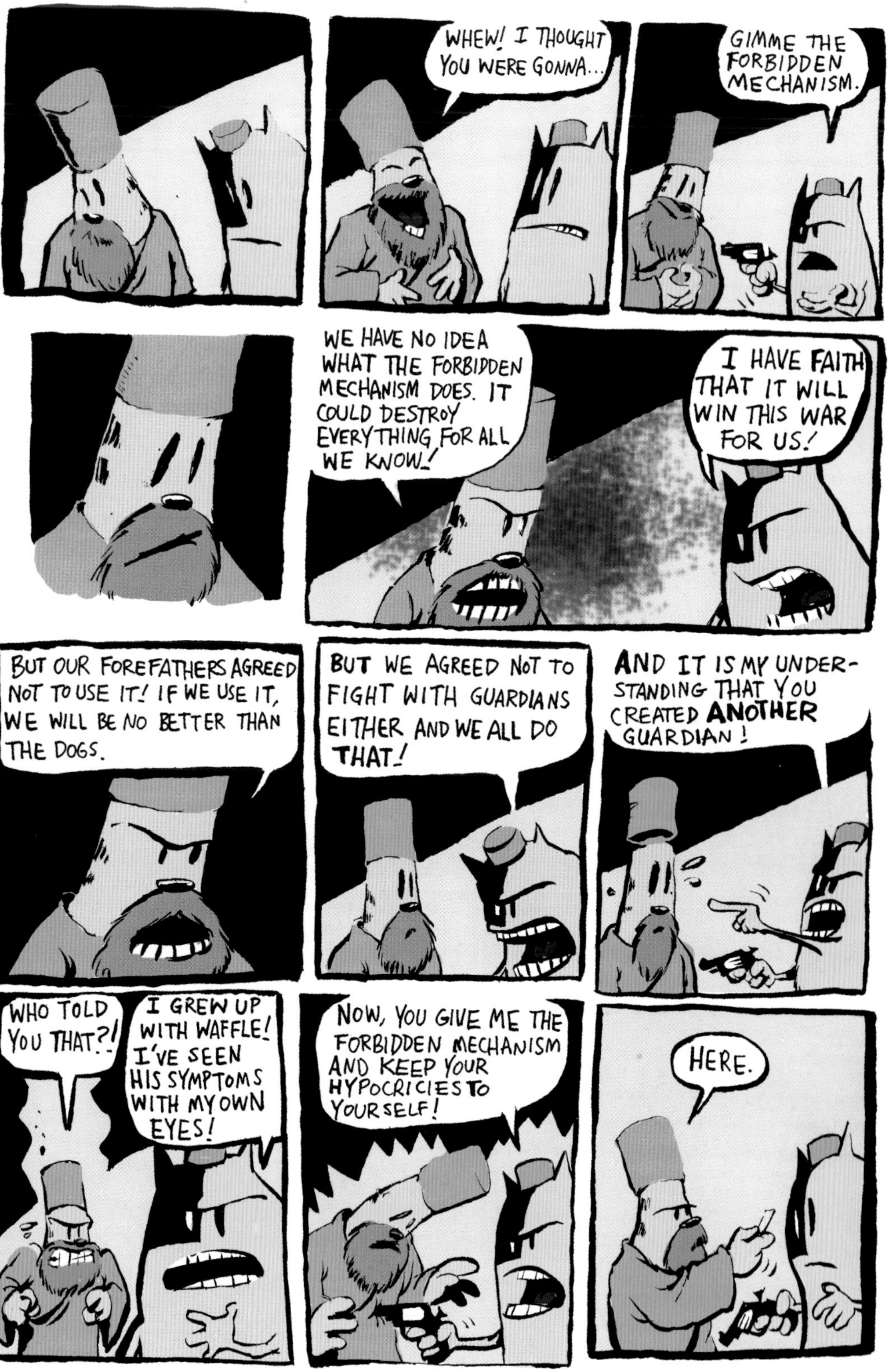
WHEW! I THOUGHT YOU WERE GONNA...
GIMME THE FORBIDDEN MECHANISM.
WE HAVE NO IDEA WHAT THE FORBIDDEN MECHANISM DOES. IT COULD DESTROY EVERYTHING FOR ALL WE KNOW!
I HAVE FAITH THAT IT WILL WIN THIS WAR FOR US!
BUT OUR FOREFATHERS AGREED NOT TO USE IT! IF WE USE IT, WE WILL BE NO BETTER THAN THE DOGS.
BUT WE AGREED NOT TO FIGHT WITH GUARDIANS EITHER AND WE ALL DO THAT!
AND IT IS MY UNDERSTANDING THAT YOU CREATED ANOTHER GUARDIAN!
WHO TOLD YOU THAT?!
I GREW UP WITH WAFFLE! I'VE SEEN HIS SYMPTOMS WITH MY OWN EYES!
NOW, YOU GIVE ME THE FORBIDDEN MECHANISM AND KEEP YOUR HYPOCRICIES TO YOURSELF!
HERE.

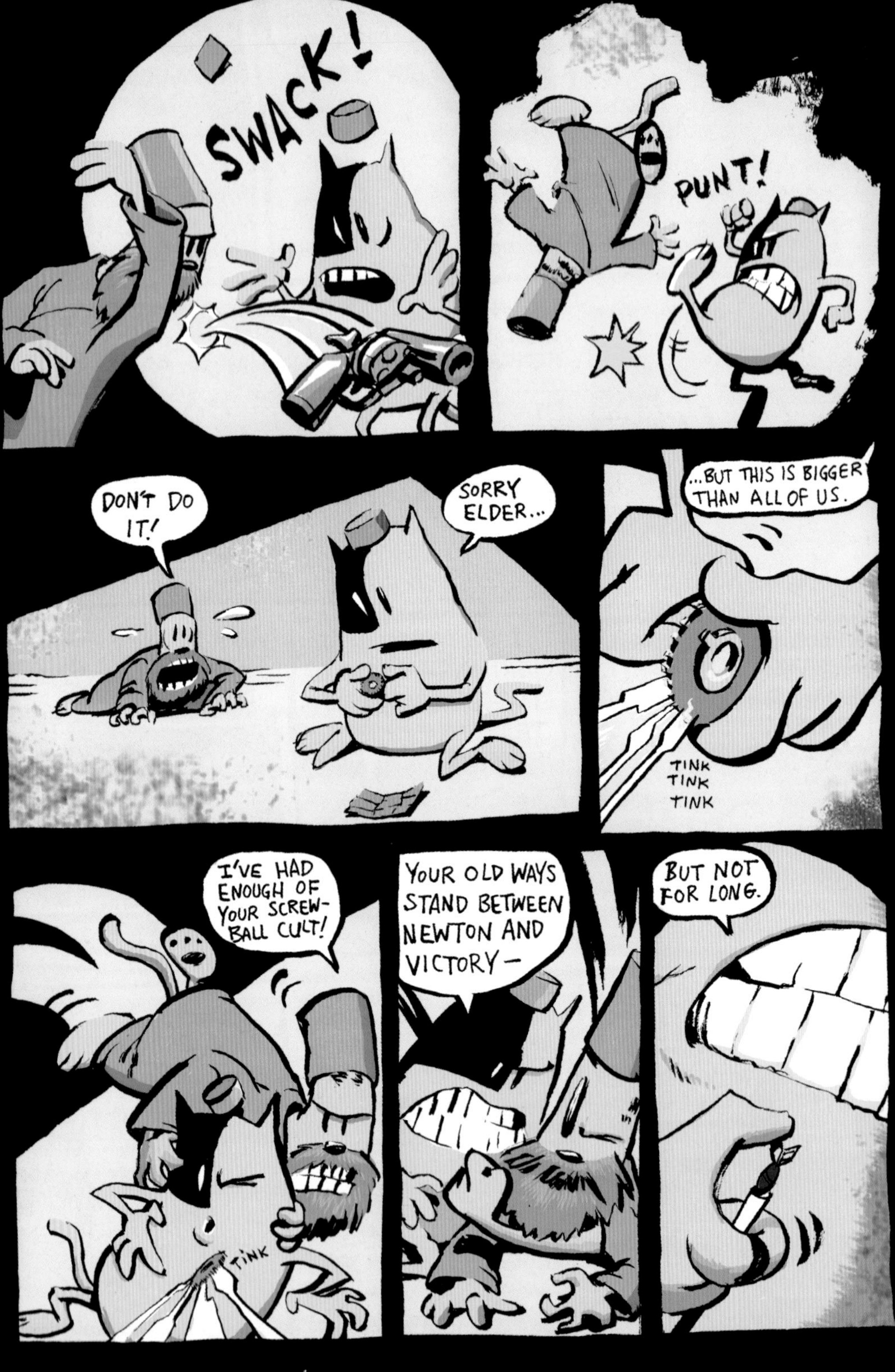
SWACK!
PUNT!
DON'T DO IT!
SORRY ELDER...
...BUT THIS IS BIGGER THAN ALL OF US.
TINK TINK TINK
I'VE HAD ENOUGH OF YOUR SCREW-BALL CULT!
TINK
YOUR OLD WAYS STAND BETWEEN NEWTON AND VICTORY—
BUT NOT FOR LONG.

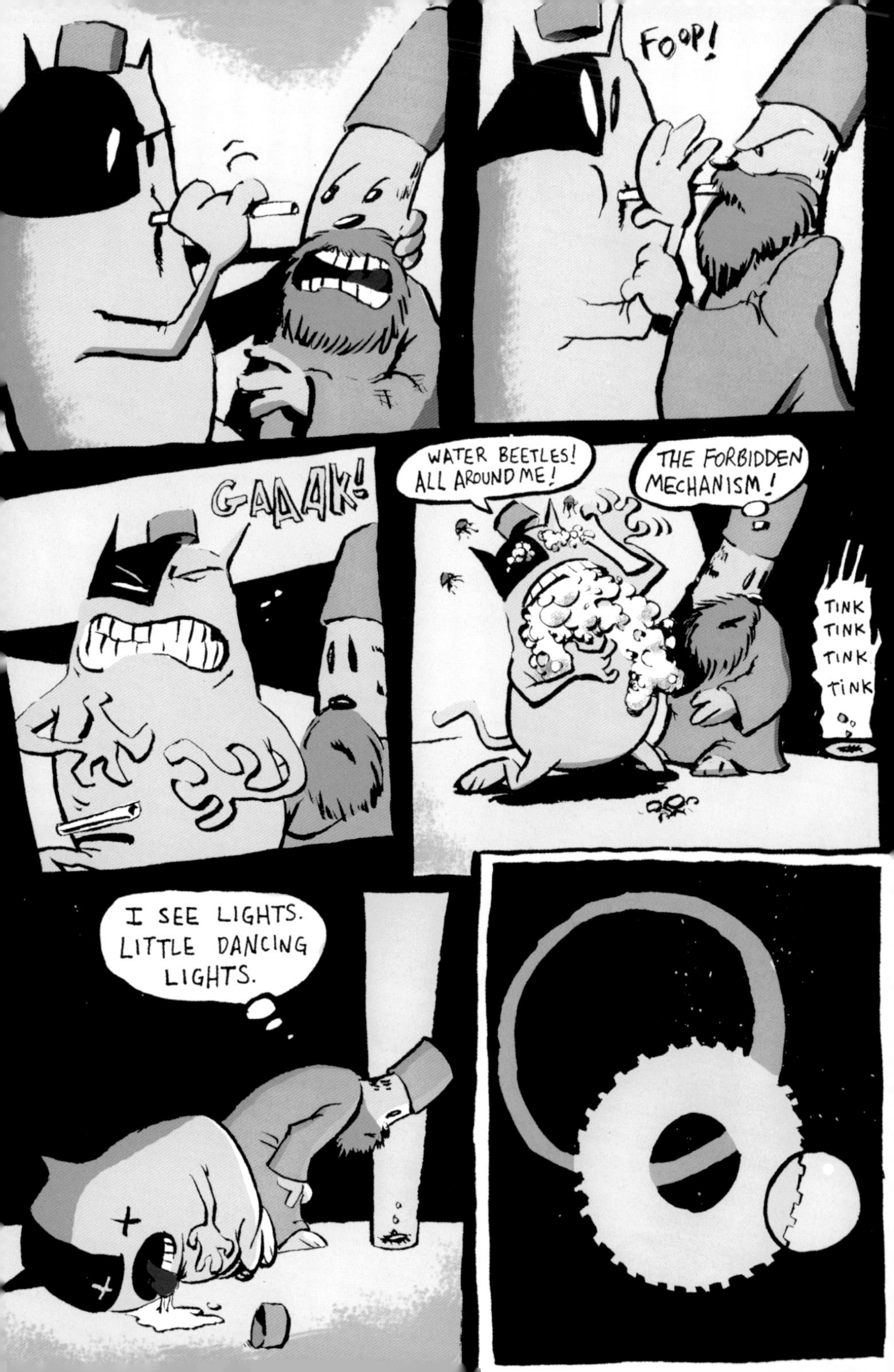
FOOP!
GAAAK!
WATER BEETLES! ALL AROUND ME!
THE FORBIDDEN MECHANISM!
TINK
TINK
TINK
TINK
I SEE LIGHTS. LITTLE DANCING LIGHTS.

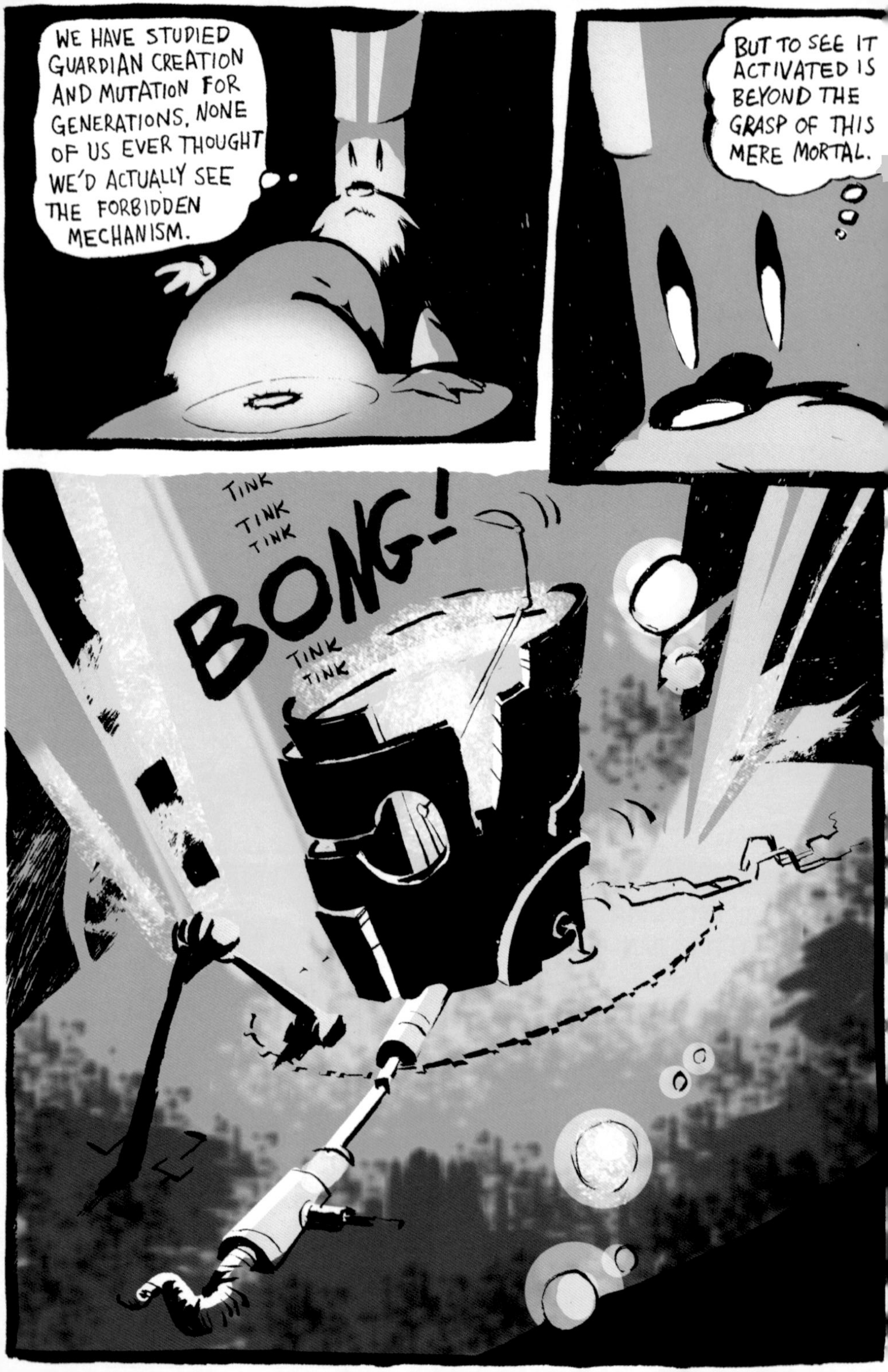

WE HAVE STUDIED GUARDIAN CREATION AND MUTATION FOR GENERATIONS. NONE OF US EVER THOUGHT WE'D ACTUALLY SEE THE FORBIDDEN MECHANISM.
BUT TO SEE IT ACTIVATED IS BEYOND THE GRASP OF THIS MERE MORTAL.
TINK TINK TINK
BONG!
TINK TINK

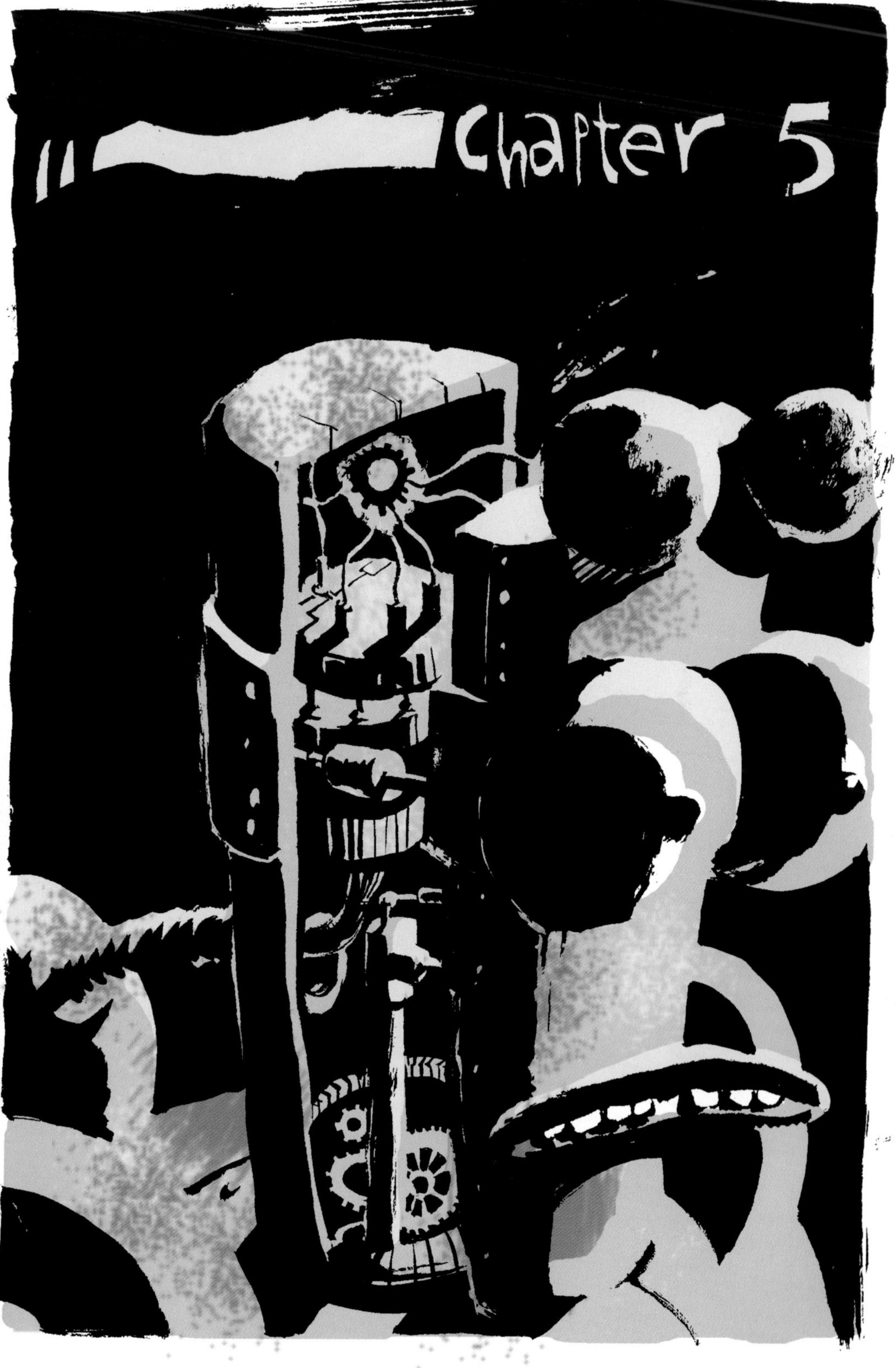
Chapter 5

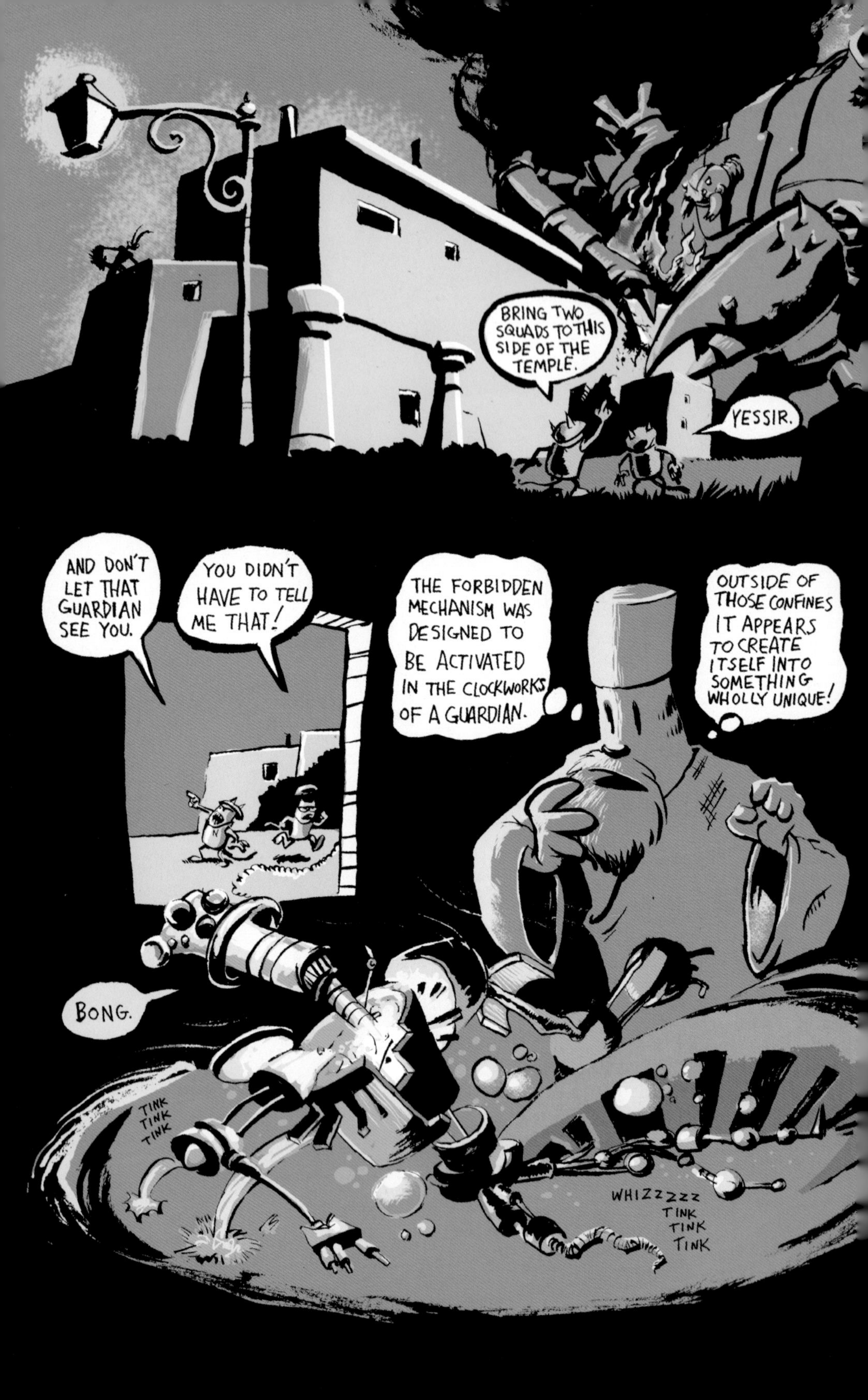
BRING TWO SQUADS TO THIS SIDE OF THE TEMPLE.
YESSIR.
AND DON'T LET THAT GUARDIAN SEE YOU.
YOU DIDN'T HAVE TO TELL ME THAT!
THE FORBIDDEN MECHANISM WAS DESIGNED TO BE ACTIVATED IN THE CLOCKWORKS OF A GUARDIAN.
OUTSIDE OF THOSE CONFINES IT APPEARS TO CREATE ITSELF INTO SOMETHING WHOLLY UNIQUE!
BONG.
TINK TINK TINK
WHIZZZZZ
TINK TINK TINK

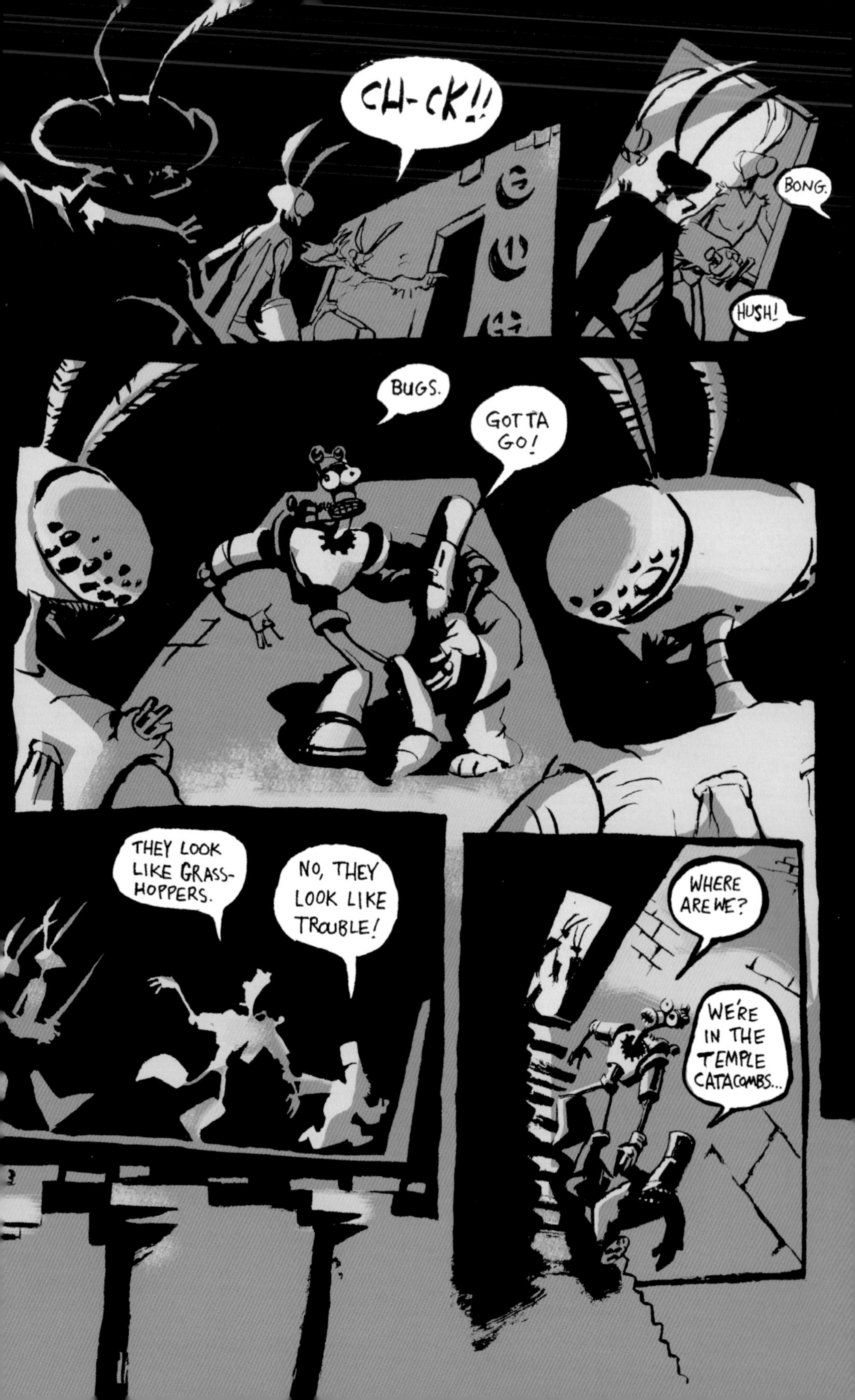
CH-CK!!
BONG.
HUSH!
BUGS.
GOTTA GO!
THEY LOOK LIKE GRASS-HOPPERS.
NO, THEY LOOK LIKE TROUBLE!
WHERE ARE WE?
WE'RE IN THE TEMPLE CATACOMBS...

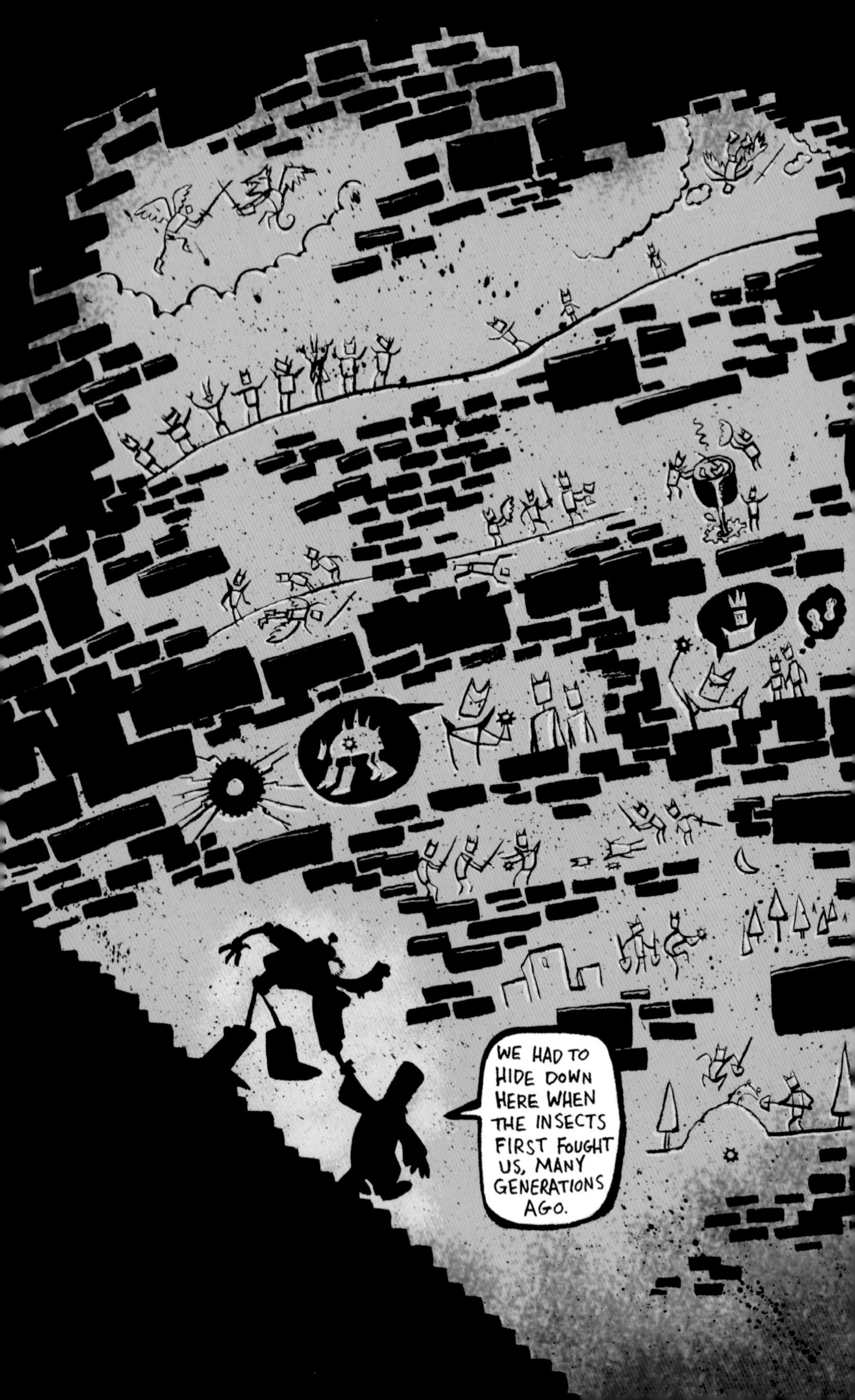
WE HAD TO HIDE DOWN HERE WHEN THE INSECTS FIRST FOUGHT US, MANY GENERATIONS AGO.

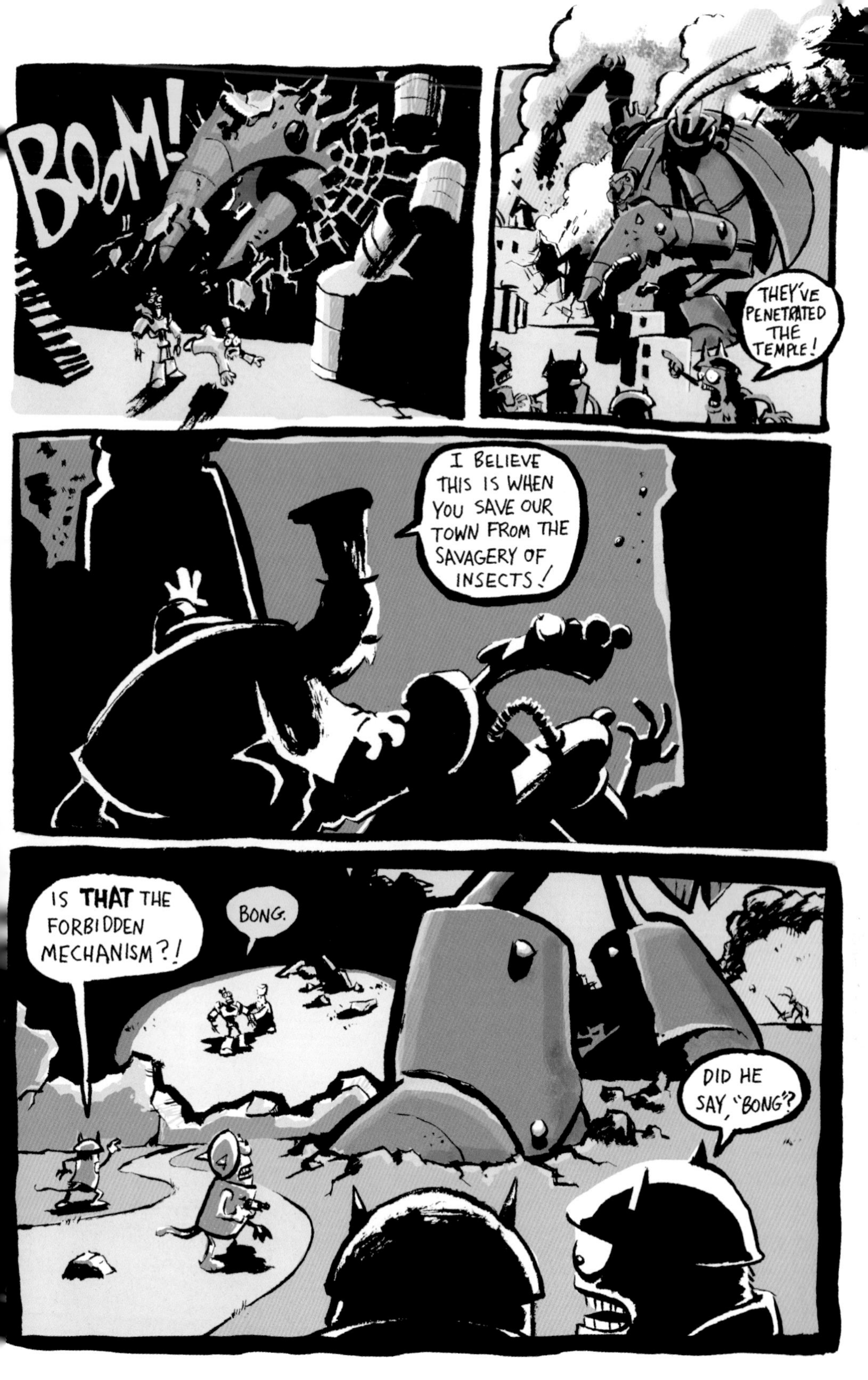
BOOM!
THEY'VE PENETRATED THE TEMPLE!
I BELIEVE THIS IS WHEN YOU SAVE OUR TOWN FROM THE SAVAGERY OF INSECTS!
IS **THAT** THE FORBIDDEN MECHANISM?!
BONG.
DID HE SAY, "BONG"?

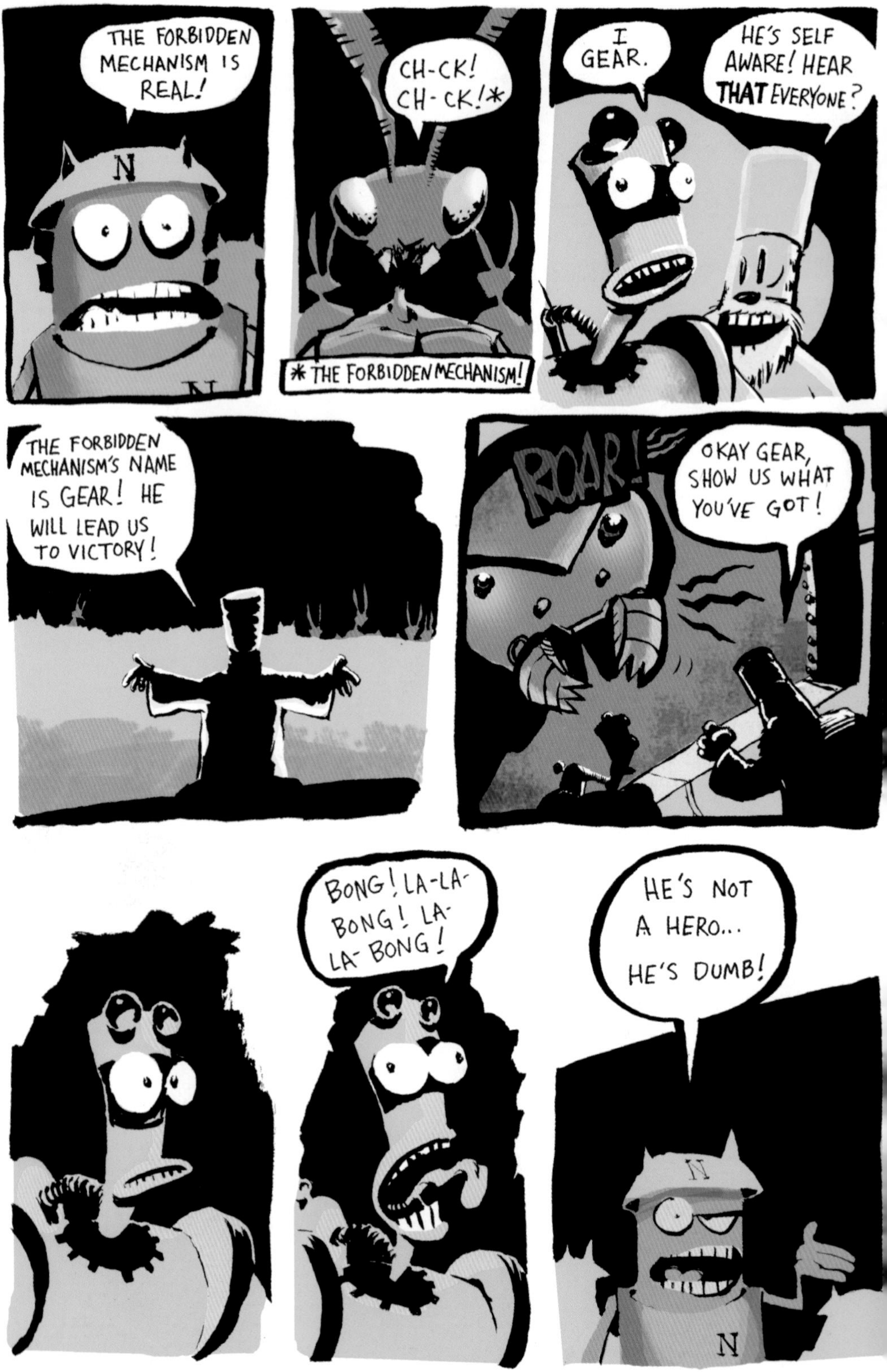
THE FORBIDDEN MECHANISM IS REAL!
CH-CK! CH-CK!*
* THE FORBIDDEN MECHANISM!
I GEAR.
HE'S SELF AWARE! HEAR THAT EVERYONE?
THE FORBIDDEN MECHANISM'S NAME IS GEAR! HE WILL LEAD US TO VICTORY!
ROAR!
OKAY GEAR, SHOW US WHAT YOU'VE GOT!
BONG! LA-LA-BONG! LA-LA-BONG!
HE'S NOT A HERO...
HE'S DUMB!

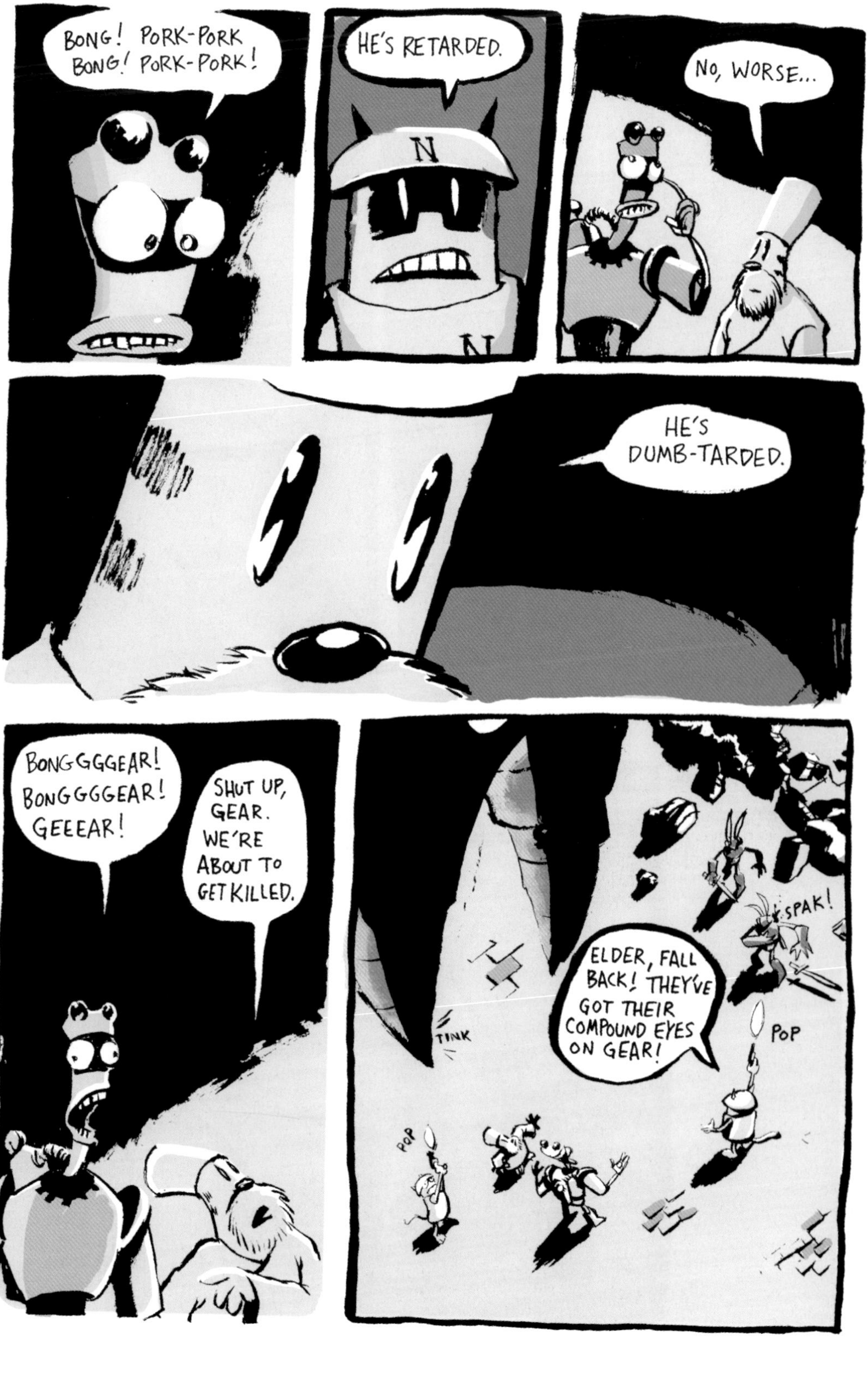
BONG! PORK-PORK BONG! PORK-PORK!
HE'S RETARDED.
NO, WORSE...
HE'S DUMB-TARDED.
BONGGGGEAR! BONGGGGEAR! GEEEAR!
SHUT UP, GEAR. WE'RE ABOUT TO GET KILLED.
SPAK!
ELDER, FALL BACK! THEY'VE GOT THEIR COMPOUND EYES ON GEAR!
TINK
POP
POP

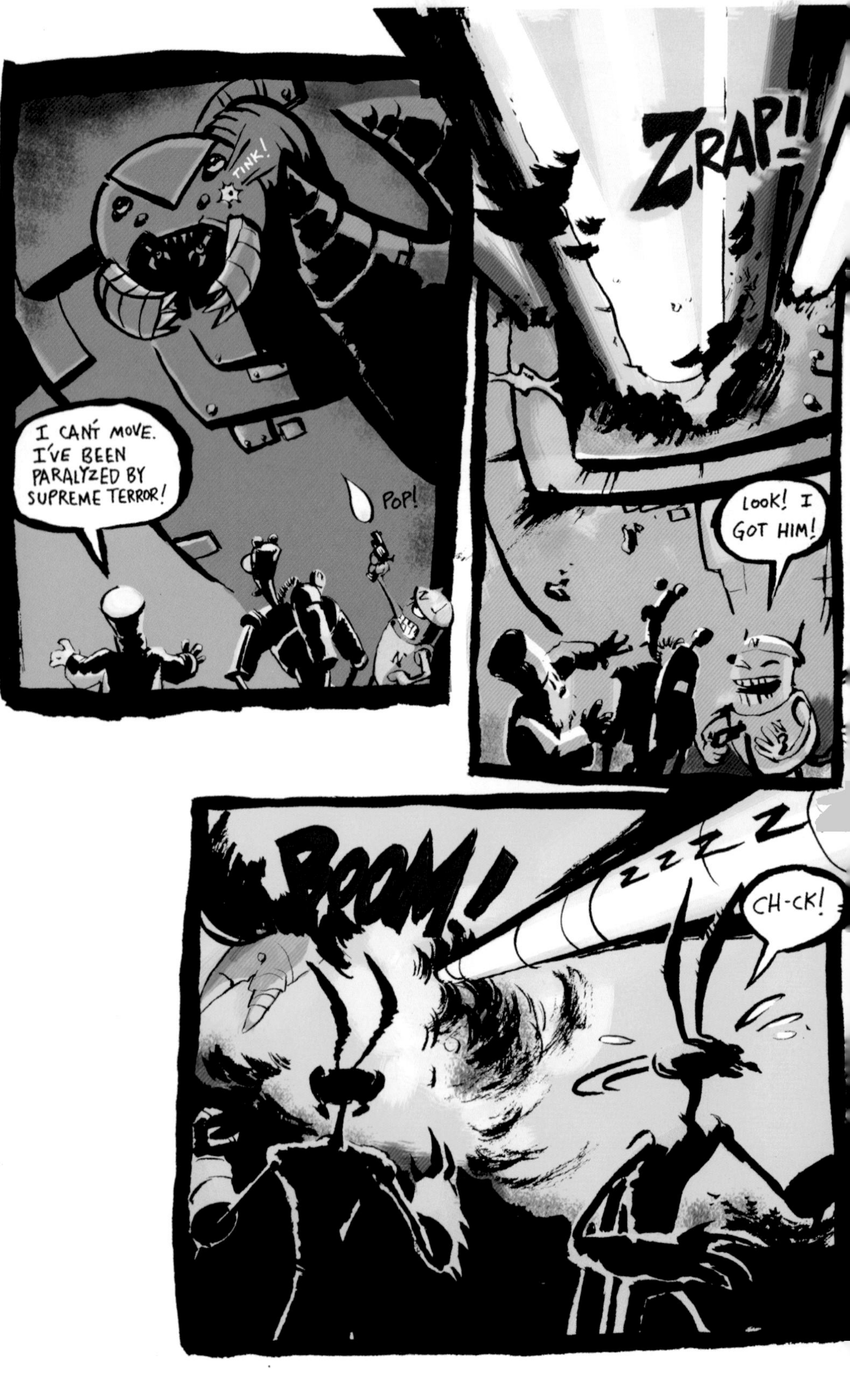
TINK!
I CAN'T MOVE. I'VE BEEN PARALYZED BY SUPREME TERROR!
POP!
ZRAP!!
LOOK! I GOT HIM!
BOOM!
Z Z Z Z Z
CH-CK!

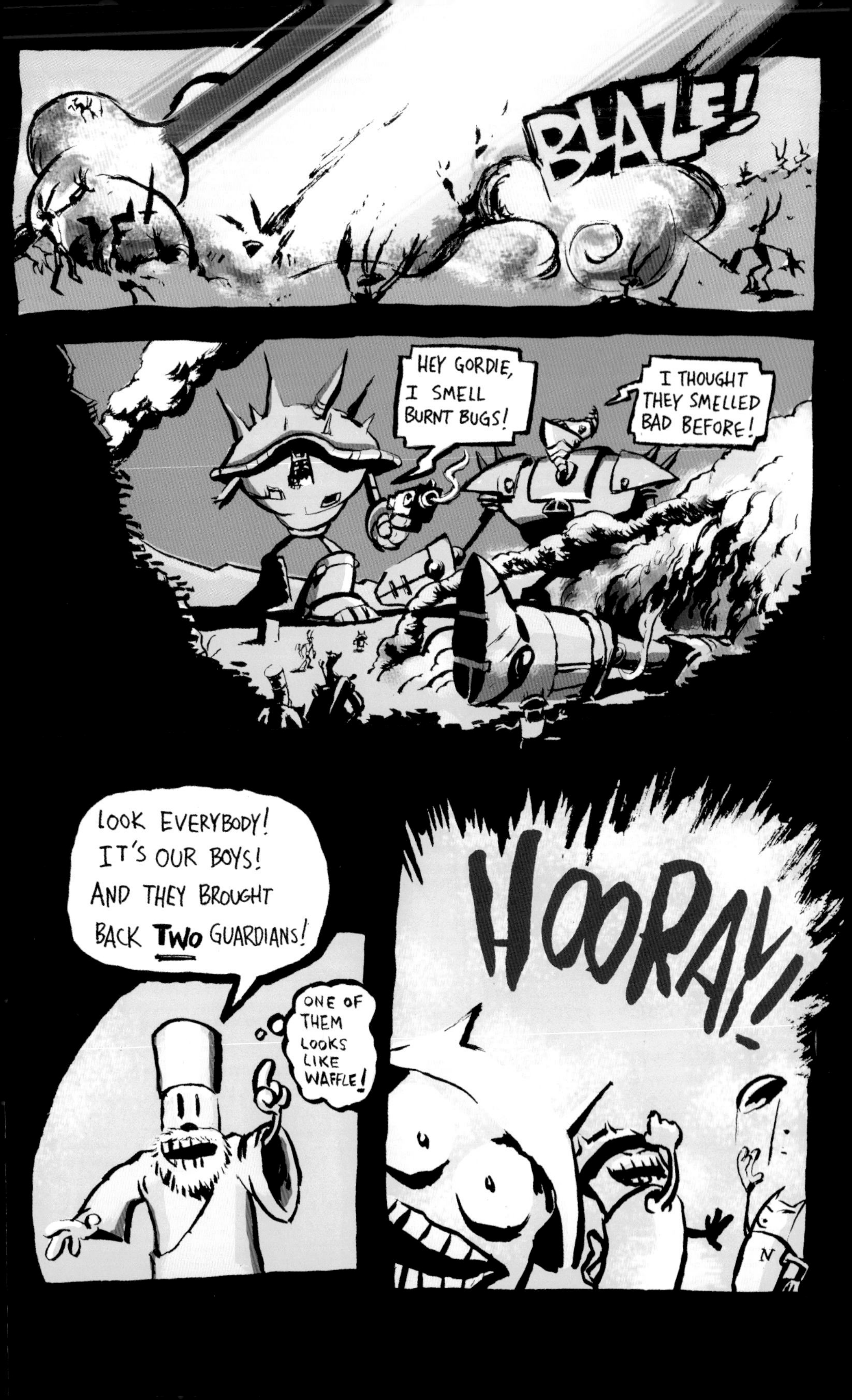
BLAZE!
HEY GORDIE, I SMELL BURNT BUGS!
I THOUGHT THEY SMELLED BAD BEFORE!
LOOK EVERYBODY! IT'S OUR BOYS! AND THEY BROUGHT BACK TWO GUARDIANS!
ONE OF THEM LOOKS LIKE WAFFLE!
HOORAY!

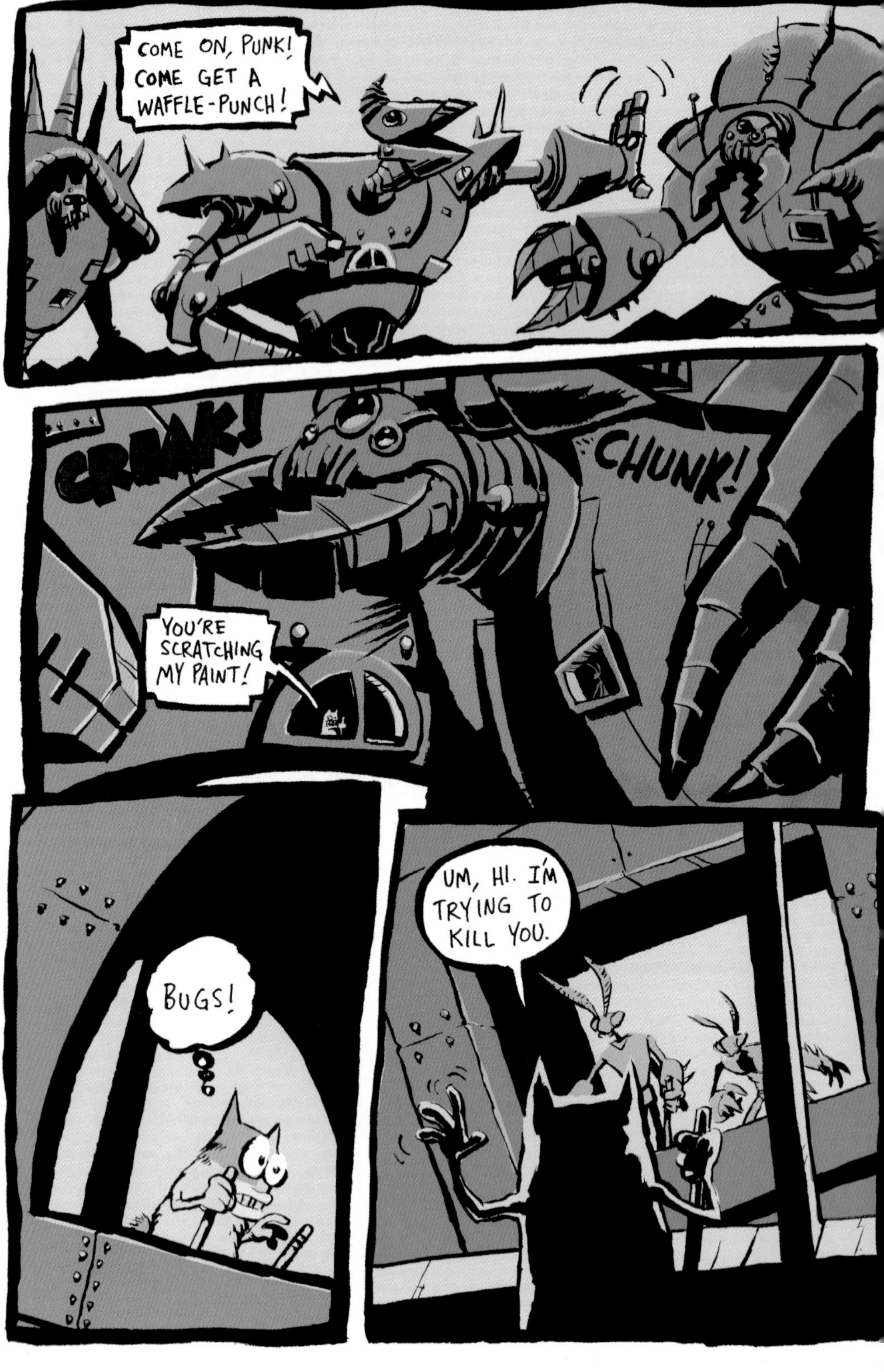
COME ON, PUNK! COME GET A WAFFLE-PUNCH!
CREAK!
CHUNK!
YOU'RE SCRATCHING MY PAINT!
BUGS!
UM, HI. I'M TRYING TO KILL YOU.

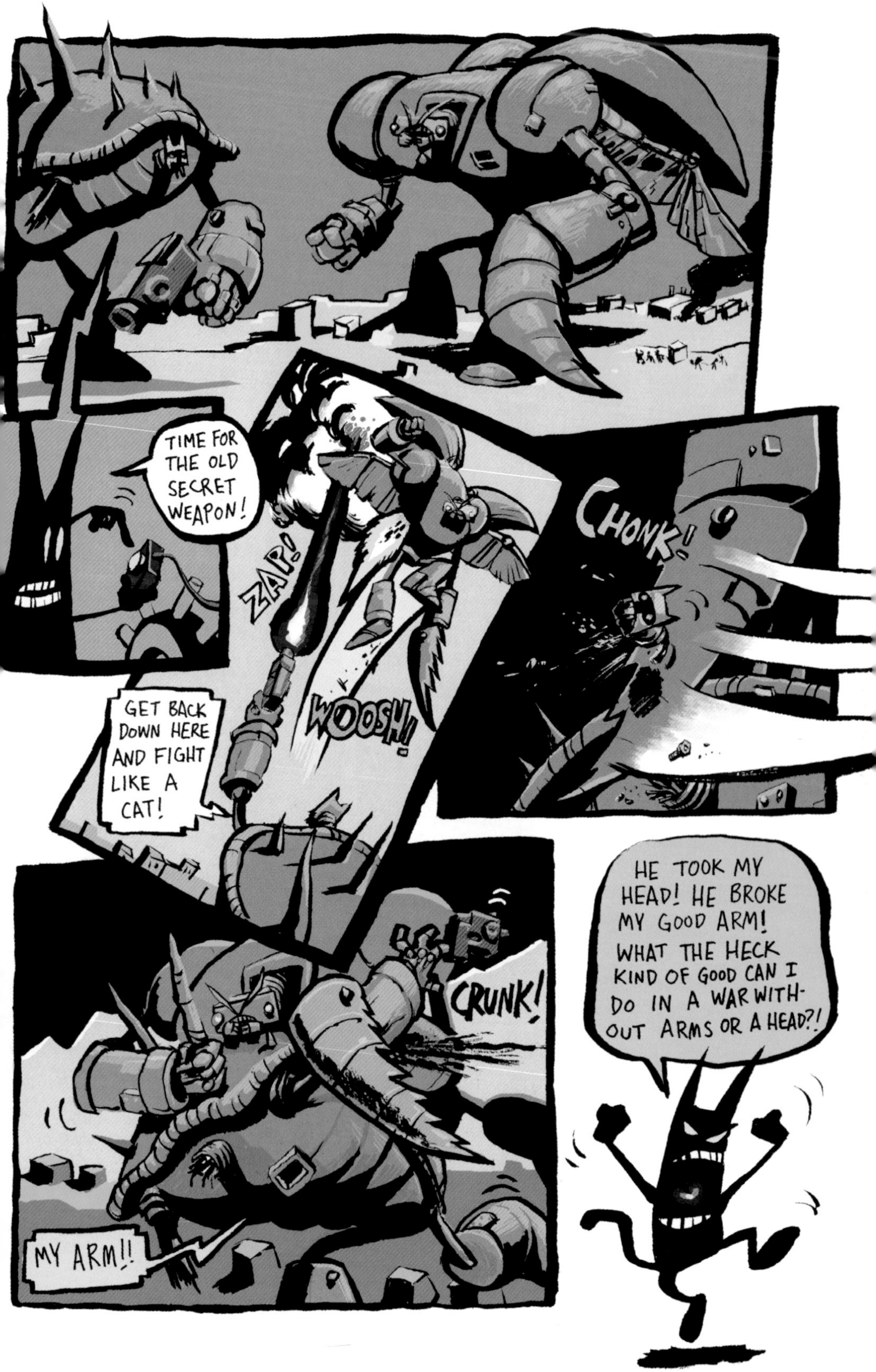
TIME FOR THE OLD SECRET WEAPON!
ZAP!
CHONK!
WOOSH!!
GET BACK DOWN HERE AND FIGHT LIKE A CAT!
CRUNK!
MY ARM!!
HE TOOK MY HEAD! HE BROKE MY GOOD ARM! WHAT THE HECK KIND OF GOOD CAN I DO IN A WAR WITHOUT ARMS OR A HEAD?!

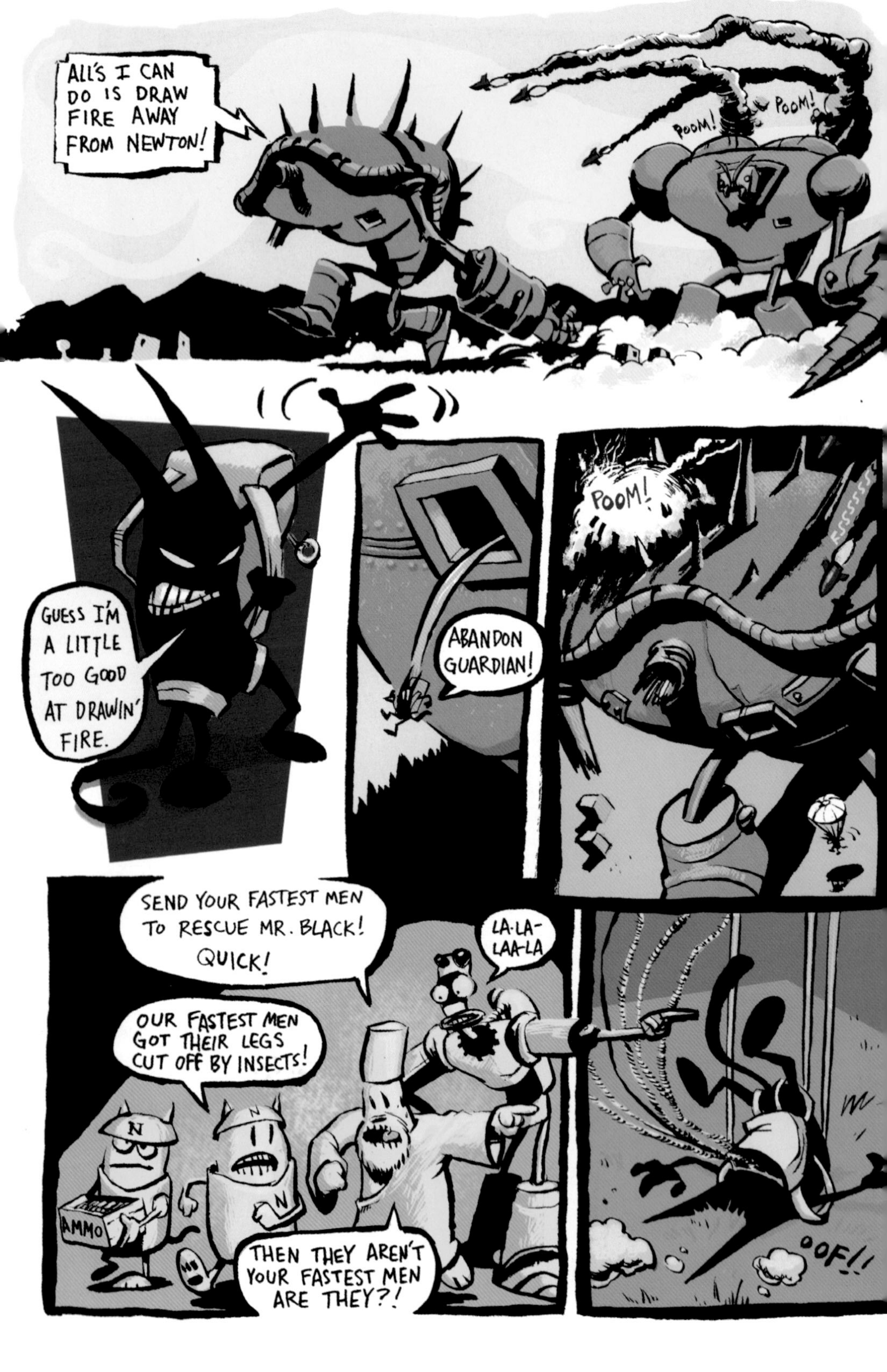
ALL'S I CAN DO IS DRAW FIRE AWAY FROM NEWTON!
POOM!
POOM!
GUESS I'M A LITTLE TOO GOOD AT DRAWIN' FIRE.
ABANDON GUARDIAN!
POOM!
FSSSSSS
SEND YOUR FASTEST MEN TO RESCUE MR. BLACK! QUICK!
LA-LA-LAA-LA
OUR FASTEST MEN GOT THEIR LEGS CUT OFF BY INSECTS!
AMMO
THEN THEY AREN'T YOUR FASTEST MEN ARE THEY?!
OOF!!

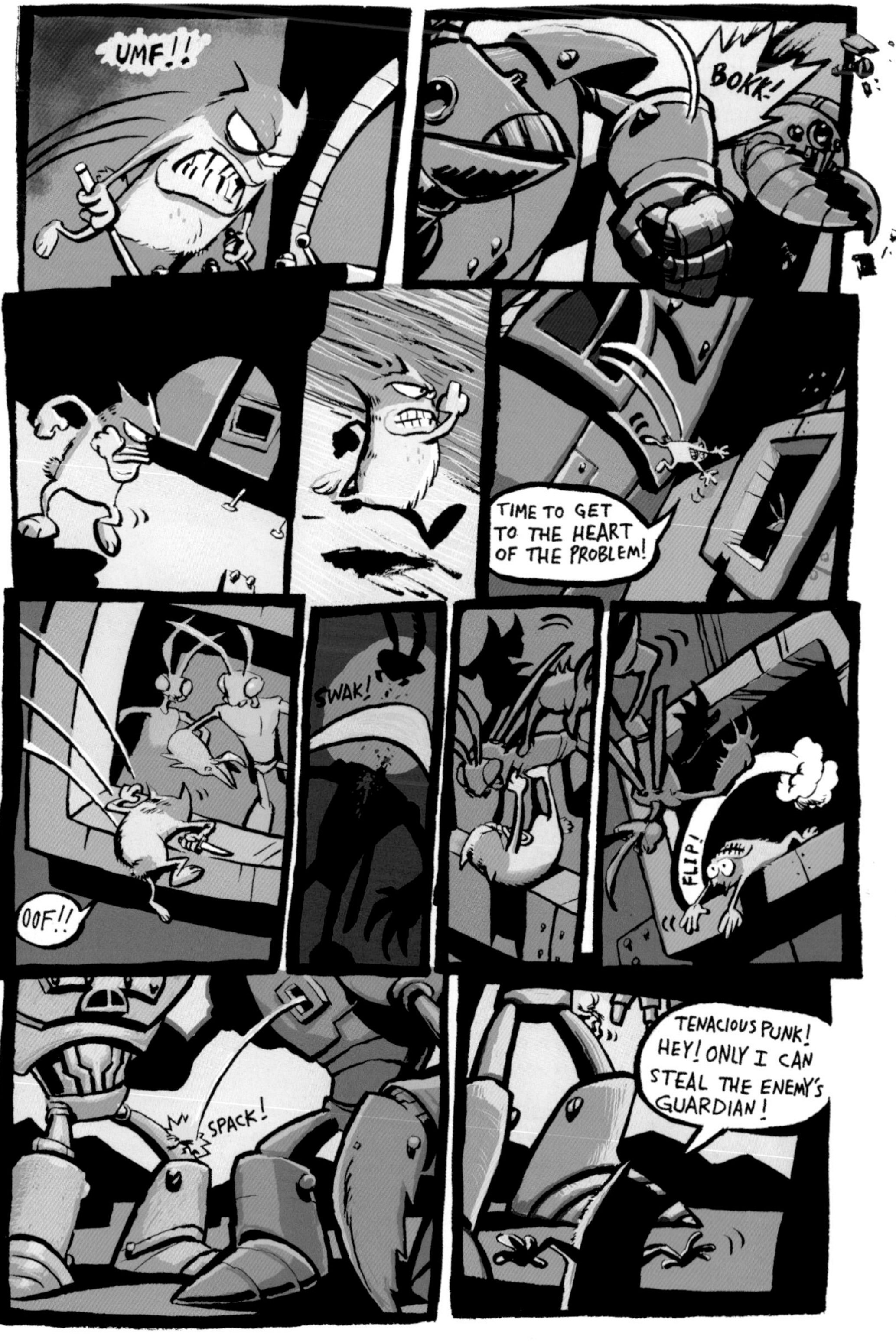
UMF!!
BOKK!
TIME TO GET TO THE HEART OF THE PROBLEM!
OOF!!
SWAK!
FLIP!
SPACK!
TENACIOUS PUNK! HEY! ONLY I CAN STEAL THE ENEMY'S GUARDIAN!

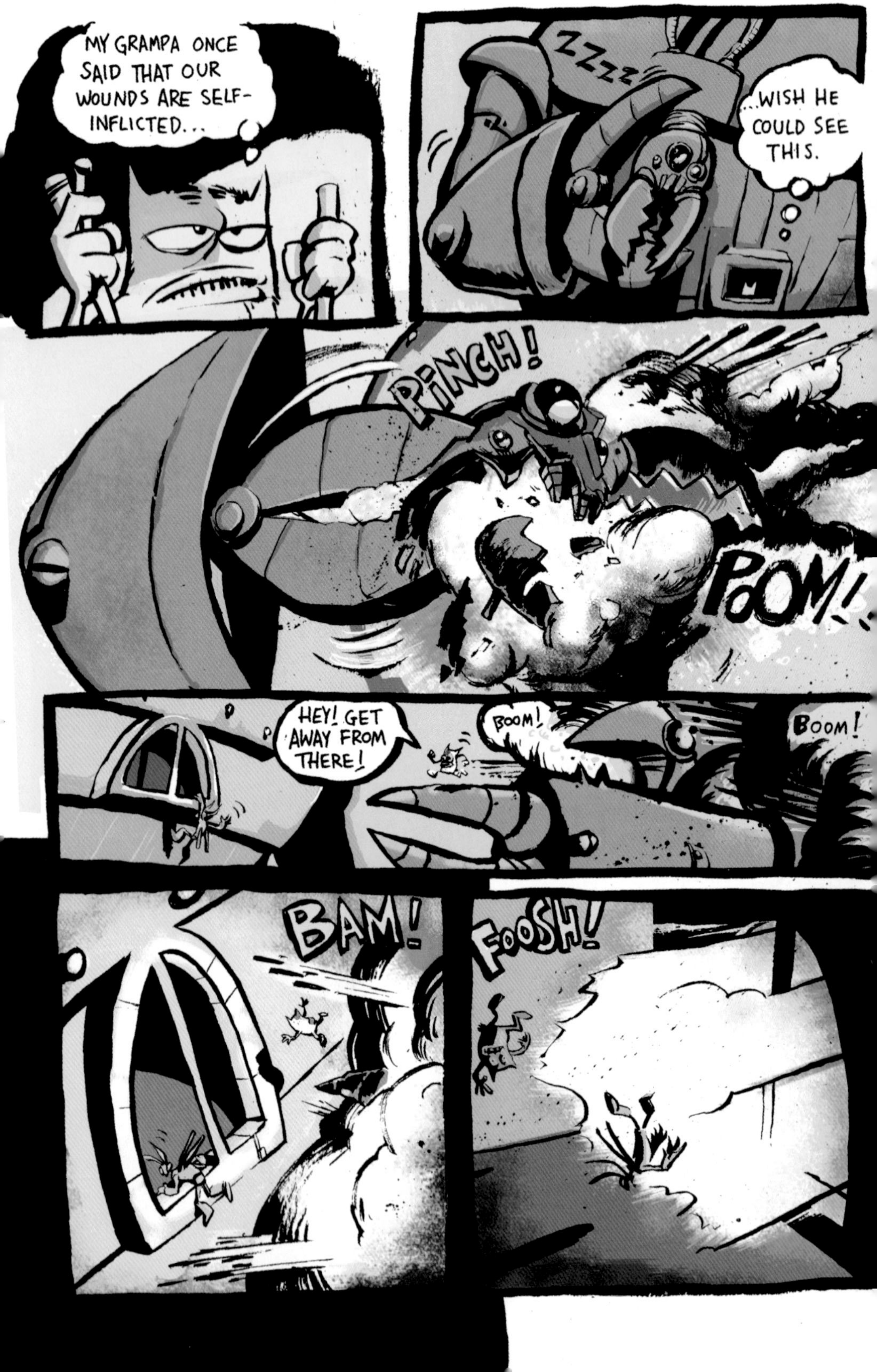
MY GRAMPA ONCE SAID THAT OUR WOUNDS ARE SELF-INFLICTED...
ZZZZZ
...WISH HE COULD SEE THIS.
PINCH!
POOM!
HEY! GET AWAY FROM THERE!
BOOM!
BOOM!
BAM!
FOOSH!

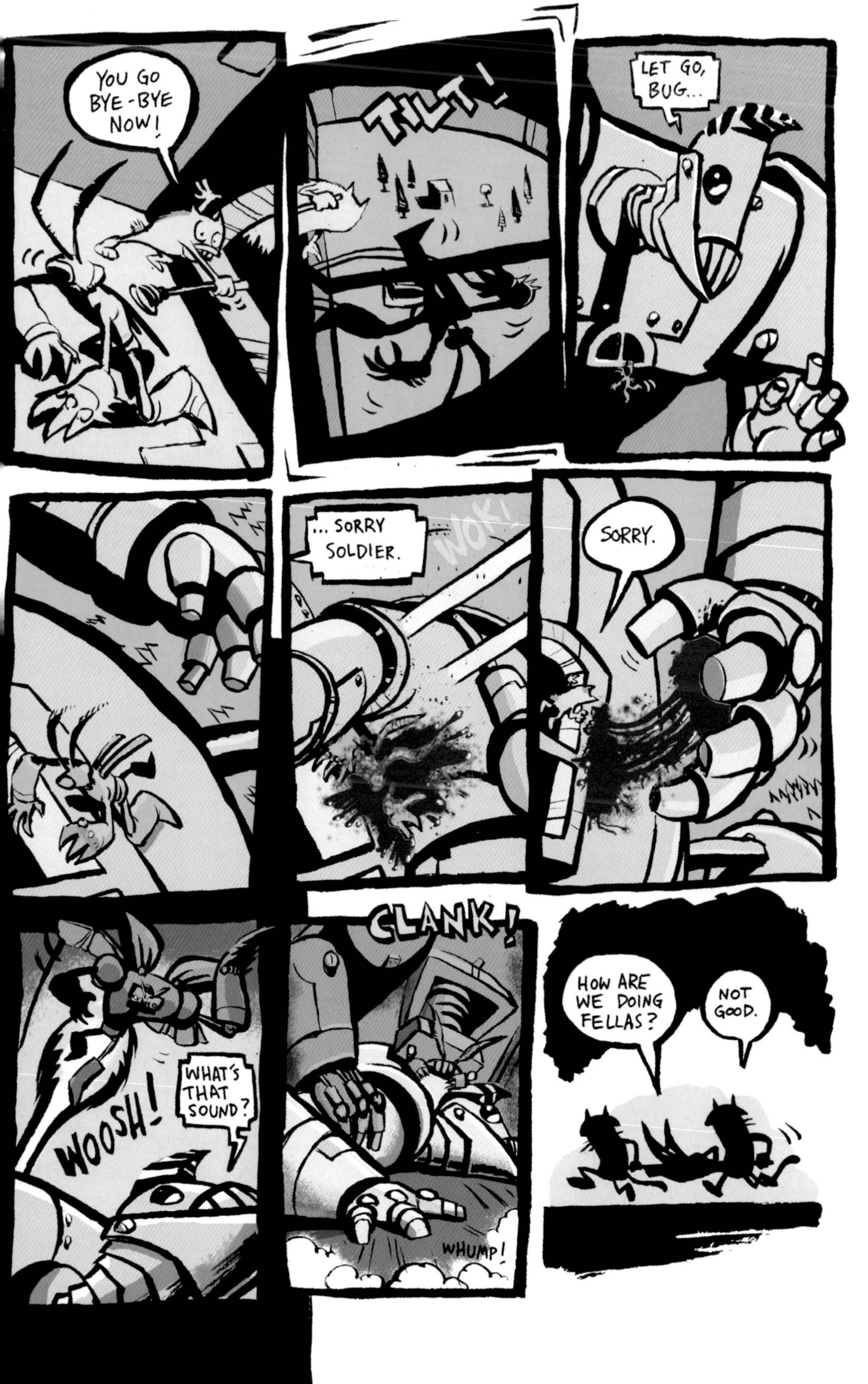
YOU GO BYE-BYE NOW!
TILT!
LET GO, BUG...
...SORRY SOLDIER.
WOK!
SORRY.
WOOSH!
WHAT'S THAT SOUND?
CLANK!
WHUMP!
HOW ARE WE DOING FELLAS?
NOT GOOD.

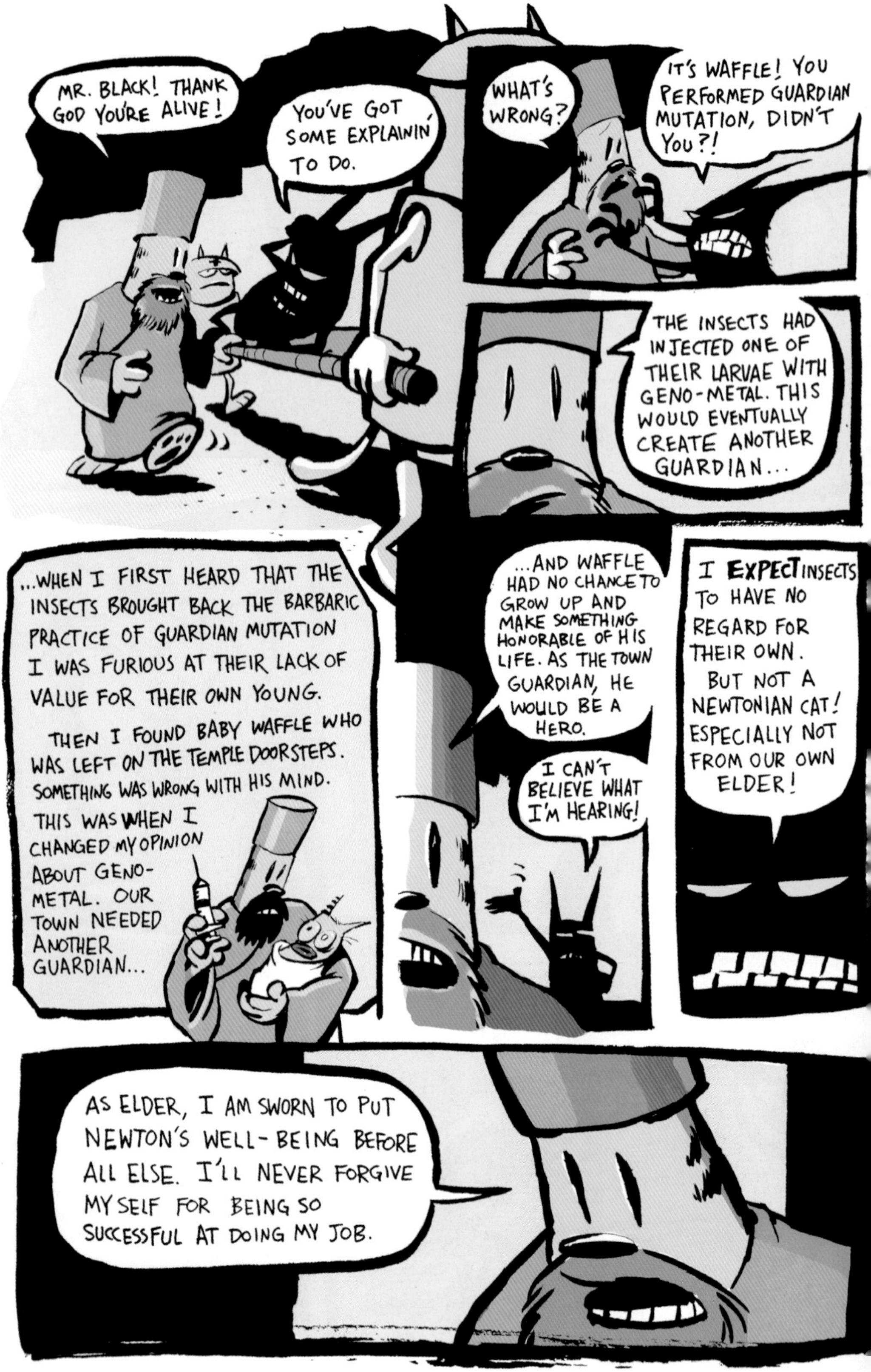
MR. BLACK! THANK GOD YOU'RE ALIVE!
YOU'VE GOT SOME EXPLAININ' TO DO.
WHAT'S WRONG?
IT'S WAFFLE! YOU PERFORMED GUARDIAN MUTATION, DIDN'T YOU?!
THE INSECTS HAD INJECTED ONE OF THEIR LARVAE WITH GENO-METAL. THIS WOULD EVENTUALLY CREATE ANOTHER GUARDIAN...
...WHEN I FIRST HEARD THAT THE INSECTS BROUGHT BACK THE BARBARIC PRACTICE OF GUARDIAN MUTATION I WAS FURIOUS AT THEIR LACK OF VALUE FOR THEIR OWN YOUNG.
THEN I FOUND BABY WAFFLE WHO WAS LEFT ON THE TEMPLE DOORSTEPS. SOMETHING WAS WRONG WITH HIS MIND.
THIS WAS WHEN I CHANGED MY OPINION ABOUT GENO-METAL. OUR TOWN NEEDED ANOTHER GUARDIAN...
...AND WAFFLE HAD NO CHANCE TO GROW UP AND MAKE SOMETHING HONORABLE OF HIS LIFE. AS THE TOWN GUARDIAN, HE WOULD BE A HERO.
I CAN'T BELIEVE WHAT I'M HEARING!
I **EXPECT** INSECTS TO HAVE NO REGARD FOR THEIR OWN. BUT NOT A NEWTONIAN CAT! ESPECIALLY NOT FROM OUR OWN ELDER!
AS ELDER, I AM SWORN TO PUT NEWTON'S WELL-BEING BEFORE ALL ELSE. I'LL NEVER FORGIVE MYSELF FOR BEING SO SUCCESSFUL AT DOING MY JOB.

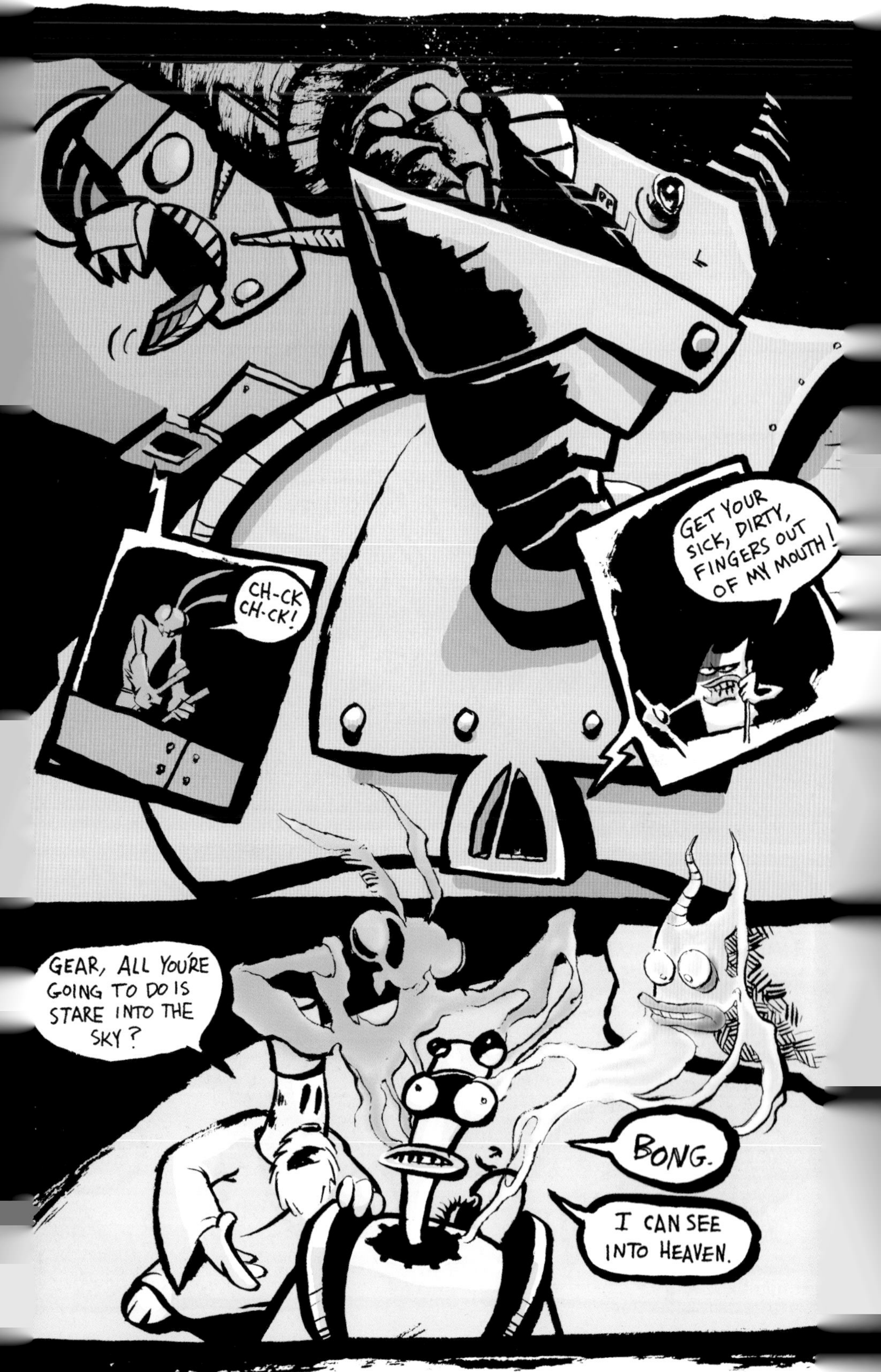
CH-CK
CH-CK!
GET YOUR SICK, DIRTY, FINGERS OUT OF MY MOUTH!
GEAR, ALL YOU'RE GOING TO DO IS STARE INTO THE SKY?
BONG.
I CAN SEE INTO HEAVEN.

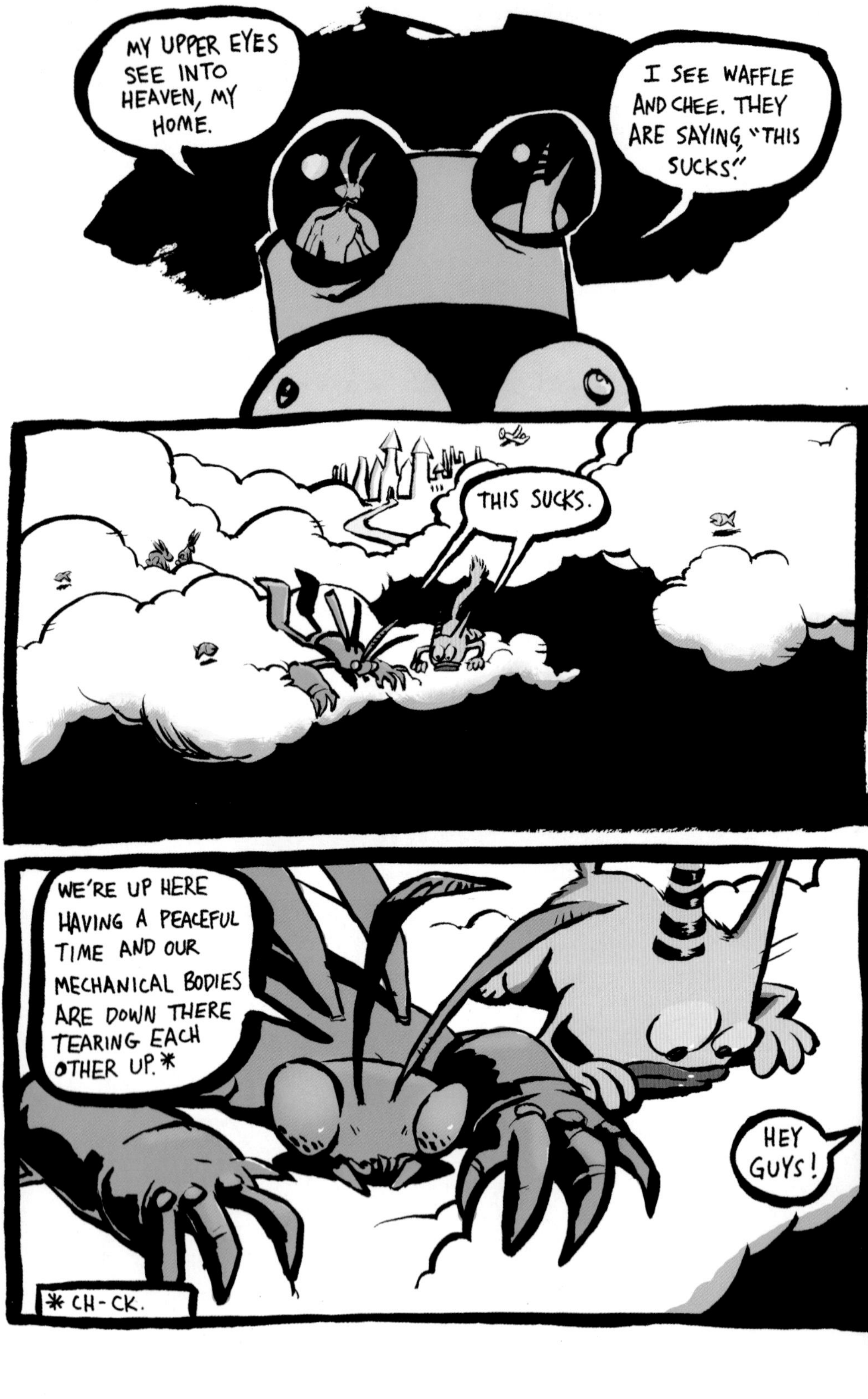
MY UPPER EYES SEE INTO HEAVEN, MY HOME.
I SEE WAFFLE AND CHEE. THEY ARE SAYING, "THIS SUCKS."
THIS SUCKS.
WE'RE UP HERE HAVING A PEACEFUL TIME AND OUR MECHANICAL BODIES ARE DOWN THERE TEARING EACH OTHER UP.*
HEY GUYS!
* CH-CK.

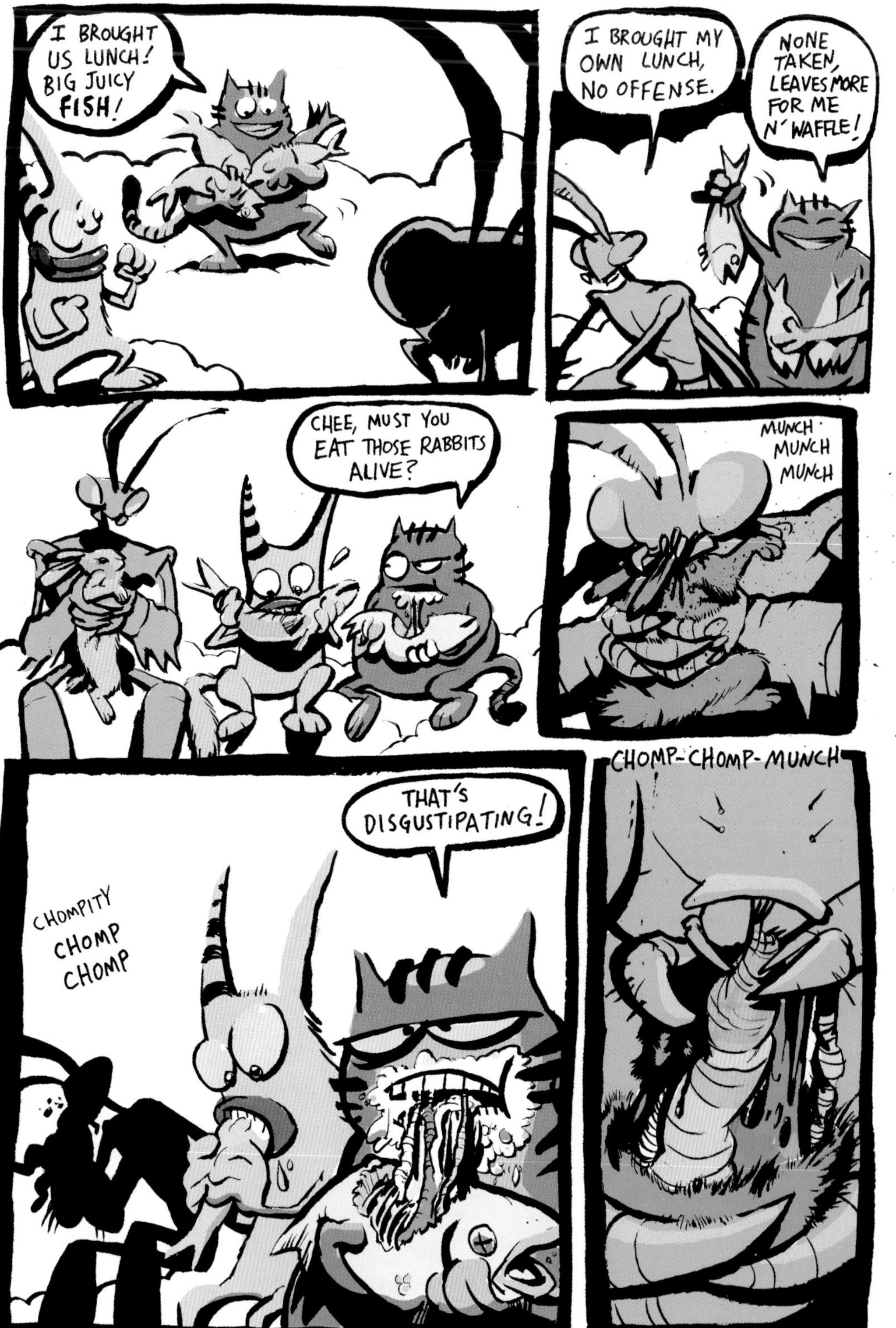
I BROUGHT US LUNCH! BIG JUICY FISH!
I BROUGHT MY OWN LUNCH, NO OFFENSE.
NONE TAKEN, LEAVES MORE FOR ME N' WAFFLE!
CHEE, MUST YOU EAT THOSE RABBITS ALIVE?
MUNCH MUNCH MUNCH
THAT'S DISGUSTIPATING!
CHOMPITY CHOMP CHOMP
CHOMP-CHOMP-MUNCH

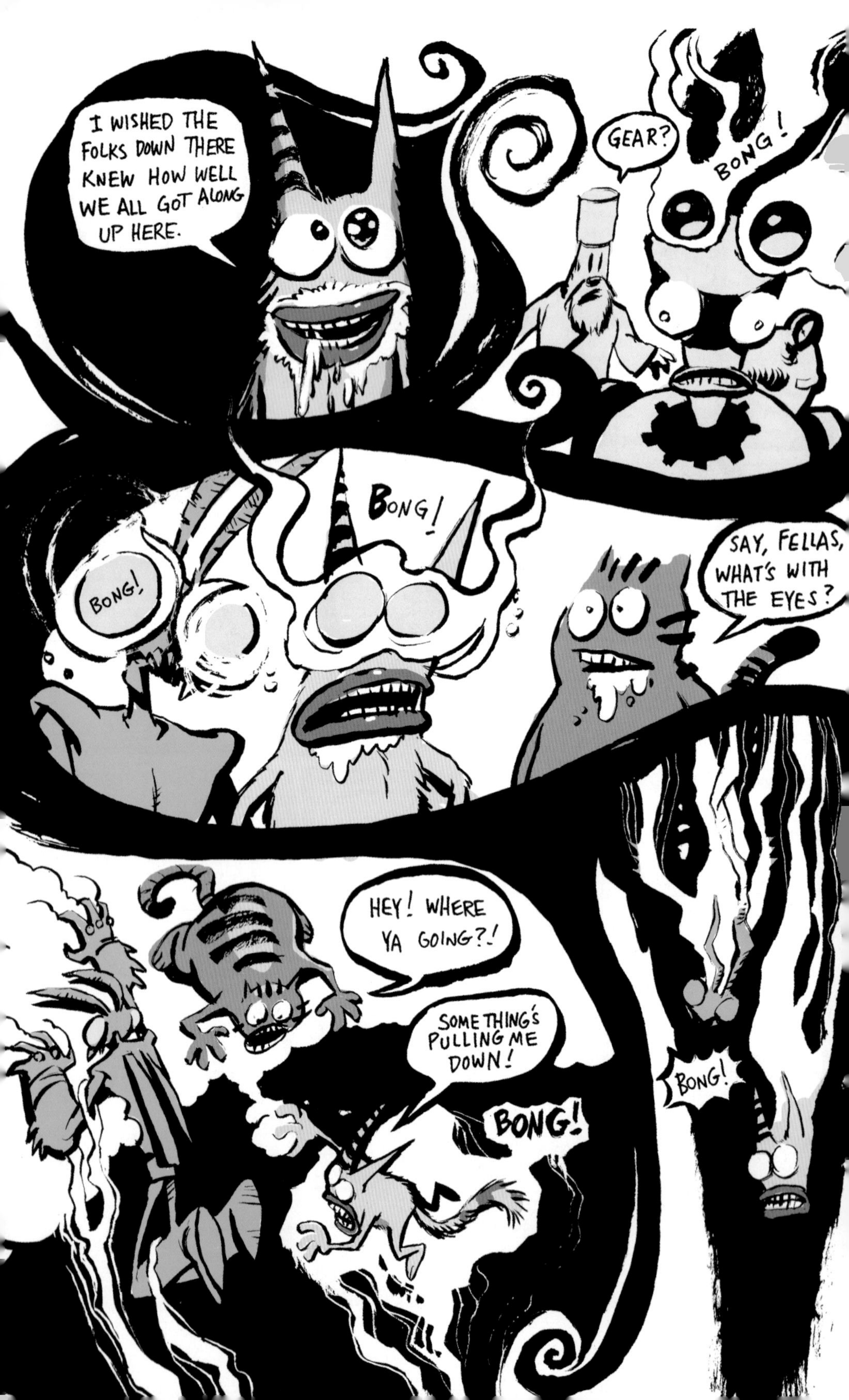
I WISHED THE FOLKS DOWN THERE KNEW HOW WELL WE ALL GOT ALONG UP HERE.
GEAR?
BONG!
BONG!
BONG!
SAY, FELLAS, WHAT'S WITH THE EYES?
HEY! WHERE YA GOING?!
SOMETHING'S PULLING ME DOWN!
BONG!
BONG!

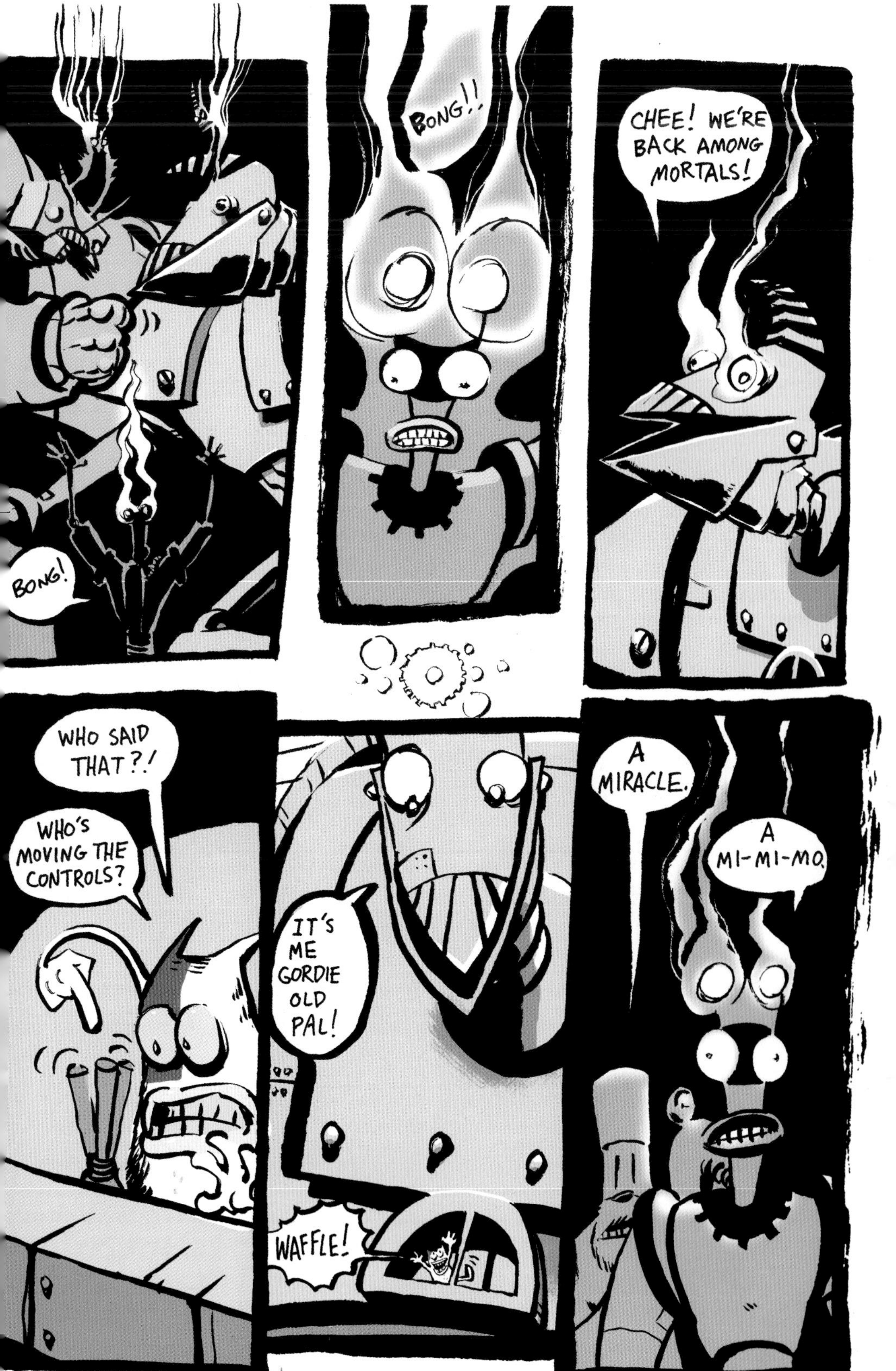
BONG!
BONG!!
CHEE! WE'RE BACK AMONG MORTALS!
WHO SAID THAT?!
WHO'S MOVING THE CONTROLS?
IT'S ME GORDIE OLD PAL!
WAFFLE!
A MIRACLE.
A MI-MI-MO.

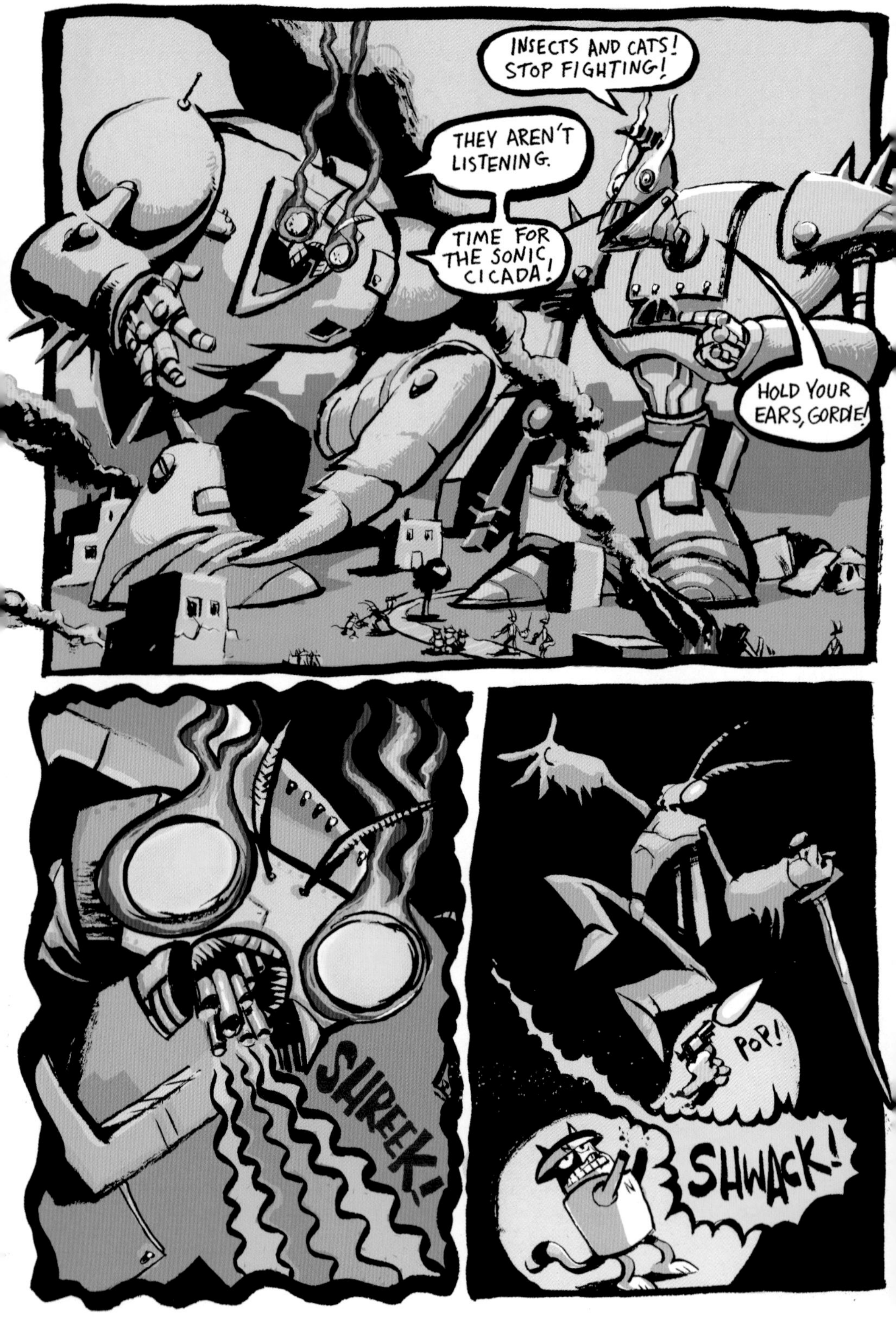
INSECTS AND CATS! STOP FIGHTING!
THEY AREN'T LISTENING.
TIME FOR THE SONIC CICADA!
HOLD YOUR EARS, GORDIE!
SHREEK!
POP!
SHWACK!

SOUTHPLATE INSECTS! I AM YOUR BROTHER, CHEE. FOR GENERATIONS, OUR PEOPLE HAVE SOUGHT TO TAKE OVER NEWTON, TO EXPAND OUR NEST.*

*CH-CK-CH-CH-CHEE!

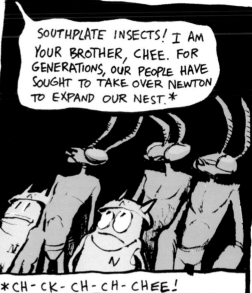

...WE MUST STOP THIS! TODAY! THE FIRST INSECT WHO RAISES SWORD AGAINST NEWTON WILL REAP MY WRATH!

OUR PEOPLE LIVED IN SYMBIOTIC HARMONY BEFORE THE TIME OF GUARDIANS...

...MY FRIENDSHIP WITH CHEE ALLOWS US TO SEE A LARGER COMMON FOE...

...A GREATER EVIL RISES IN THE EAST, AGAINST BOTH NEWTON AND SOUTH PLATE INSECTS.

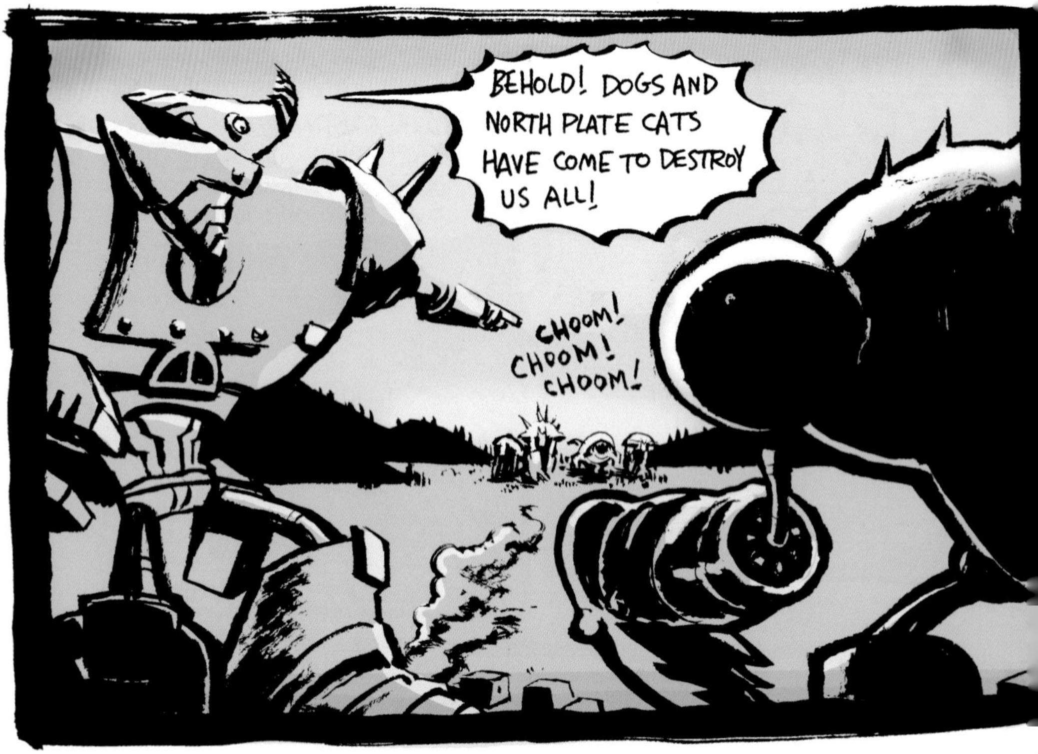
BEHOLD! DOGS AND NORTH PLATE CATS HAVE COME TO DESTROY US ALL!
CHOOM! CHOOM! CHOOM!

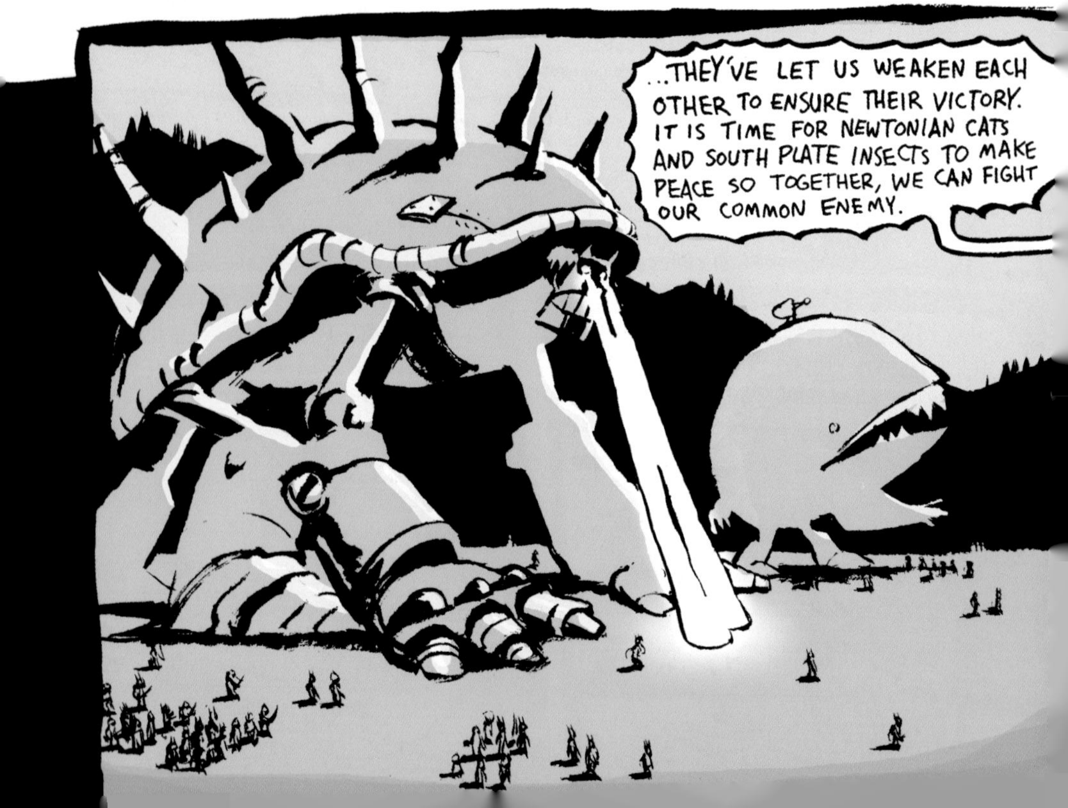
...THEY'VE LET US WEAKEN EACH OTHER TO ENSURE THEIR VICTORY. IT IS TIME FOR NEWTONIAN CATS AND SOUTH PLATE INSECTS TO MAKE PEACE SO TOGETHER, WE CAN FIGHT OUR COMMON ENEMY.

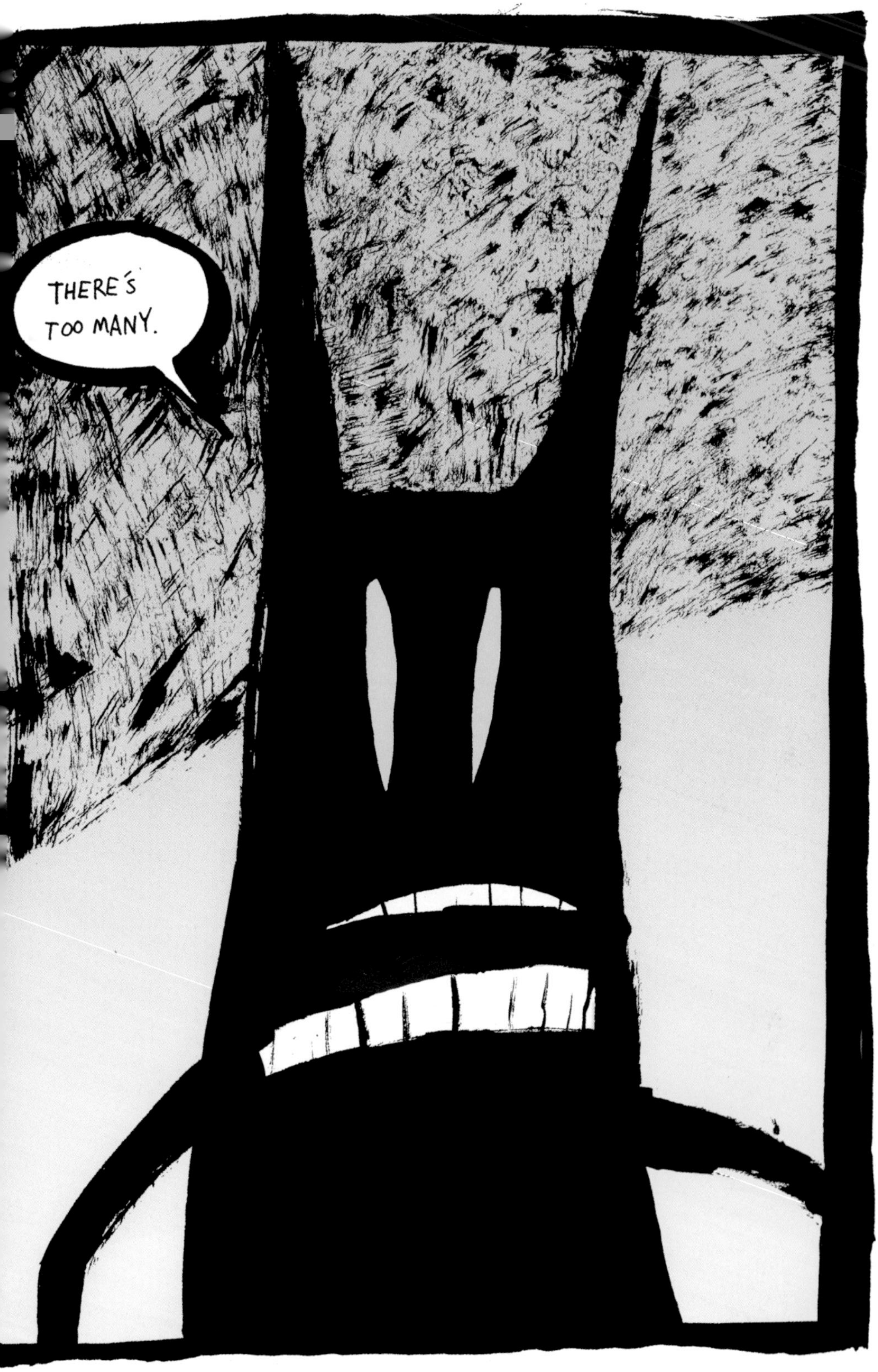
THERE'S TOO MANY.

# chapter 6

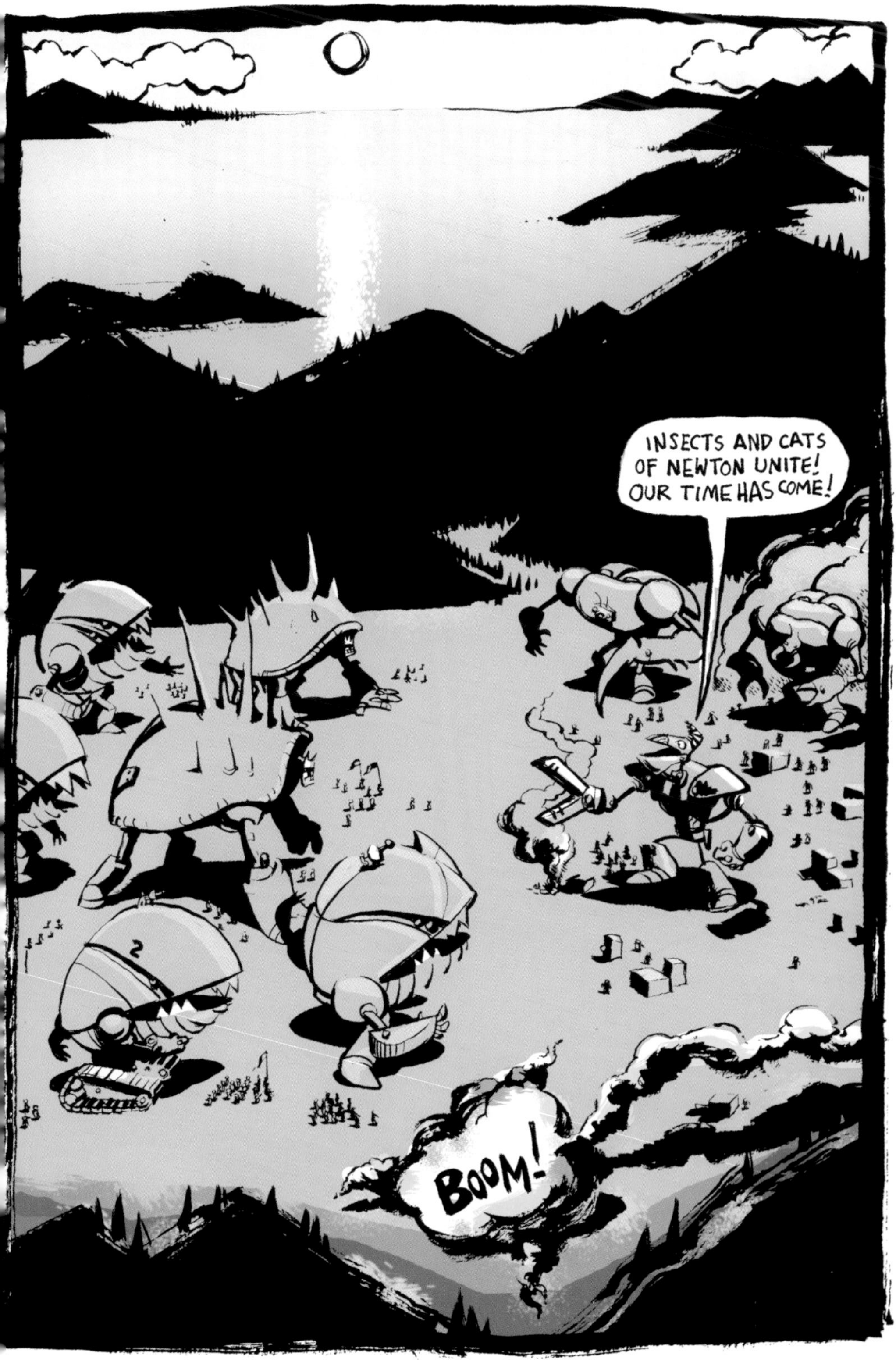
INSECTS AND CATS OF NEWTON UNITE! OUR TIME HAS COME!
2
BOOM!

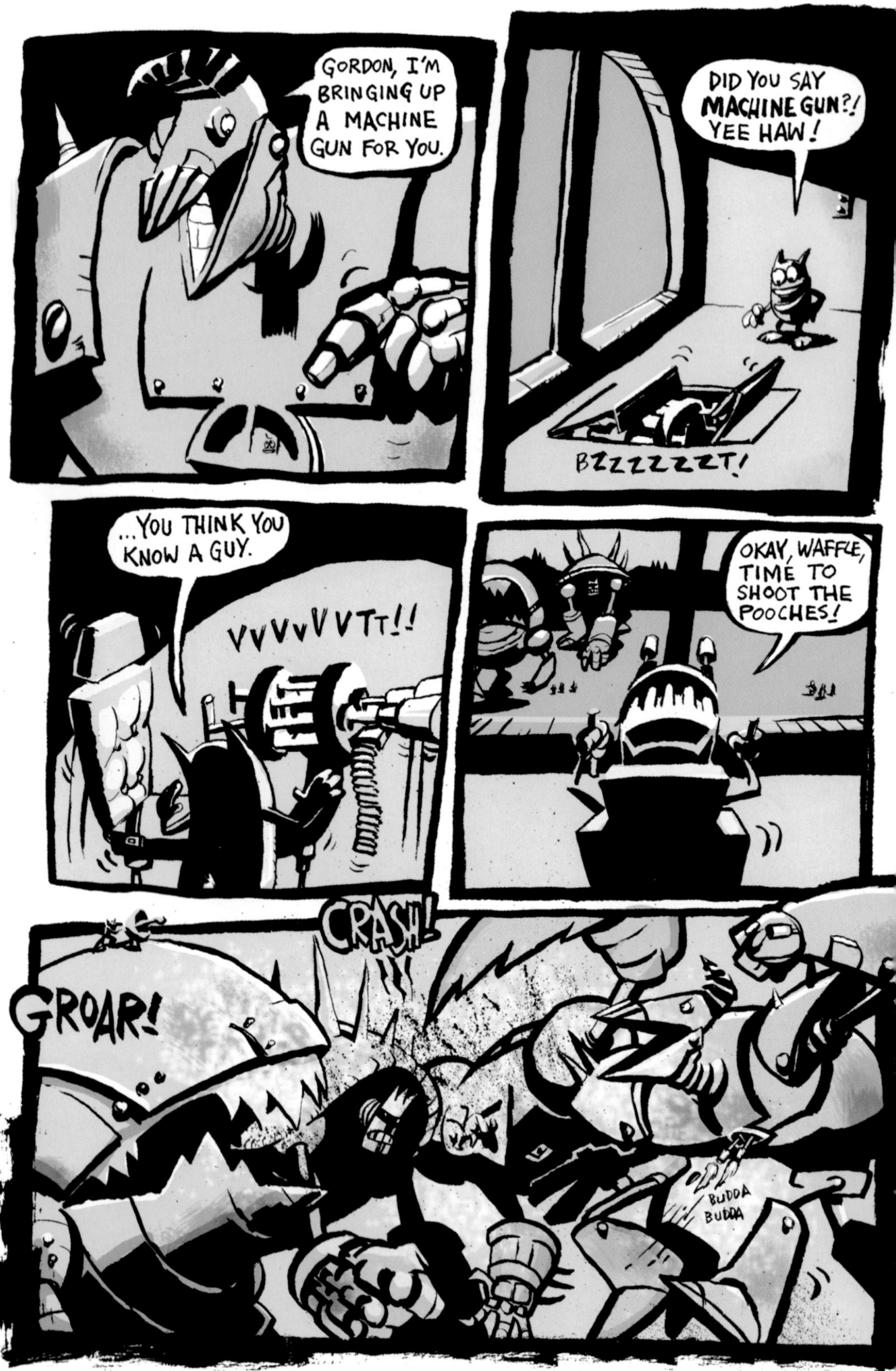
GORDON, I'M BRINGING UP A MACHINE GUN FOR YOU.
DID YOU SAY MACHINE GUN?! YEE HAW!
BZZZZZZZT!
...YOU THINK YOU KNOW A GUY.
VVVVVVTTT!!
OKAY, WAFFLE, TIME TO SHOOT THE POOCHES!
CRASH!
GROAR!
BUDDA BUDDA

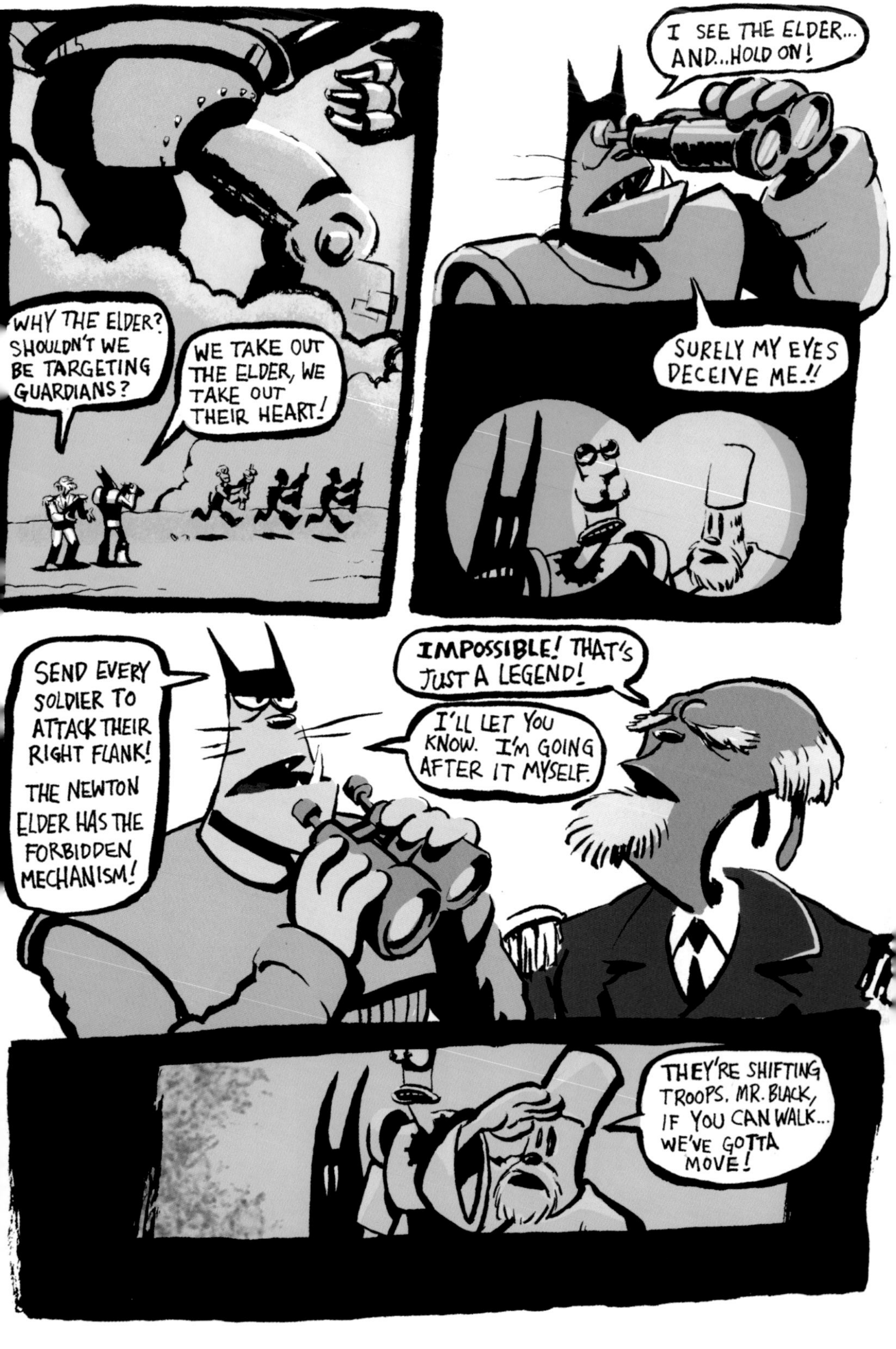
WHY THE ELDER? SHOULDN'T WE BE TARGETING GUARDIANS?
WE TAKE OUT THE ELDER, WE TAKE OUT THEIR HEART!
I SEE THE ELDER... AND...HOLD ON!
SURELY MY EYES DECEIVE ME.!!
SEND EVERY SOLDIER TO ATTACK THEIR RIGHT FLANK!
THE NEWTON ELDER HAS THE FORBIDDEN MECHANISM!
IMPOSSIBLE! THAT'S JUST A LEGEND!
I'LL LET YOU KNOW. I'M GOING AFTER IT MYSELF.
THEY'RE SHIFTING TROOPS. MR. BLACK, IF YOU CAN WALK... WE'VE GOTTA MOVE!

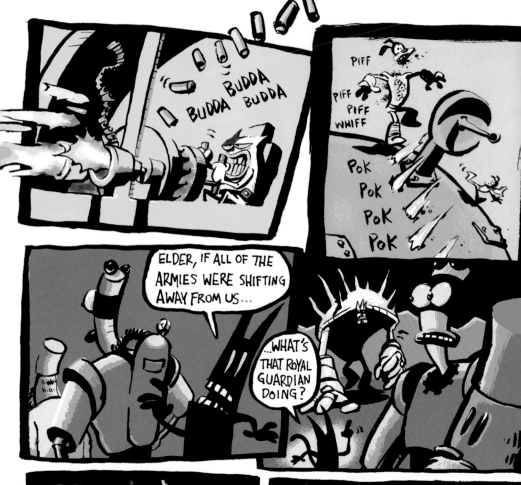

BUDDA BUDDA BUDDA

PIFF
PIFF
PIFF
WHIFF

POK
POK
POK
POK

ELDER, IF ALL OF THE ARMIES WERE SHIFTING AWAY FROM US...

...WHAT'S THAT ROYAL GUARDIAN DOING?

WHICH ONE IS THE FORBIDDEN MECHANISM?

HE'S THE ROBOT WITH THE GOOGLIE EYES.

OUR TROOPS HAVE BEEN DECOYED! THEY'RE REALLY AFTER GEAR!

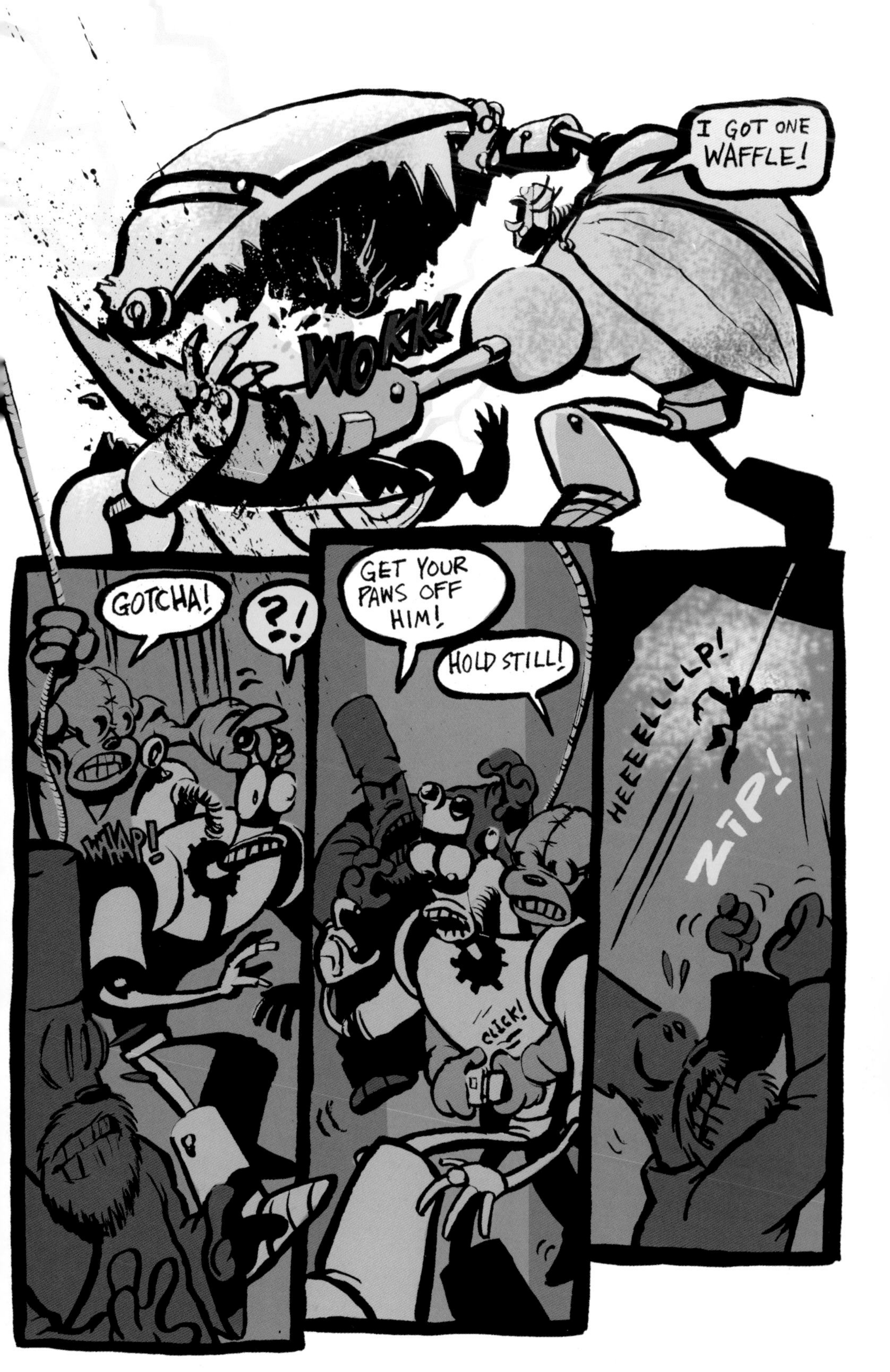

I GOT ONE WAFFLE!
WOKK!
GOTCHA!
?!
WHAP!
GET YOUR PAWS OFF HIM!
HOLD STILL!
CLICK!
HEEEELLLLLP!
ZIP!

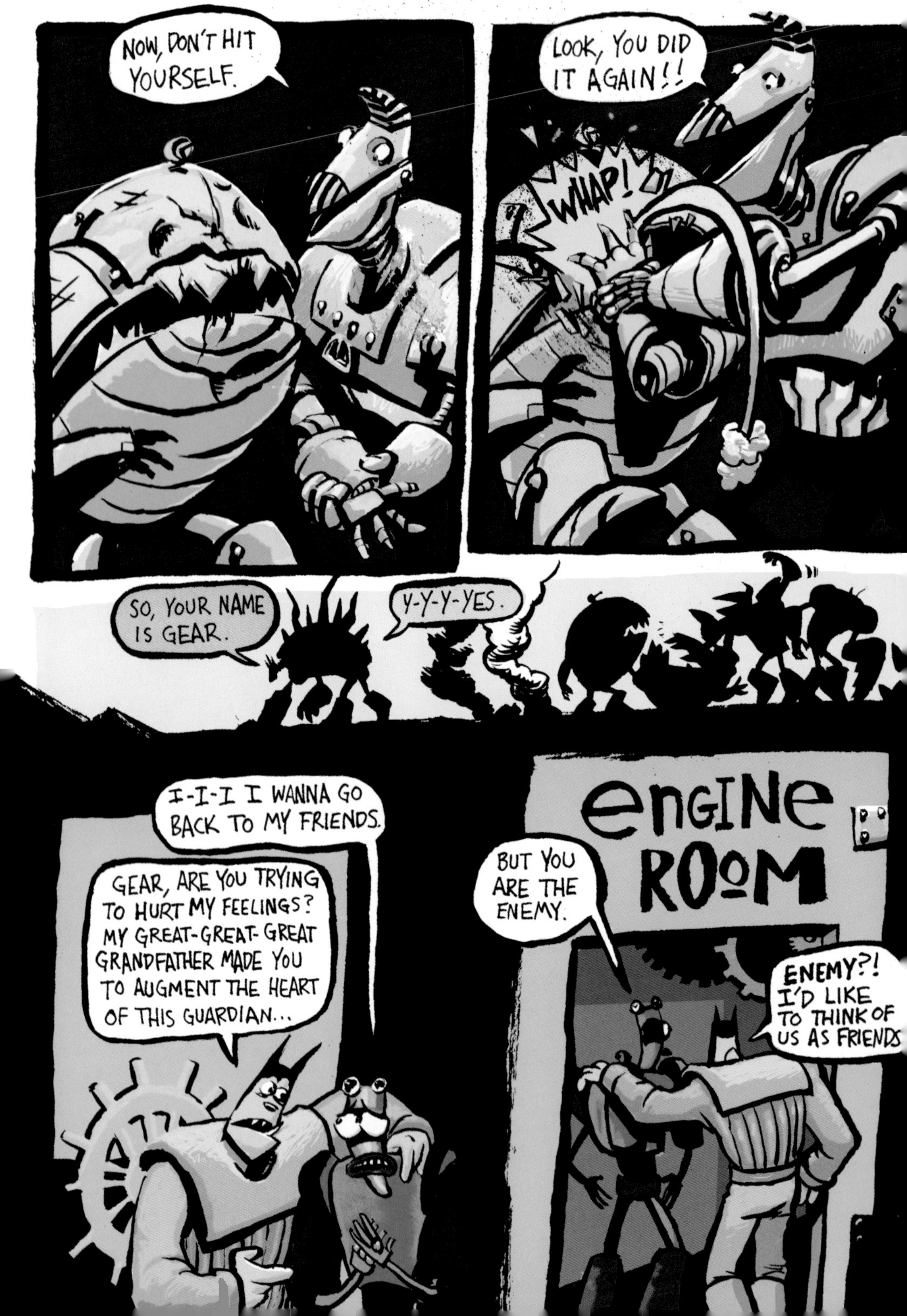
NOW, DON'T HIT YOURSELF.
LOOK, YOU DID IT AGAIN!!
WHAP!
SO, YOUR NAME IS GEAR.
Y-Y-Y-YES.
I-I-I I WANNA GO BACK TO MY FRIENDS.
GEAR, ARE YOU TRYING TO HURT MY FEELINGS? MY GREAT-GREAT-GREAT GRANDFATHER MADE YOU TO AUGMENT THE HEART OF THIS GUARDIAN...
ENGINE ROOM
BUT YOU ARE THE ENEMY.
ENEMY?! I'D LIKE TO THINK OF US AS FRIENDS

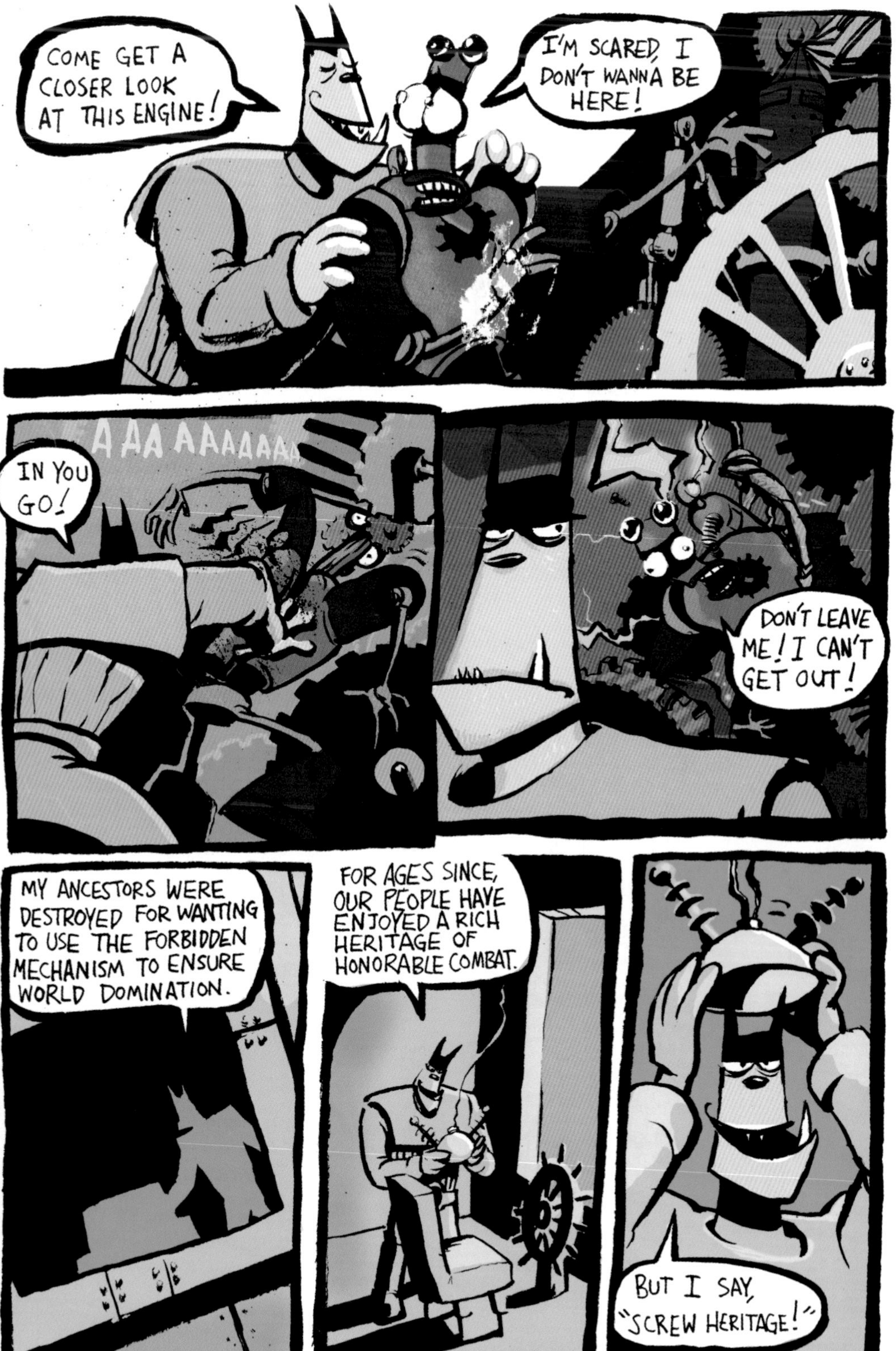
COME GET A CLOSER LOOK AT THIS ENGINE!
I'M SCARED, I DON'T WANNA BE HERE!
AAAAAAAAA
IN YOU GO!
DON'T LEAVE ME! I CAN'T GET OUT!
MY ANCESTORS WERE DESTROYED FOR WANTING TO USE THE FORBIDDEN MECHANISM TO ENSURE WORLD DOMINATION.
FOR AGES SINCE, OUR PEOPLE HAVE ENJOYED A RICH HERITAGE OF HONORABLE COMBAT.
BUT I SAY, "SCREW HERITAGE!"

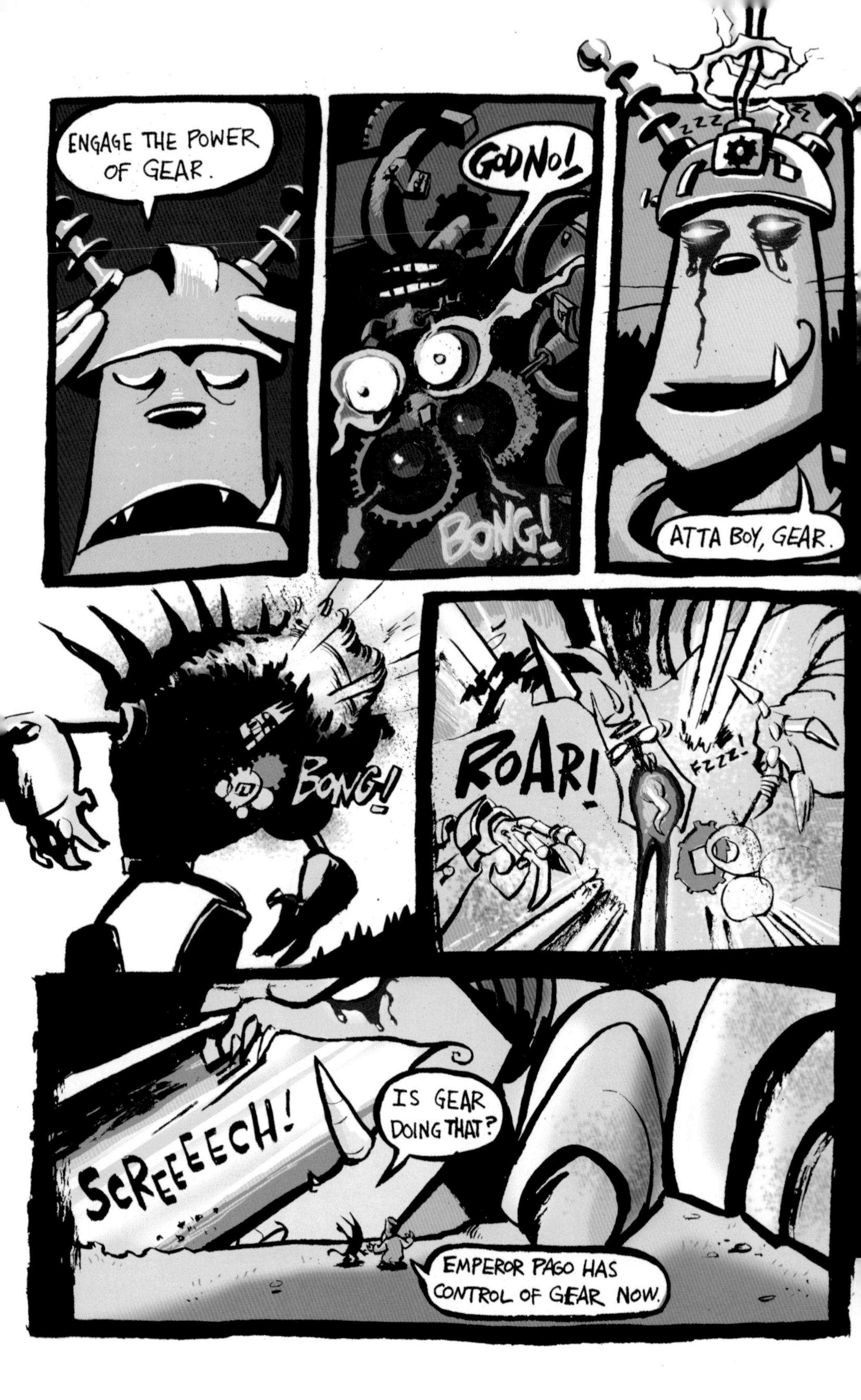
ENGAGE THE POWER OF GEAR.
GOD NO!
BONG!
ZZZ
ATTA BOY, GEAR.
BONG!
ROAR!
FZZZ!
SCREEEEECH!
IS GEAR DOING THAT?
EMPEROR PAGO HAS CONTROL OF GEAR NOW.

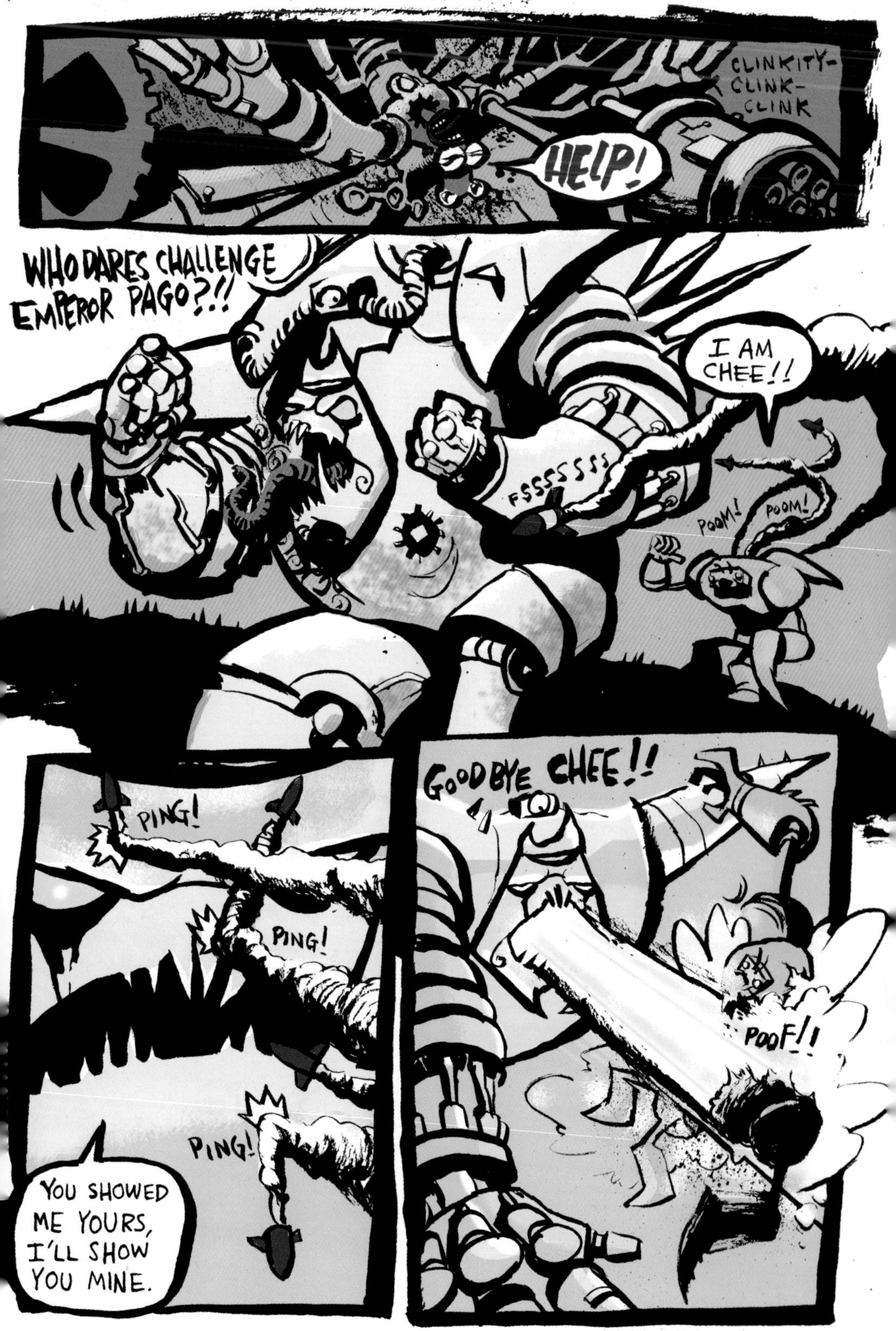

CLINKITY-CLINK-CLINK
HELP!
WHO DARES CHALLENGE EMPEROR PAGO?!!
I AM CHEE!!
FSSSSSSS
POOM! POOM!
PING!
PING!
PING!
YOU SHOWED ME YOURS, I'LL SHOW YOU MINE.
GOODBYE CHEE!!
POOF!!

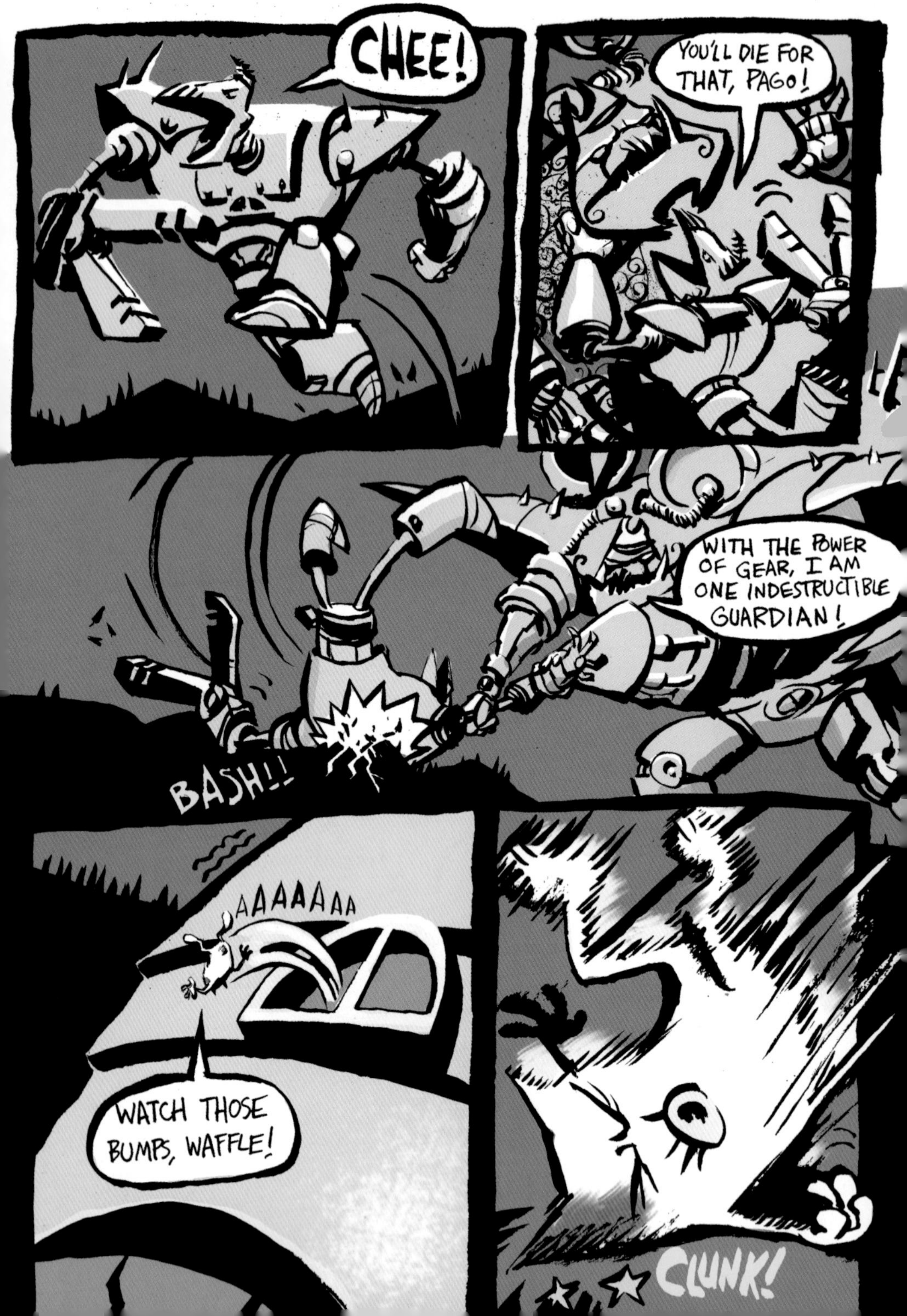
CHEE!
YOU'LL DIE FOR THAT, PAGO!
WITH THE POWER OF GEAR, I AM ONE INDESTRUCTIBLE GUARDIAN!
BASH!!
AAAAAAA
WATCH THOSE BUMPS, WAFFLE!
CLUNK!

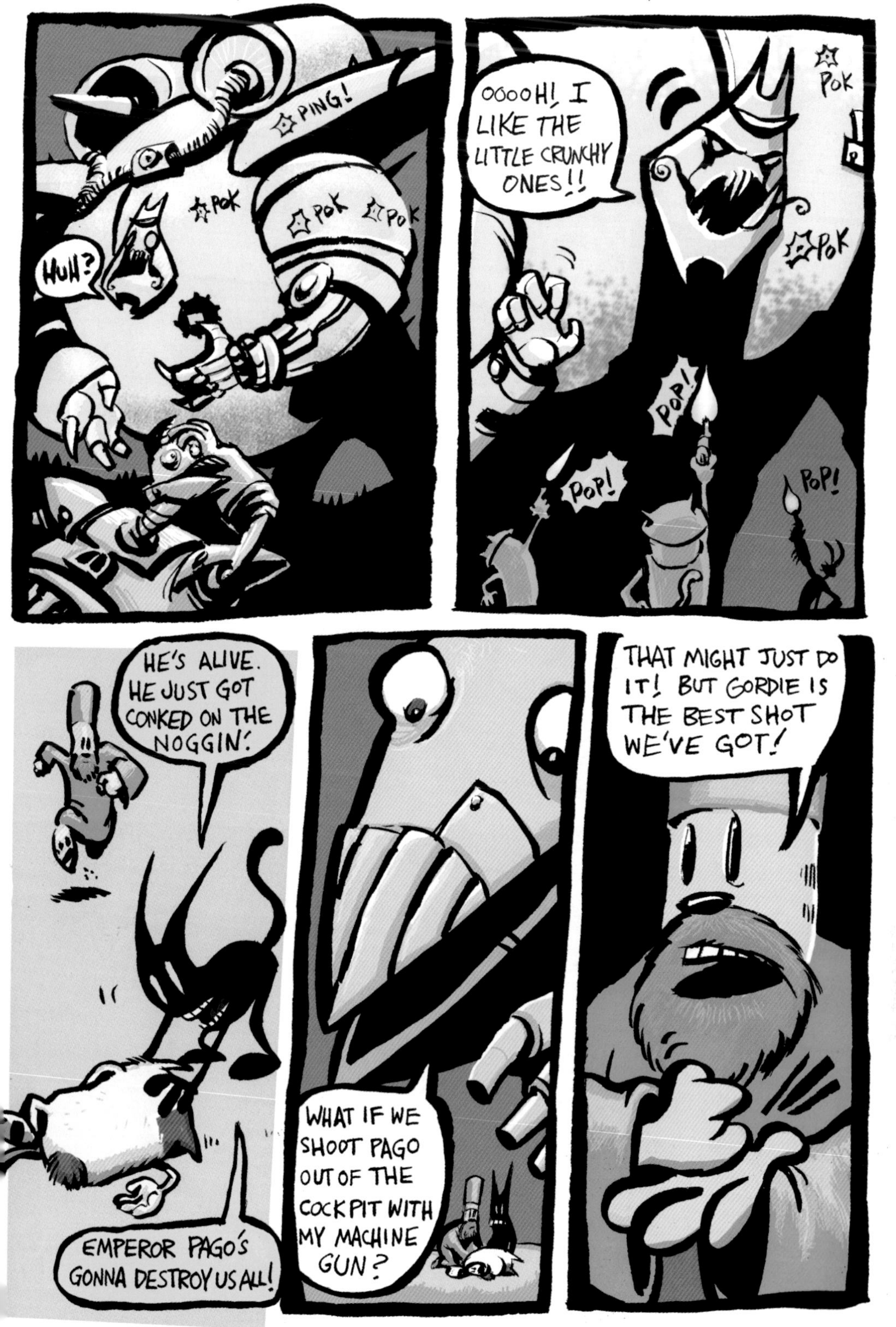
PING!
POK
POK
POK
HUH?
OOOOH! I LIKE THE LITTLE CRUNCHY ONES!!
POK
POK
POP!
POP!
POP!
HE'S ALIVE. HE JUST GOT CONKED ON THE NOGGIN!
EMPEROR PAGO'S GONNA DESTROY US ALL!
WHAT IF WE SHOOT PAGO OUT OF THE COCKPIT WITH MY MACHINE GUN?
THAT MIGHT JUST DO IT! BUT GORDIE IS THE BEST SHOT WE'VE GOT!

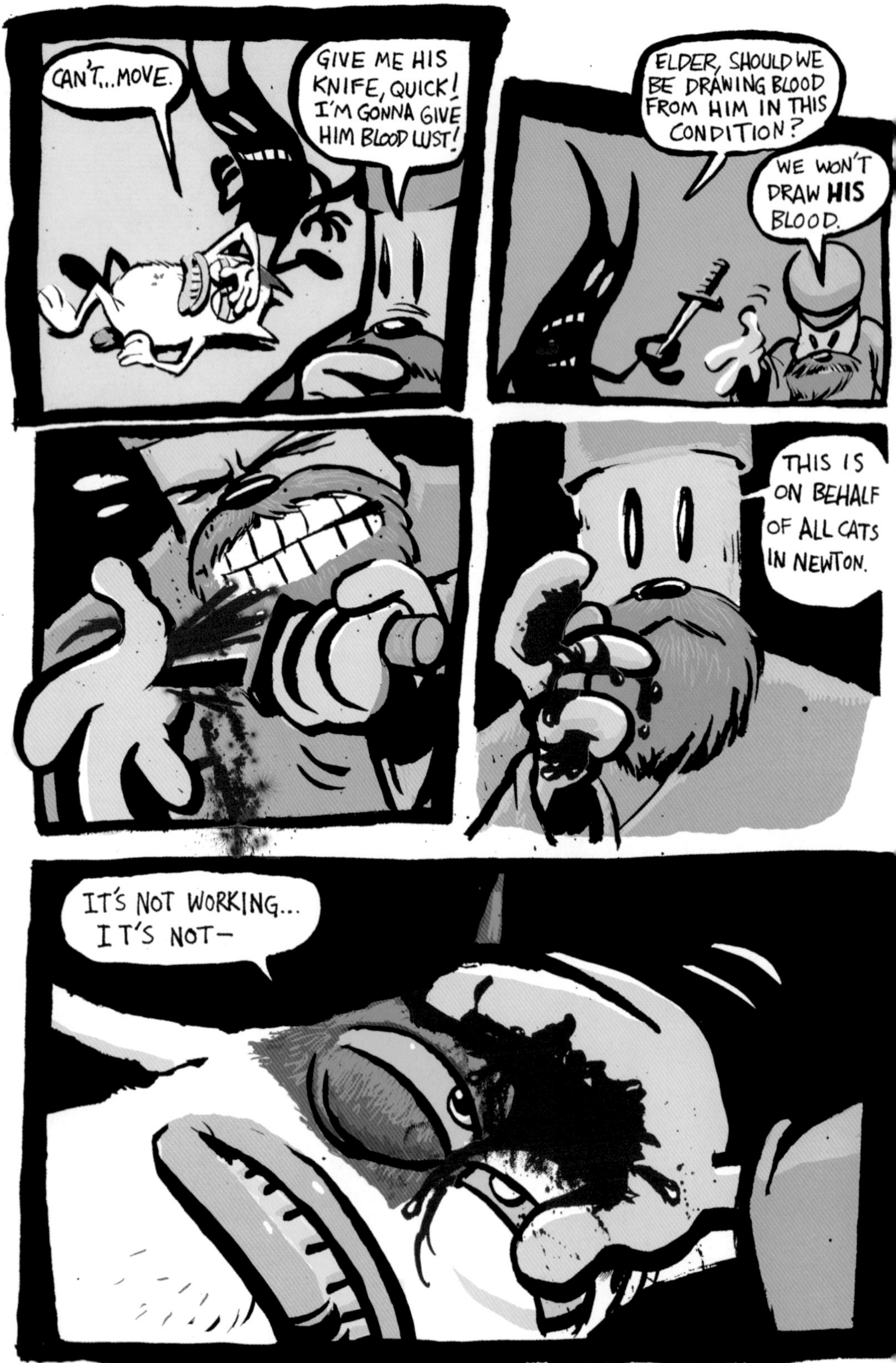
CAN'T...MOVE.
GIVE ME HIS KNIFE, QUICK! I'M GONNA GIVE HIM BLOOD LUST!
ELDER, SHOULD WE BE DRAWING BLOOD FROM HIM IN THIS CONDITION?
WE WON'T DRAW HIS BLOOD.
THIS IS ON BEHALF OF ALL CATS IN NEWTON.
IT'S NOT WORKING... IT'S NOT-

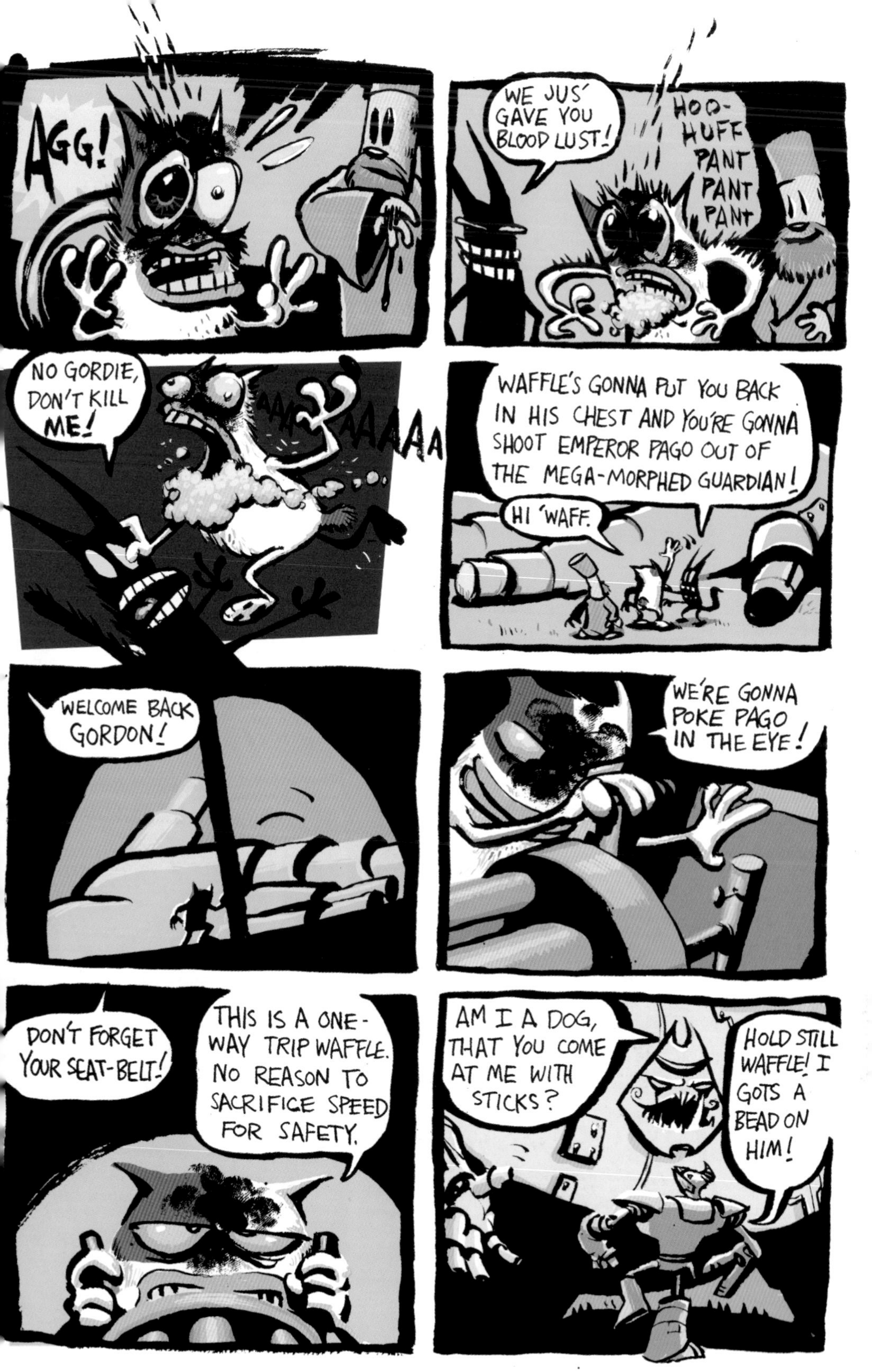
AGG!
WE JUS' GAVE YOU BLOOD LUST!
HOO-HUFF PANT PANT PANT
NO GORDIE, DON'T KILL ME!
AAAAAAAAA
WAFFLE'S GONNA PUT YOU BACK IN HIS CHEST AND YOU'RE GONNA SHOOT EMPEROR PAGO OUT OF THE MEGA-MORPHED GUARDIAN!
HI 'WAFF.
WELCOME BACK GORDON!
WE'RE GONNA POKE PAGO IN THE EYE!
DON'T FORGET YOUR SEAT-BELT!
THIS IS A ONE-WAY TRIP WAFFLE. NO REASON TO SACRIFICE SPEED FOR SAFETY.
AM I A DOG, THAT YOU COME AT ME WITH STICKS?
HOLD STILL WAFFLE! I GOTS A BEAD ON HIM!

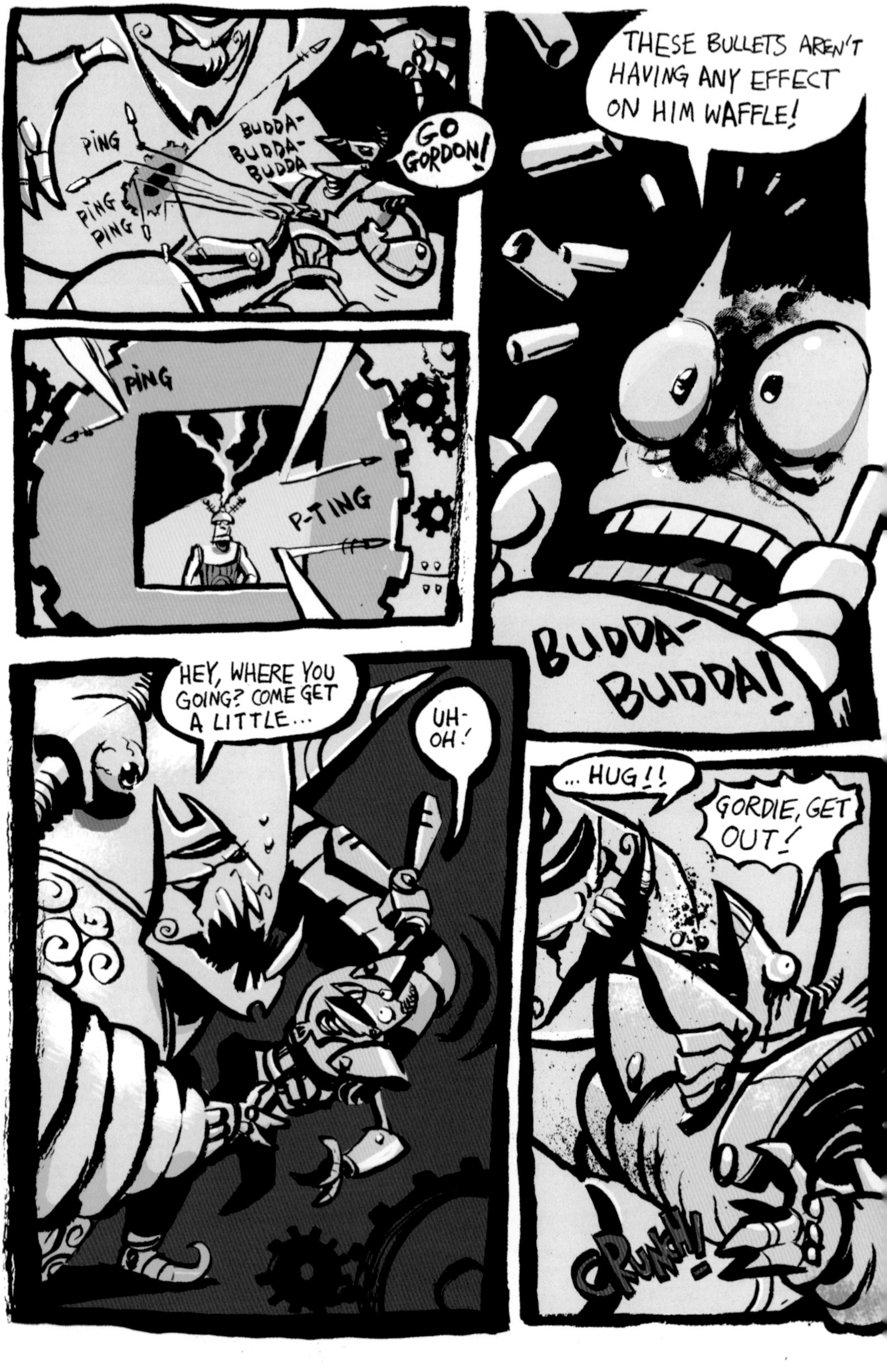
PING
PING PING
BUDDA-BUDDA-BUDDA
GO GORDON!
THESE BULLETS AREN'T HAVING ANY EFFECT ON HIM WAFFLE!
PING
P-TING
BUDDA-BUDDA!
HEY, WHERE YOU GOING? COME GET A LITTLE...
UH-OH!
...HUG!!
GORDIE, GET OUT!
CRUNCH!

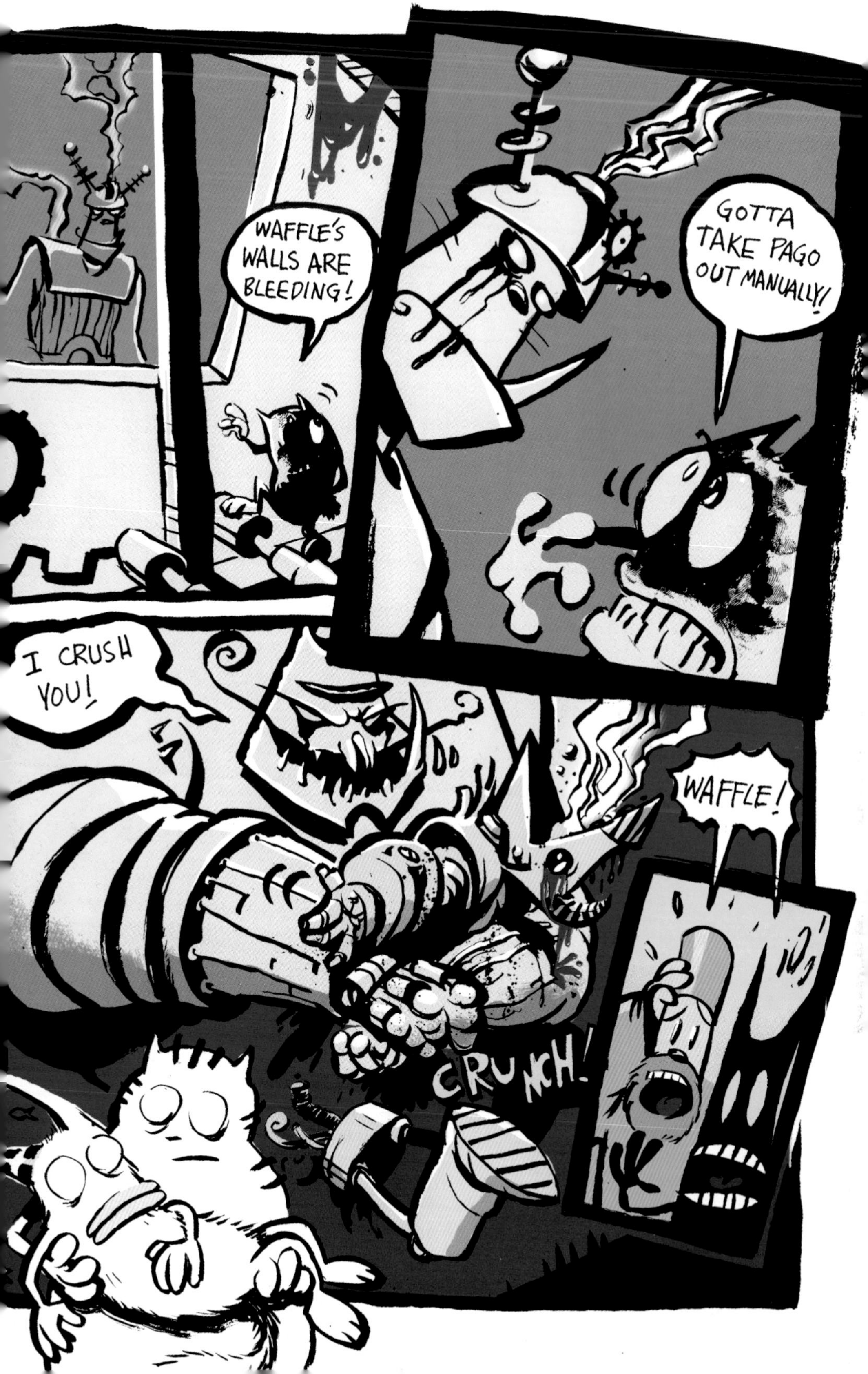
WAFFLE'S WALLS ARE BLEEDING!
GOTTA TAKE PAGO OUT MANUALLY!
I CRUSH YOU!
WAFFLE!
CRUNCH!

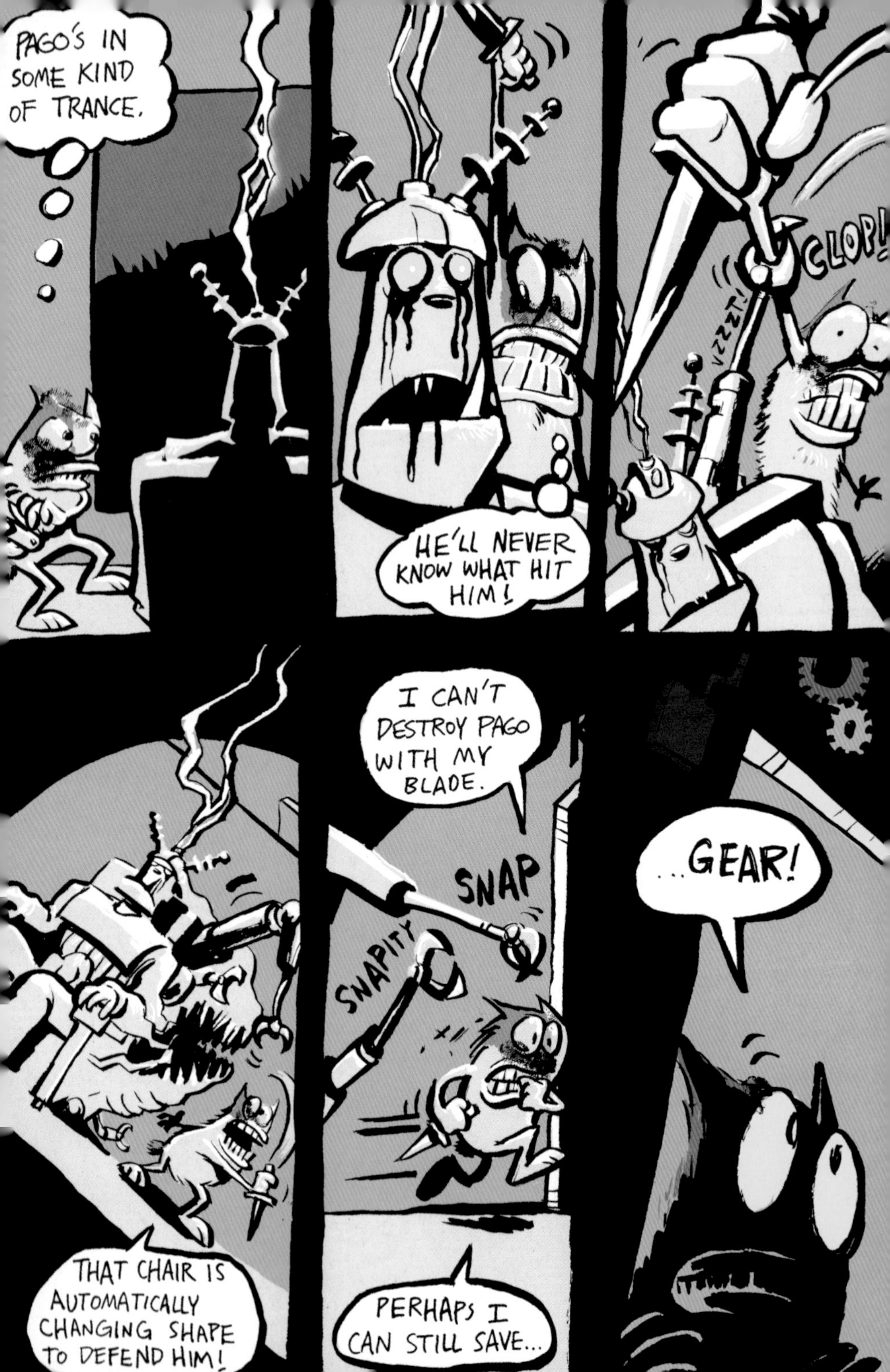
PAGO'S IN SOME KIND OF TRANCE.
HE'LL NEVER KNOW WHAT HIT HIM!
CLOP!
VZZZT!
THAT CHAIR IS AUTOMATICALLY CHANGING SHAPE TO DEFEND HIM!
I CAN'T DESTROY PAGO WITH MY BLADE.
SNAP
SNAPITY
PERHAPS I CAN STILL SAVE...
...GEAR!

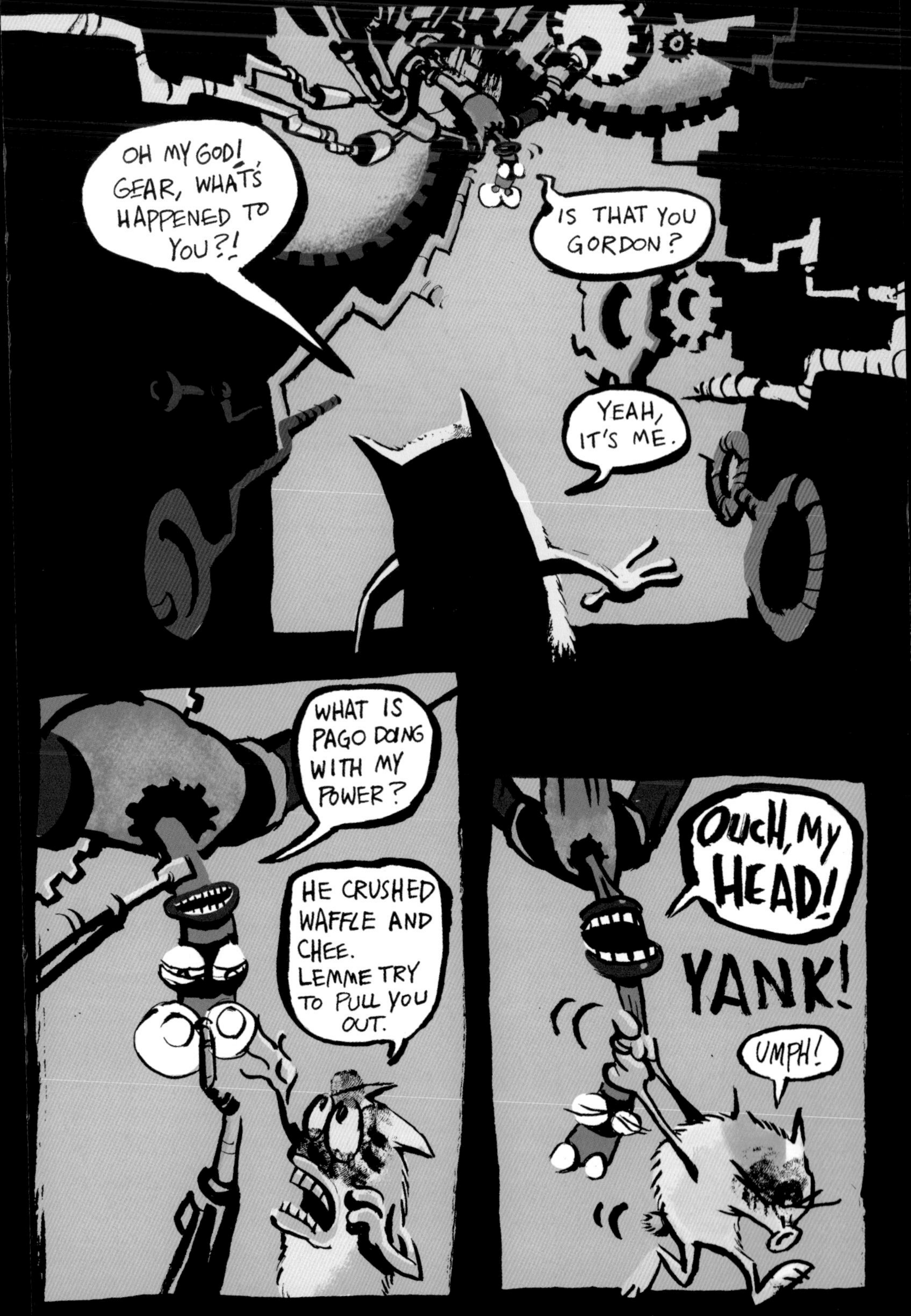
OH MY GOD! GEAR, WHAT'S HAPPENED TO YOU?!
IS THAT YOU GORDON?
YEAH, IT'S ME.
WHAT IS PAGO DOING WITH MY POWER?
HE CRUSHED WAFFLE AND CHEE. LEMME TRY TO PULL YOU OUT.
OUCH, MY HEAD!
YANK!
UMPH!

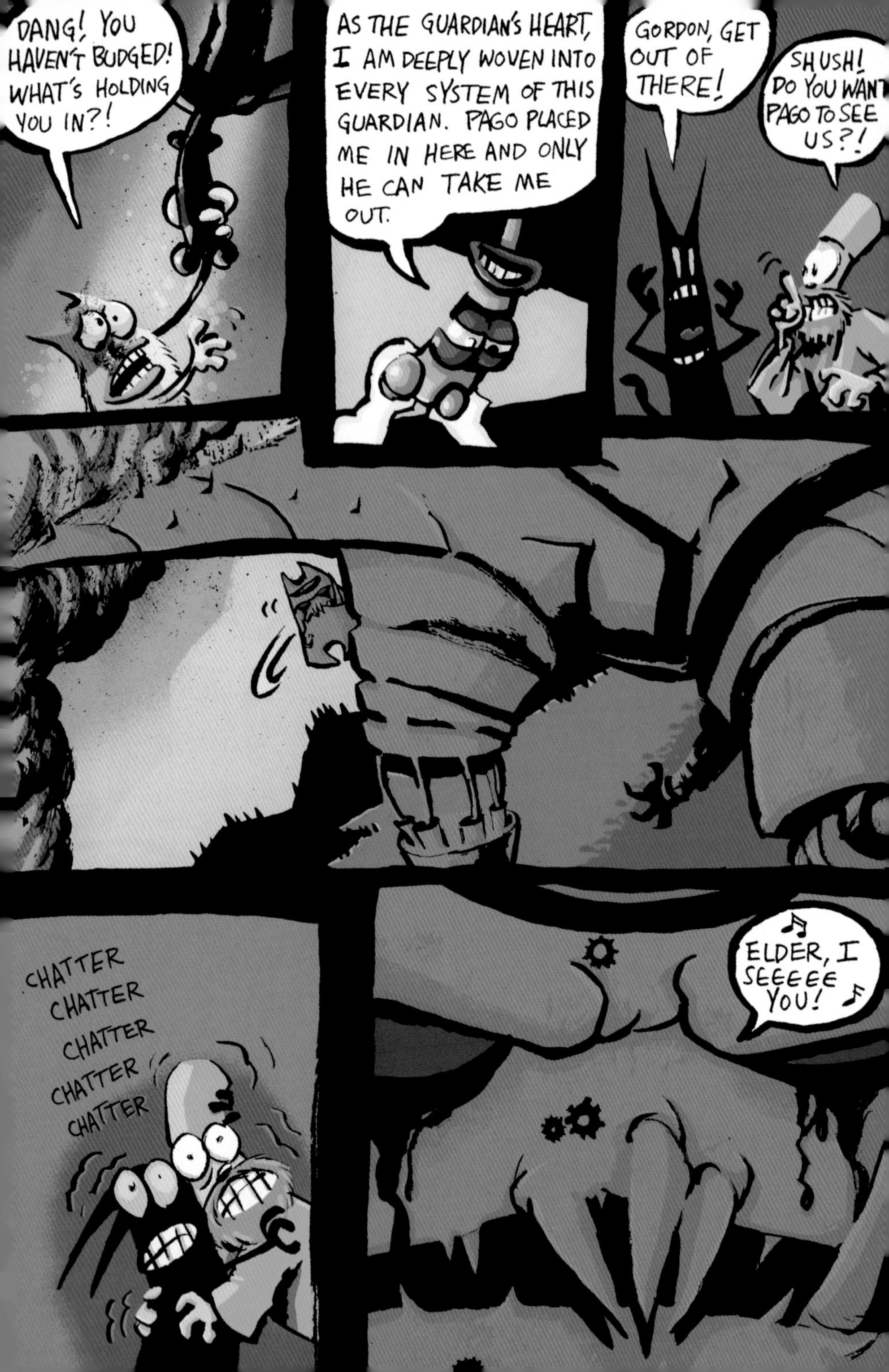
DANG! YOU HAVEN'T BUDGED! WHAT'S HOLDING YOU IN?!
AS THE GUARDIAN'S HEART, I AM DEEPLY WOVEN INTO EVERY SYSTEM OF THIS GUARDIAN. PAGO PLACED ME IN HERE AND ONLY HE CAN TAKE ME OUT.
GORDON, GET OUT OF THERE!
SHUSH! DO YOU WANT PAGO TO SEE US?!
CHATTER
CHATTER
CHATTER
CHATTER
CHATTER
ELDER, I SEEEEE YOU!

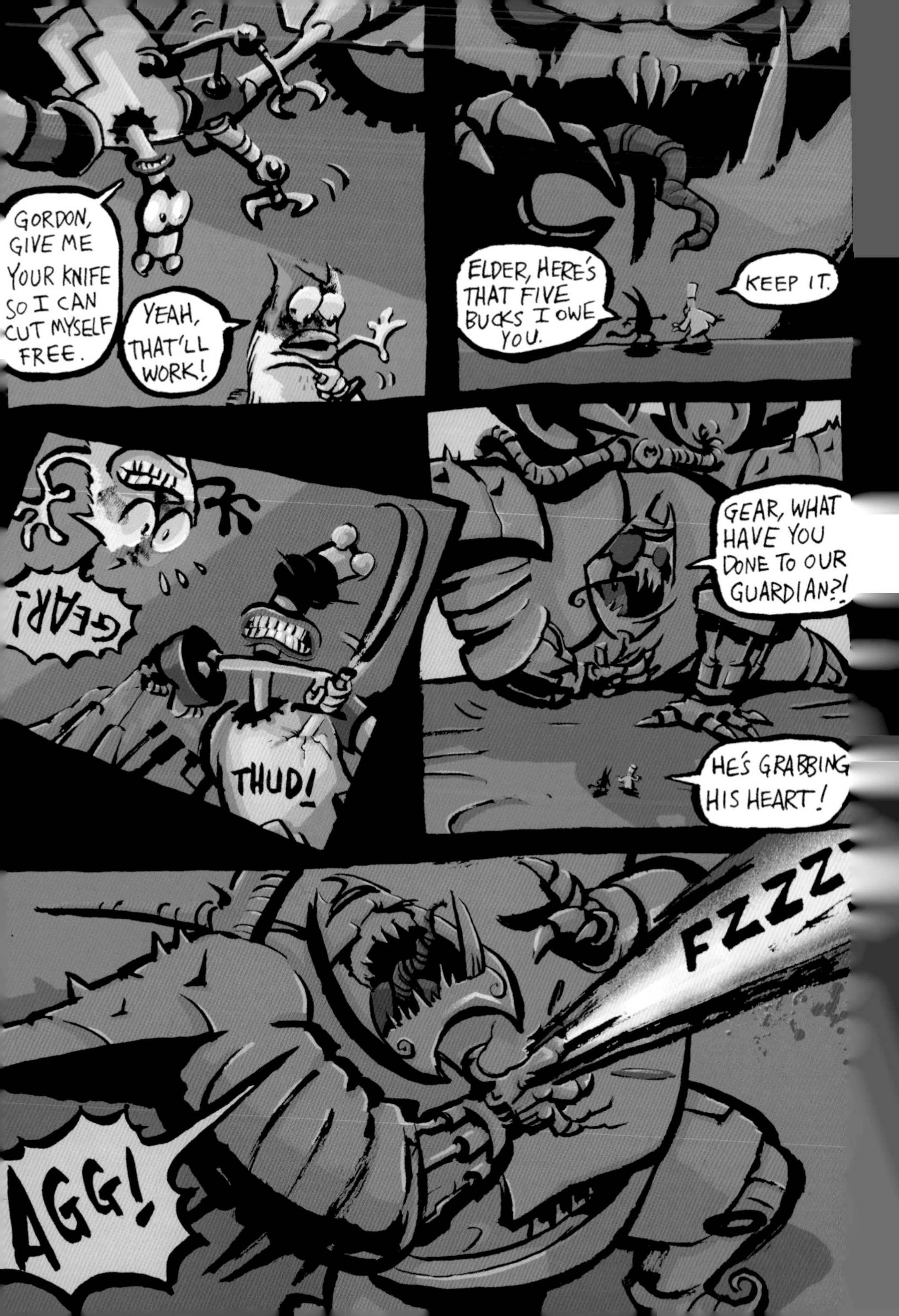
GORDON, GIVE ME YOUR KNIFE SO I CAN CUT MYSELF FREE.
YEAH, THAT'LL WORK!
ELDER, HERE'S THAT FIVE BUCKS I OWE YOU.
KEEP IT.
GEAR!
THUD!
GEAR, WHAT HAVE YOU DONE TO OUR GUARDIAN?!
HE'S GRABBING HIS HEART!
FZZZZ
AGG!

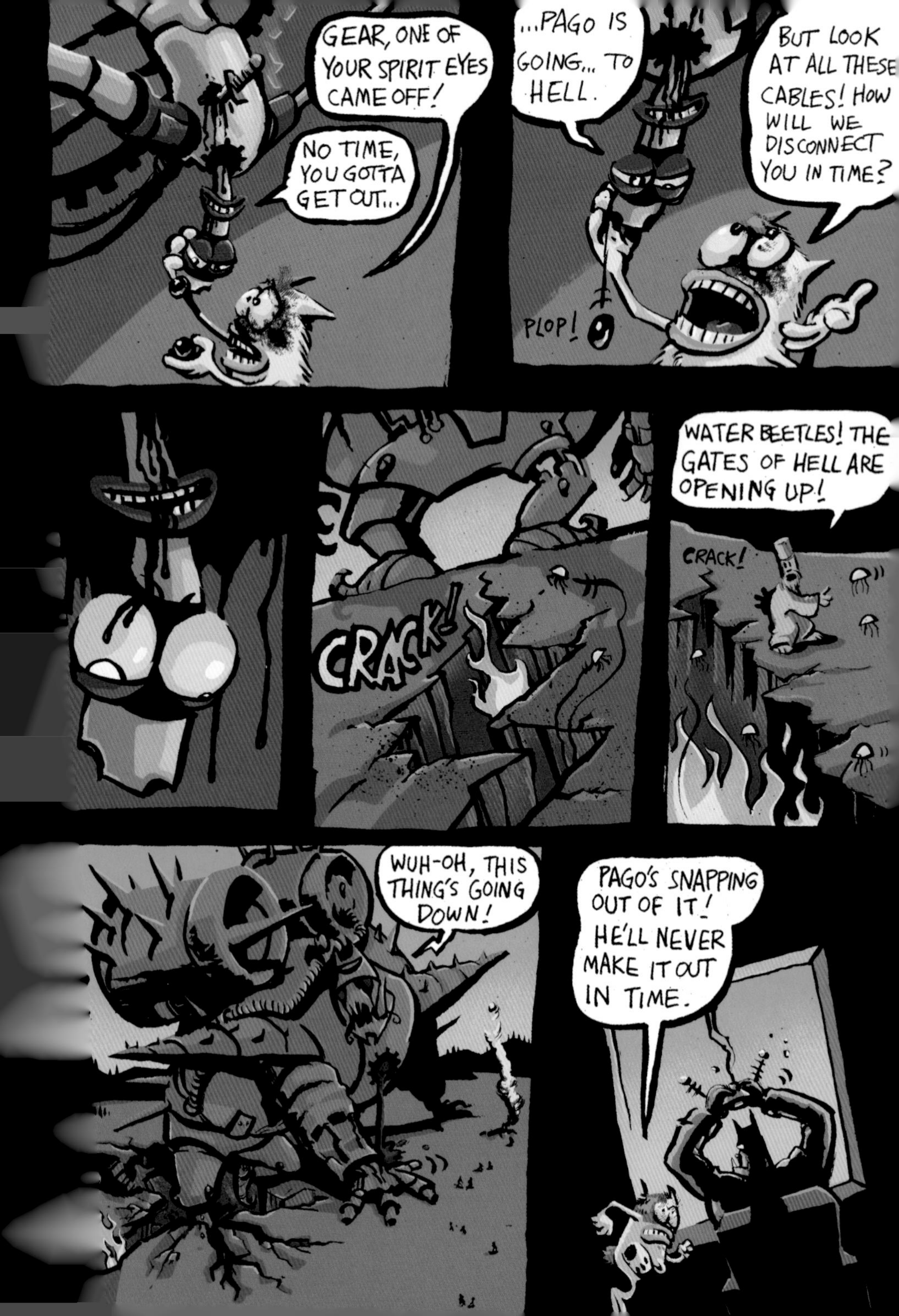
GEAR, ONE OF YOUR SPIRIT EYES CAME OFF!
NO TIME, YOU GOTTA GET OUT...
...PAGO IS GOING... TO HELL.
BUT LOOK AT ALL THESE CABLES! HOW WILL WE DISCONNECT YOU IN TIME?
PLOP!
CRACK!
WATER BEETLES! THE GATES OF HELL ARE OPENING UP!
CRACK!
WUH-OH, THIS THING'S GOING DOWN!
PAGO'S SNAPPING OUT OF IT! HE'LL NEVER MAKE IT OUT IN TIME.

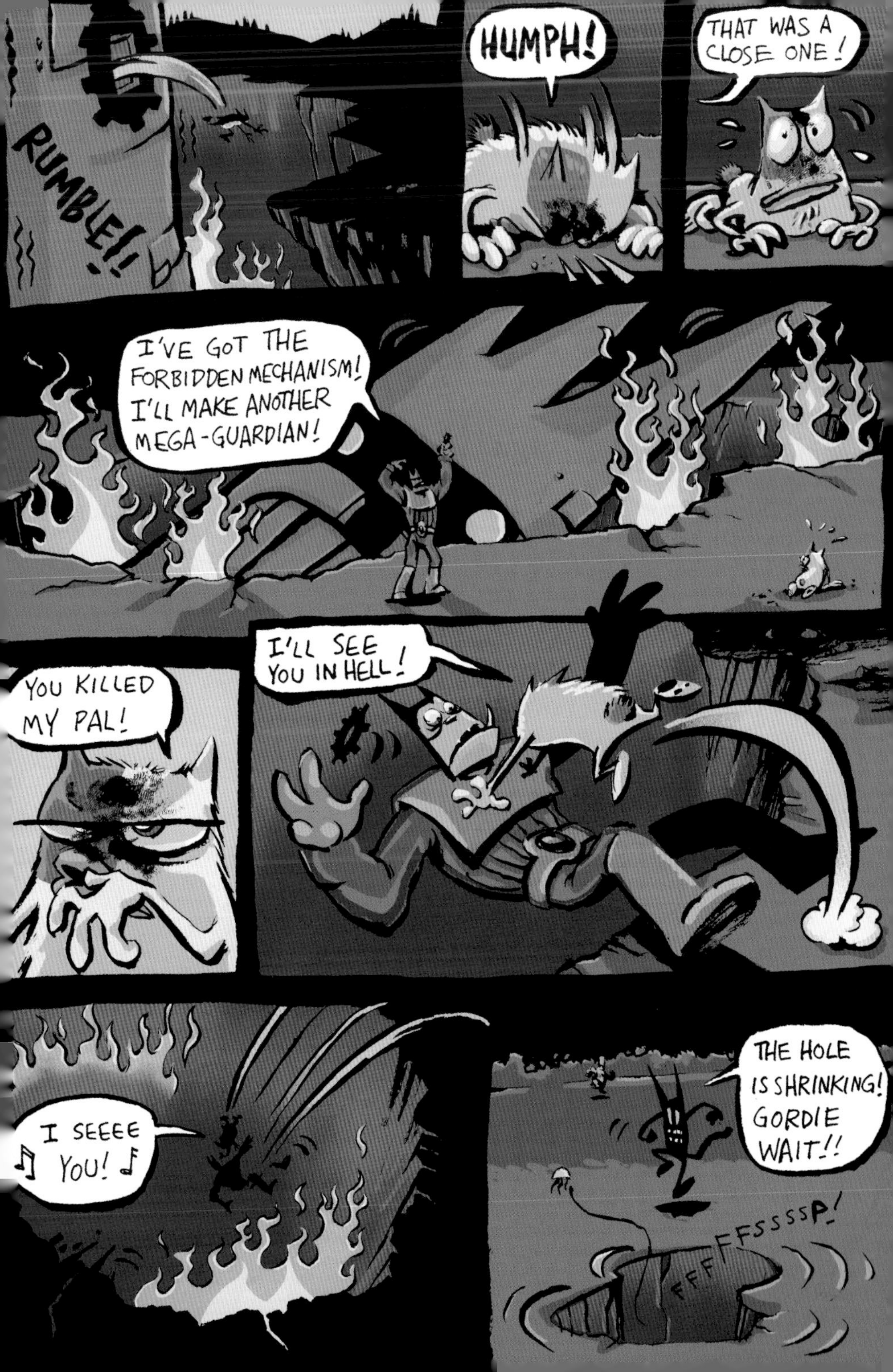
RUMBLE!!
HUMPH!
THAT WAS A CLOSE ONE!
I'VE GOT THE FORBIDDEN MECHANISM! I'LL MAKE ANOTHER MEGA-GUARDIAN!
YOU KILLED MY PAL!
I'LL SEE YOU IN HELL!
I SEEEE YOU!
THE HOLE IS SHRINKING! GORDIE WAIT!!
FFFFFSSSSSP!

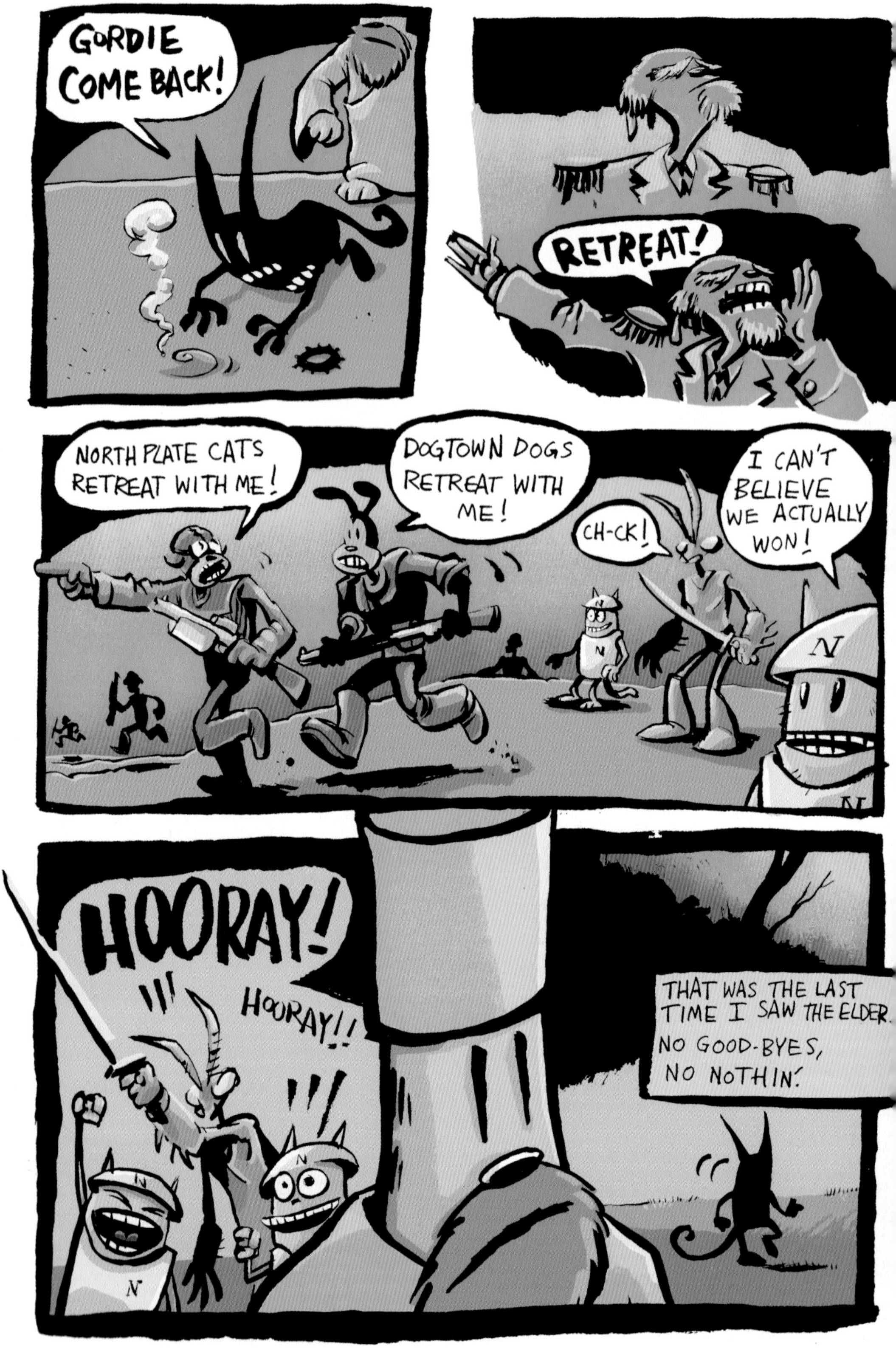
GORDIE COME BACK!
RETREAT!
NORTH PLATE CATS RETREAT WITH ME!
DOGTOWN DOGS RETREAT WITH ME!
CH-CK!
I CAN'T BELIEVE WE ACTUALLY WON!
HOORAY!
HOORAY!!
THAT WAS THE LAST TIME I SAW THE ELDER.
NO GOOD-BYES, NO NOTHIN'.

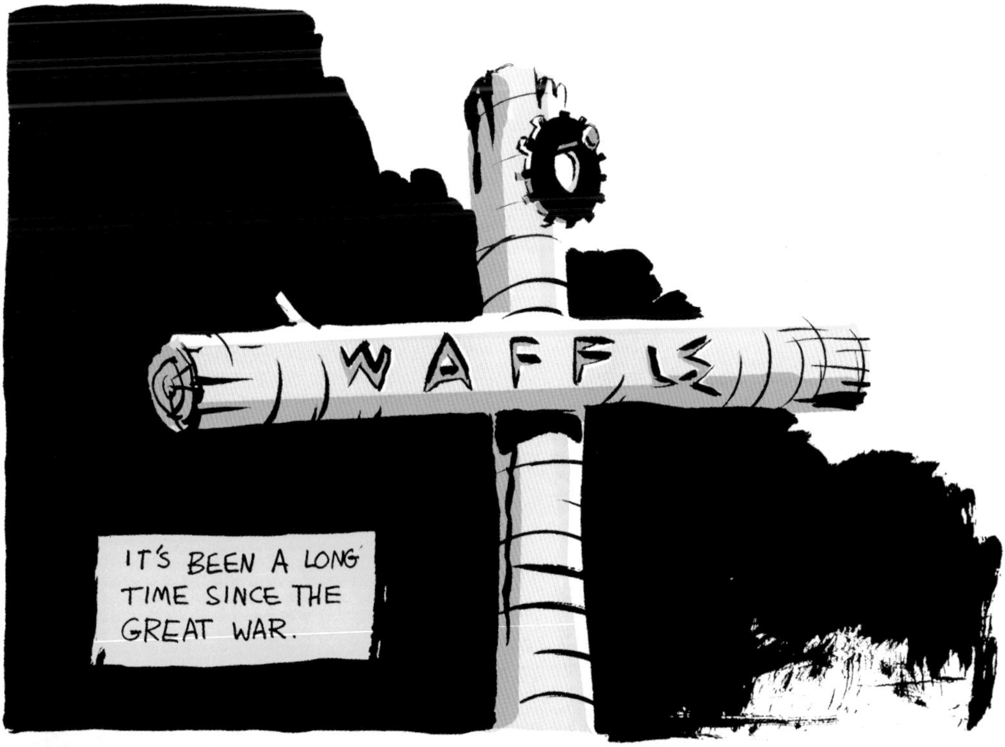
WAFFLE
IT'S BEEN A LONG TIME SINCE THE GREAT WAR.

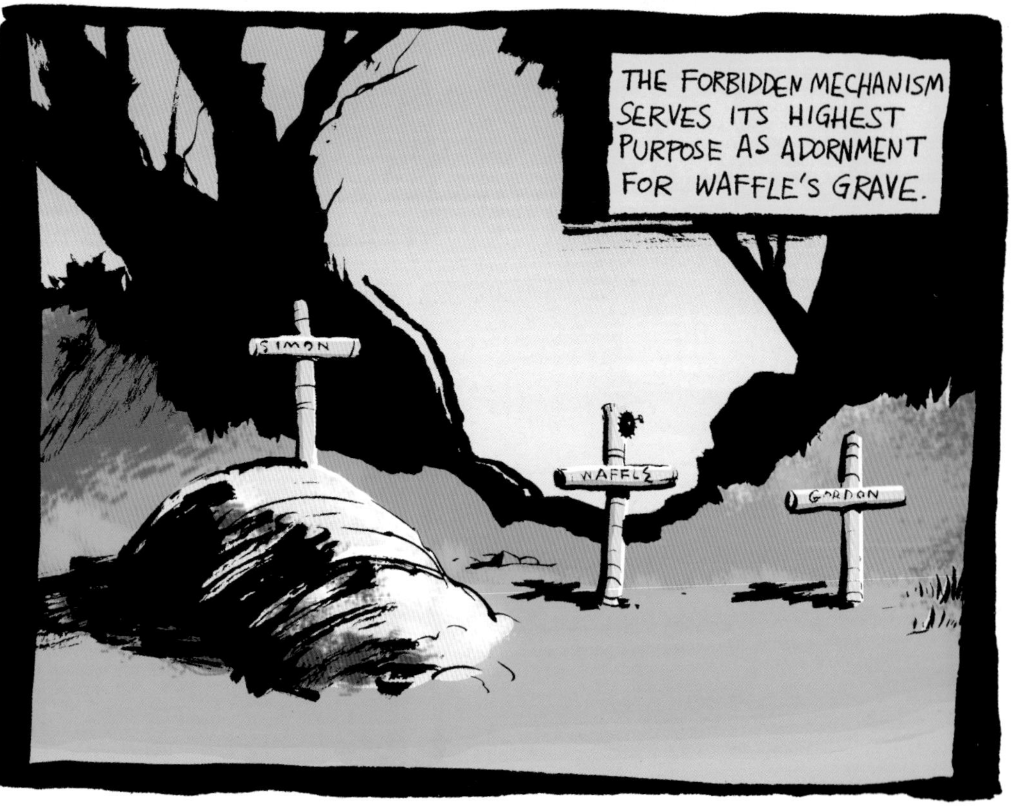
THE FORBIDDEN MECHANISM SERVES ITS HIGHEST PURPOSE AS ADORNMENT FOR WAFFLE'S GRAVE.
SIMON
WAFFLE
GORDON

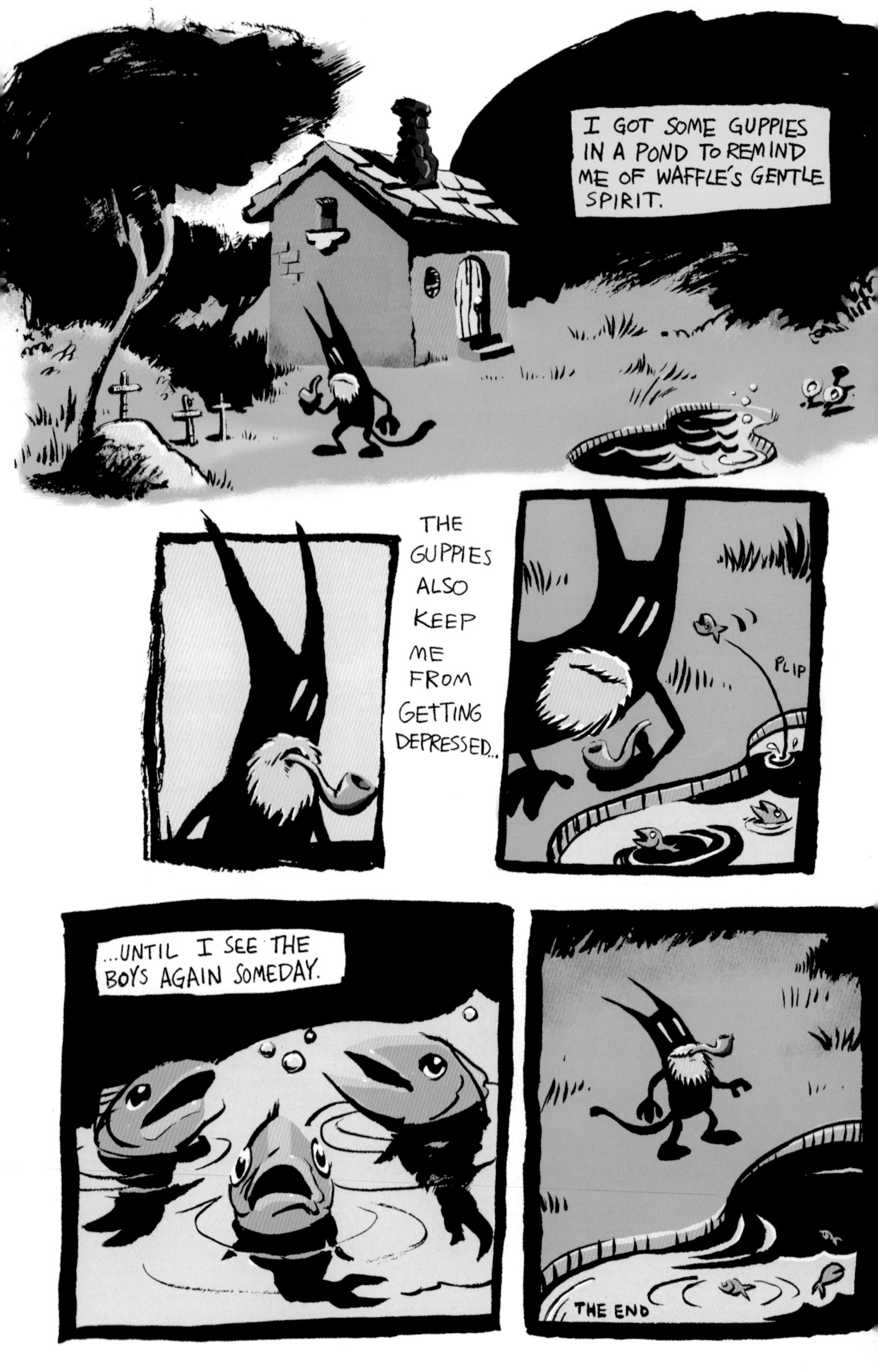
I GOT SOME GUPPIES IN A POND TO REMIND ME OF WAFFLE'S GENTLE SPIRIT.
THE GUPPIES ALSO KEEP ME FROM GETTING DEPRESSED...
PLIP
...UNTIL I SEE THE BOYS AGAIN SOMEDAY.
THE END

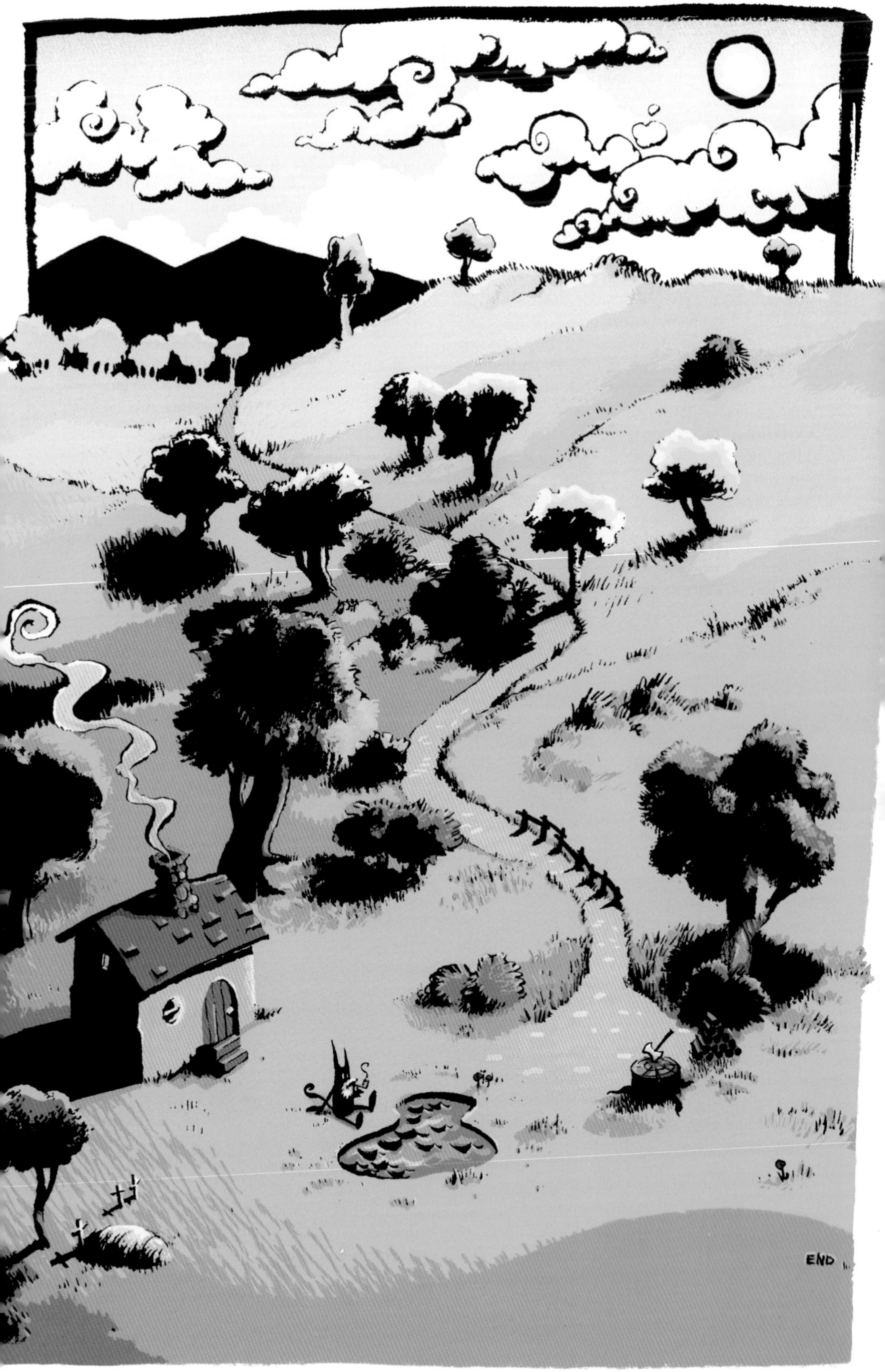
END

I have a TV show on Nickelodeon called Catscratch. If I didn't make the GEAR graphic novel over eight years ago, there would be no tv show. This graphic novel came to symbolize the way my life works and the way my successes appear to be the end of a long string of happy accidents.

When I was in first grade, I found a kitten on the street and brought it home. My father, who wisely knew that this kitten probably belonged to somebody else, probably was diseased, and that I probably wasn't going to take care of it forbid me from keeping him. In my undeveloped narcissistic mind, my father was evil for this, which is pretty much how I painted my parents regarding everything they didn't give me. My reasons for wanting something were always noble and their reason for not giving it too me were always unreasonable. But this lack of cat put a fire in my belly…a love for cats that would endure for the rest of my life. Now, when I get a cat as an adult, I'm not just judging the cat on his own merits. I'm filling a perceived gap in my childhood. Needing the world's most independent, fickle animal is the great beginning of a long cruel joke. Thus, I own a cat and can't really explain why I keep him around, even though I long to get rid of him because he poops on the bathroom tile and howls at 4am, waking up my entire family.

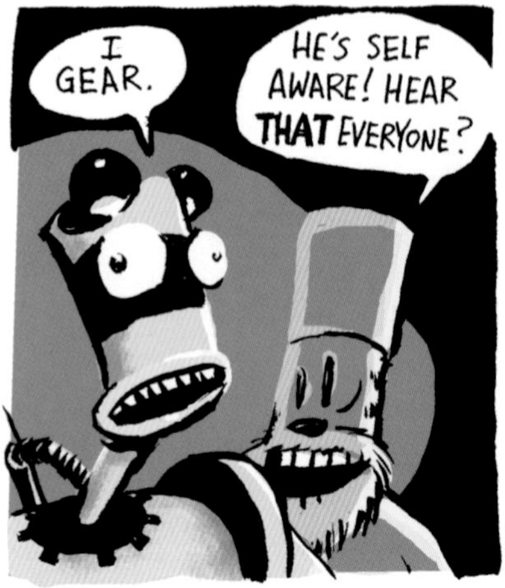
I GEAR.
HE'S SELF AWARE! HEAR THAT EVERYONE?

I became pals with three renegade gentlemen of the comics industry who worked under the name of Fireman Press—a small start-up in the mid 90s. Rob Schrab created the legendary character SCUD and Dan Harmon was the writer/editor while Peter Alberts was the publisher. I served as a guest artist/writer for SCUD: Tales From The Vending Machine and was anxious to do my own title. They asked me to submit an idea. and the gears started turning (sorry).

Working on GEAR was the first time I used a Japanese bamboo and horsehair brush. I had seen greats like Scott Morse and Jon J. Muth use this brush with great results. I had taken a few business trips to Japan to promote my video game. The Neverhood. and I liked to walk the streets of Japan alone at night to people-watch. While in Japan. I saw many artists use the bamboo brush for their form of calligraphy sumi (meaning, "ink"). I went to an art store in Tokyo's famous Ginza shopping district and bought my first bamboo brush with a bottle of sumi ink. Returning to my hotel I sat at the pond behind the lobby and inked a drawing of koi from life. I instantly fell in love with the medium.

I like mixing genres. so I wanted to make a comic book that used the ancient tools of bamboo/sumi but mix it with my modern cartoon sensibilities. I sat down and just started drawing pages of (what else?) cats. My cats. The good guys would be based on my real cats—Simon, Waffle, Gordon and Mr. Black. It was pretty easy to write, since I wasn't getting paid to do the book, so I had no boss. The personality of my main characters would mimic those of my real cats. The main bad guy, PAGO, was named after Peter Albert's cat of the same name. I did four to eight pages a day until I got the first 24 pages done. My wife marveled at how much fun I was having! I was literally singing while doing the pages. The bamboo brush and crude artwork gave me permission to really throw some ink around. I didn't want to focus on perfection or technique. I went for raw expression.

I submitted the first 24 pages of GEAR to Fireman Press, and they were on the brink of splitting up as a company. I released the first chapter of GEAR on their label as a mini at the San Diego Comic-Con. Schrab made these funky hand silk-screened covers that made every book a one of a kind collector's item. The book did well enough to start on the second chapter of GEAR. These pages came fast, since now I had a deadline to put out a 24-page book every other month. The style was so loose and silly that I could bang out a 4-8 pages a night, and the sloppiness appeared to be part of the GEAR style.

By the end of the second book, I was having story problems. This is the first and only story I ever started where I didn't know where it would end before I started. I had to sit down and write the rest of the story in thumbnail form so I had the confidence that it would resolve in a satisfying way.

Prophetically, just after the cat character Simon died in the comic book, my real life Simon the cat died of an enlarged heart. I gave Gordon away to my uncle Jim. Waffle was eviscerated by a coyote on a neighbor's lawn in 2004. Mr. Black is still with us today.

The original black and white GEAR graphic novel came out in 1998 and did pretty well, though it was a relatively unknown book. The editor of The Simpsons comics, Terry Delegeane, liked the book so much that he let me write and illustrate a Simpson's Treehouse of Horror story. I tried to do the Simpson's using the GEAR style of black and white while another colorist applied color to my black and white. The result was amazing…the black and white gained electricity with the garish colors and I kept that in the back of my mind that GEAR would work well in color some day.

GEAR drew the attention of a Nickelodeon newbie named Claudia Spinelli. She loved comics and took GEAR in to her boss Doug Greiff, who liked the book…then left Nickelodeon. This happens a lot at these entertainment companies where individuals get switched around, fired, quit or just plain forget about your work. I assumed GEAR was pretty much over. Little did I know that Claudia was working with another Nickelodeon executive, Eric Coleman, and they invited me in to discuss developing the book into an animated tv show.

Most kids who draw dream of having a TV show or movie of their work but have no idea what

happens behind the scenes. It ain't pretty. The acceptance of the first pitch is the end of the easy part, and the real work begins once a project walks through the front doors of an entertainment conglomerate. Mr. Black gained pupils and became Mr. Blik, we changed the name of the cartoon to Catscratch and we removed all of the giant robots, gun-fights, insect armies and just kept the three main cats.

I got my first office at Nickelodeon in 2001. The Catscratch Bible and support materials weren't finished until late in 2002. Nick officially ordered a pilot in 2003, which is when I got my first real pay check. They decided to go to series in 2004. Went on the air in summer of 2005, and here I am writing this at the end of 2006, and the series is pretty much finished around here. This is the way the series ends. Not with a bang but a whimper.

*Doug signs Catscratch posters at San Diego Comic-Con 2006.*

The thing I love about making comics is what you're holding in your hands… it's liquid lightning to a storyteller like me. The fun part is exercising the thing out of my mind and into your head. We both know there's no such thing as cats at war with insects who shoot pistols and drive giant robots to battle over a mechanical Christ figure, yet something rings true about their mission, their personality, their existence. These stories aren't about cats after all. They're about us.

I'm a pretty happy guy, but I can't credit all of my happiness to my own efforts. I was born in America, raised by good parents I didn't get to choose, I married an amazing woman and have 3 kids with one on the way…I couldn't go back and find the one thing that made everything click. The same with GEAR becoming Catscratch, it just happened. I wrote a cute little comic as a basically selfish exercise and now there's a McDonald's Happy Meal with my characters all over it.

**Douglas TenNapel**
*December 15, 2006*

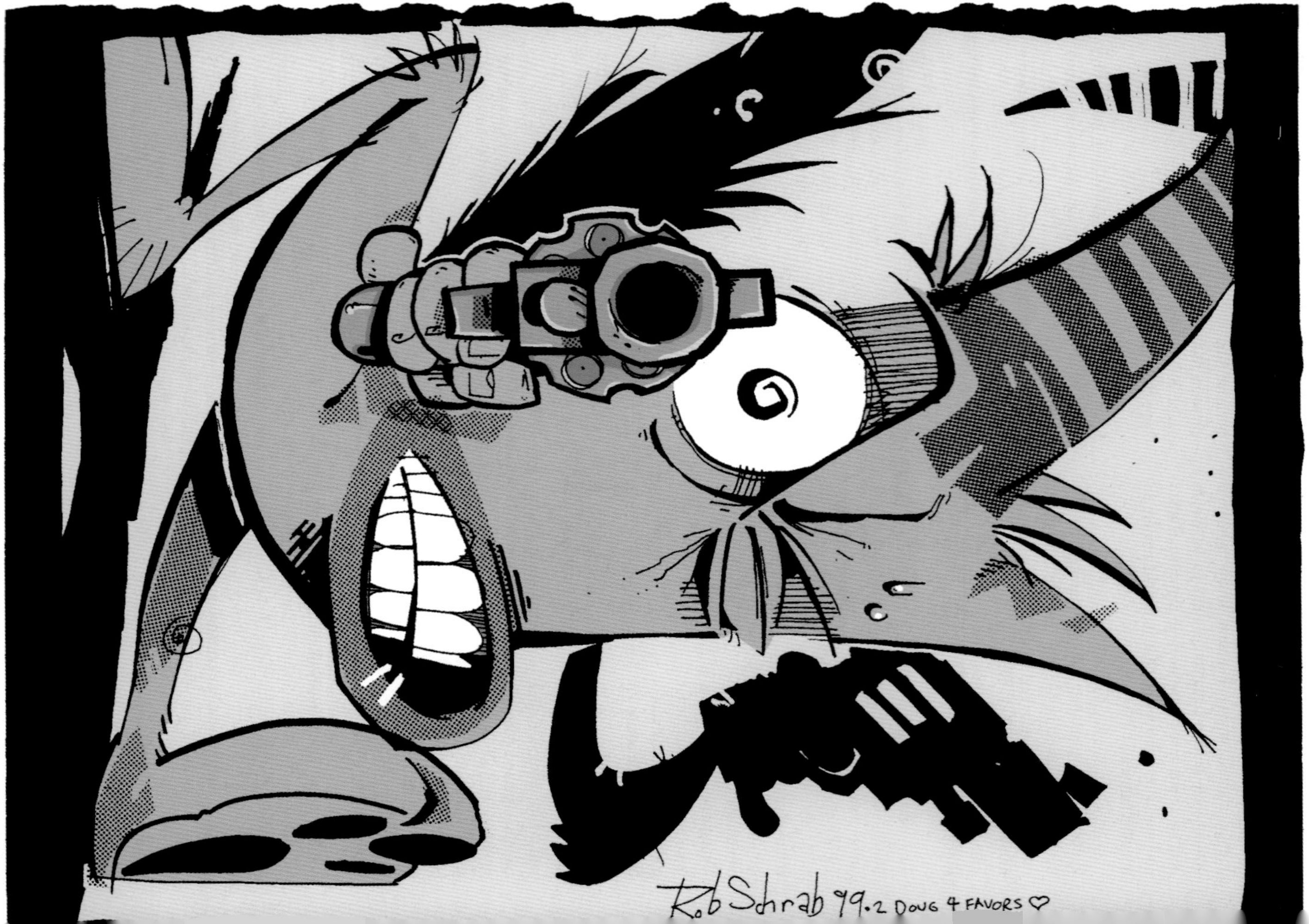
Rob Schrab 99.2 DOUG 4 FAVORS ♡

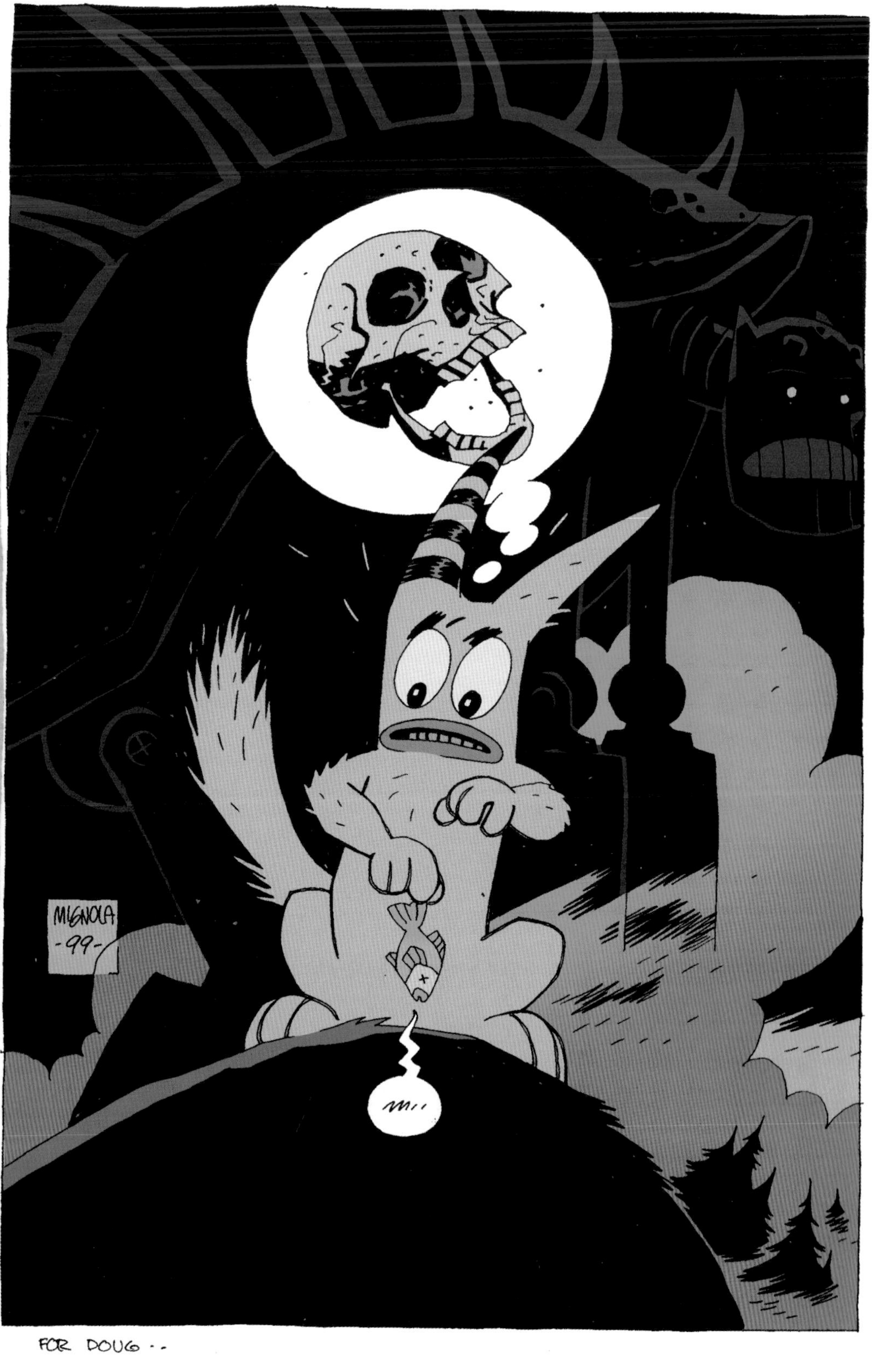
MIGNOLA
-99-

FOR DOUG --

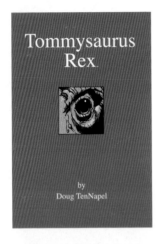
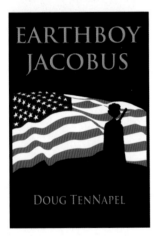